FAVORITE FAMILIES OF TV

by
Christopher Paul Denis

and
Michael Denis

A Citadel Press Book

Published by Carol Publishing Group

For their help and cooperation, thanks to: Al Rosenberg, Roger Glazer, Anne Marie Allocca, Alvin H. Marill, Jerry Vermilye, and Allan Wilson. Special thanks to Lyle Stuart.

Photos courtesy Denis Archives

A Citadel Press Book
Published by Carol Publishing Group

Citadel Press is a registered trademark of Carol Communications, Inc.

Editorial Offices: 600 Madison Avenue, New York, N.Y. 10022
Sales & Distribution Offices: 120 Enterprise Avenue, Secaucus, N.J. 07094
In Canada: Canadian Manda Group, P.O. Box 920, Station U,
    Toronto, Ontario M8Z 5P9

DESIGNED BY LESTER GLASSNER

Queries regarding rights and permissions should be addressed to Carol Publishing Group, 600 Madison Avenue, New York, N.Y. 10022

Carol Publishing Group books are available at special discounts for bulk purchases, for sales promotions, fund raising, or educational purposes. Special editions can be created to specifications. For details contact: Special Sales Department, Carol Publishing Group, 120 Enterprise Avenue, Secaucus, N.J. 07094

Manufactured in the United States of America

10   9   8   7   6   5   4   3   2   1

Library of Congress Cataloging-in-Publication Data

Denis, Christopher.
    Favorite families of TV / by Christopher Paul Denis and Michael Denis.
        p.   cm.
    "A Citadel Press book."
    ISBN 0-8065-1255-5 (pbk.)
    1. Television and family—United States.   2. Television serials—United States.   I. Denis, Michael.   II. Title.   III. Title:
Favorite families of television.
PN1992.8.F33D46   1991
791.45'75'0973—dc20   91-41116
                                                           CIP

WITH LOVE AND ADMIRATION
TO PAUL DENIS AND
HELEN MARTIN DENIS

The authors, Christopher (left), age four, and Michael Denis, age seven, ready themselves for the exhaustive research experience of watching classic primetime family TV shows circa 1953.

Contents

INTRODUCTION

The adult in all of us readily acknowledges an imperfect world, but the child within keeps those icons from the past in the silver box of memory and recalls them from time to time, their sweetness ever intact. No sooner do I think of The Beaver than a myriad of images flood the TV screen in my mind, and I am swept away. The same emotions I felt back then arise, a bit creaky through the gauze of memory, but the same nevertheless. If The Beaver is being tortured by some "creepy" girl, or Bud is being lectured by a father who thought he knew best, or Mama is taking care of her brood, I have absorbed all that information and stored it, and it *has* made a difference.

The gray world we pass through today is a shabby substitute for the safety of those strong black and white images from the past. The archetypes of heroes and heroines and their lessons bequeathed hold fast and color our perceptions of the present. Life's complex problems were resolved in twenty-six minutes—what a magical reality! And it was real, happening right before our eyes. No one in any TV family was ever struck, beaten or bloodied, and rarely did anyone die.

It is to the fairy tale endings and more pleasant aspects of the experience of viewing programs about families that this book is dedicated. This book is meant to revive warm memories of those twenty or so programs which over the years best represented, for good or bad, a Cyclopian vision of family life in modern day U.S.A. Not only have we recounted some of the programs in each individual series, but we have strived to include anecdotal and biographical material on players, origins of the series, and various and sundry trivia which we hope will entertain and offer a balm against the woes of the day, much as did many of these beloved programs. Some of the commentary on the shows may include criticism by either author and/or cast member (for instance, Billy Gray's angry assessments on the impact of *Father Knows Best* on viewers' perceptions of family relationships). We hope that this book will be more a celebration than an indictment of those favorite TV families.

This book is respectfully dedicated to our father, Paul Denis, first television editor of the *New York Post,* a pioneer show business journalist whose columns, articles, and books covered every aspect of show business beginning with vaudeville reporting in 1926 (he was the first journalist ever to review a chubby Brooklyn nightclub comic named Jackie Gleason), radio, movies, and legitimate stage, to television—up through and including daytime soap operas. He is a living gold mine of show business lore, having met, interviewed, and reported on just about anyone who was anyone in entertainment over the last six decades. He remembers interviewing Ozzie and Harriet in Hollywood at their house and finding them to be exactly as they were on the show, "middle class and upwardly mobile." Tony Dow (Wally) of *Leave It to Beaver* was a "nice kid, well-mannered and polite." Don Grady of *My Three Sons* roared through midtown Manhattan traffic on a motor scooter while our Dad held on for dear life, determined to get his interview no matter what.

Our childhood was filled with anecdotes from our father on his many adventures and misadventures with the stars. Much of the information on which this book is based was derived from the Denis Archives, the massive collection of files Paul Denis kept for more than forty years. These biographical and subject files occupied all the rooms in the basement of our home in Riverdale, New York. Our dad began his files in the 1940s as a way of verifying the accuracy of his articles. The files grew over the years (my brother and I both continue to "clip" to this day—a "disease" our father called it; we can't say in polite company what our mother called the avocation.)

On the set with Mama *in 1949 are Peggy Wood together with "children":
seven year-old Robin Morgan (Dagmar), Rosemary Rice (Katrin), and Dick
Van Patten (Nels).*

So, return with us now to those golden days of yesteryear…sorry, wrong channel, perhaps our next book will be one on great television Westerns. Until then, we hope you enjoy reading about these shows as much as we did writing about them. We acknowledge the shortcomings of our arbitrary decisions (fought hard between the two of us) over which shows to include. My brother and I agreed on a primary criterion that the chosen shows must include families with children, thereby qualifying them as *real* families. Therefore *The Honeymooners* isn't included even though Ralph Kramden and Ed Norton could, arguably, qualify as *big* children. To modify our arbitrariness, we have added at the end an Honorable Mention listing to include, hopefully, some of our readers' personal choices.

—Christopher Paul Denis

ROBERT YOUNG
co-starring JANE WYATT

FATHER KNOWS BEST

BIOGRAPHY

Presented by KENT cigarettes

ROBERT YOUNG

(Star of "Father Knows Best," Sundays, at 10:00 p.m., EST,
on CBS television)

A Hollywood product and one of its best exponents of
craftsmanship, Robert Young stars in his first television series when
"Father Knows Best" makes its TV debut Sunday, Oct. 3, on CBS
television at 10:00 p.m., EST. It is sponsored by the P. Lorillard
Company for Kent Cigarettes.

He was also the star of the program which was a radio favorite
from the Fall of 1949 until last year when it began to prepare for
television production.

The star's realistic acting on the program, concerned with the
poignantly amusing events of a family with three children, can be
attributed not only to his competence as an actor, but also to his
practical experience as the real life father of four.

Bob was born (Feb. 22, 1907) in Chicago and spent a short time
in Seattle, but he has lived in and around Los Angeles since he was 10
year old. One of five children of an Irish-American building
contractor and his wife, he began to accept responsibility early with a
variety of jobs. At eight he was a helper on a grocery delivery truck.
While attending school he was a clerk in a soda store, had a job in the
press-room of the "Los Angeles Times," drove a cleaning and dyeing
truck and was a service station grease monkey.

(more)

BUREAU OF INDUSTRIAL SERVICE, INC. • Subsidiary of YOUNG & RUBICAM, INC. • 285 Madison Ave., New York 17, N.Y.

Fathers Know Best—Our father, Paul Denis, with two of television's legendary dads, Fred MacMurray of My Three Sons *and Robert Young of* Father Knows Best.

This Father Knows Best *masthead for press releases about the show pictures Father as a saint in his family.*

From the first "realistic" black sitcom, Good Times: *(from left) Jimmie Walker, BernNadette Stanis, Esther Rolle and Ralph Carter.*

Michael Landon with one of his mentors, award-winning director of photography Ted Voigtlander, on the set of Little House on the Prairie *in 1979. The two also worked together on Landon's next series,* Highway to Heaven.

March 27, 1978 · 60¢

Hollywood bows to Neil Simon
How to fix dinner for 140—White House style
Will Bobby Orr ever skate again?

People weekly

Farewell to The Family
We'll miss them, and they'll miss each other

AUGUST 11, 1980 · $1.25

UNEMPLOYMENT: The Real Price

TIME

TV's *Dallas*
WHODUNIT?

Larry Hagman
as J.R.

The MIAMI HERALD
TV
November 26–December 2

Prime time's first 'Family'

GORBACHEV'S ULTIMATUM
A Blockade of Lithuania?

Newsweek

BART!

Why America Loves the Simpsons
TV's Twisted New Take On the Family

MATT GROENING

22 MORE ON THE WAY!

Reeves Entertainment Group congratulates Jane Curtin, Susan St. James and the cast and crew of

Kate & Allie

on its renewal by the CBS Television Network. This 22 show order brings the number of Kate & Allie episodes to 122.

MAMA

A family portrait of the Hansens on the front porch of their house on Steiner Street in San Francisco circa 1909. Left to right are Katrin (Rosemary Rice), Papa Hansen (Judson Laire), Mama (Peggy Wood), Nels (Dick Van Patten) and Dagmar (Robin Morgan).

Mama suffered from flimsy-looking sets, jerky camera movements, flat lighting, and an abundance of stage-trained actors who, in the early years of "live" television broadcasting, sometimes missed their marks, enunciated too loudly, or were unused to and unknowledgeable about the economical techniques required for acting in this new medium. Nevertheless, at the center of all these seeming weaknesses lay the fledgling program's greatest strength—heart. "Mama," as played by the sublime Peggy Wood, had enough to carry this sweet, simple show to glory during its eight-season run.

The idea for this comedy/drama was culled from John Van Druten's play, *I Remember Mama,* which, produced by Rodgers and Hammerstein, enjoyed a successful run on Broadway during the mid-1940s.* The play, in turn, was based upon Kathryn Forbes's popular book, *Mama's Bank Account.* The television series *Mama* had its debut on CBS at 8:00 P.M. on July 1, 1949, and was broadcast "live" until July 1956. The program, sponsored by Maxwell House Coffee, was then cancelled, much to the cast's dismay. Immediate, resounding public outcry from viewers was such that CBS revived the series, televising it for thirteen weeks, from December 1956 through March 17, 1957, before giving it the final ax. The last thirteen episodes were shot on film.

Following the play's success on Broadway, a film of it starring Irene Dunne in the title role was released in 1948. The television version that followed the next year honed the drama by calling it *Mama* and infused it with a lighter comedic tone. What endeared the program to viewers was the simplicity and consistent warmth of the storylines. If Ozzie and Harriet lived in a Hollywoodized netherworld, the faithful, closely knit immigrant Norwegian family of Hansens certainly did not. There were always morals to the stories, but those morals were more the unspoken ones, the "givens" of a simpler time—Papa says you give your word to a man to do a job, and you keep your oath.

The setting was the house of the Hansens on Steiner Street in San Francisco in 1910 (incidentally, the same year eighteen-year-old Peggy Wood made her New York stage debut in *Naughty Marietta*). Featured players in the *Mama* cast were Peggy

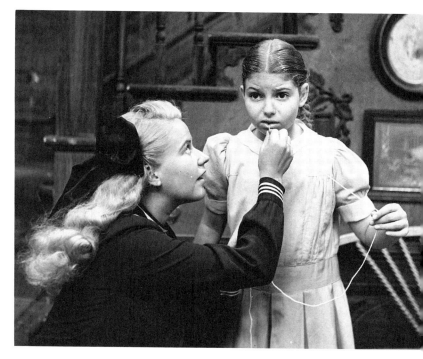

Eldest daughter Katrin (Rosemary Rice) readies younger sister Dagmar (Robin Wright) for tooth removal the old-fashioned way.

Wood as Marta (Mama) Hansen; Judson Laire as Lars (Papa) Hansen, a carpenter; Rosemary Rice as older daughter Katrin, whose off-camera narration opened and closed each episode; Dick Van Patten as son Nels (the role originated on Broadway a few years before by a young Marlon Brando); Iris Mann (1949–50), Robin Morgan (1950–56), and Toni Campbell (1957) as younger daughter Dagmar; Ruth Gates as Aunt Jenny, Mama's older sister; Malcolm Keen as Uncle Chris; Carl Frank as Uncle Gunnar; Alice Frost as Aunt Trina, Mama's younger sister; Kevin Coughlin as T. R. Ryan, child neighbor of the Hansens (1952–57), and Patty McCormack as Ingeborg, a young Norwegian child adopted by Uncle Gunnar and Aunt Trina, and playmate to T. R. Ryan (1953–57).

*It's latter-day incarnation was, ironically, as a musical by Richard Rodgers (his last) and Martin Charnin.

Kevin Coughlin, age nine, plays T. R. Ryan on Mama, *and Patty McCormack, also nine, portrays Ingeborg. Here they share a banana split between rehearsals. (1954)*

During the first season there was some fear that the new program might be cancelled because the network's lineup in those days was pretty shaky. *Mama* was given the deadly Friday-evening-at-eight time slot when most families were out seeing a double feature at the then still affordable local Bijou. However, the weekly tribulations of the humble Hansen family proved irresistible to many viewers, and *Mama* was soon firmly entrenched, much to the delight of the network and the Maxwell House Coffee people. The opening and closing scenes always took place in the kitchen over a pot of freshly brewed coffee (sponsors' product hints were anything but subliminal in those early TV days). The plots were simple, identifiable to all viewers. The stories never portrayed Papa as a bumbling idiot or Mama as a whiny shrew or the kids as either perfect little angels or as midget agents of Satan. The simple stories spoke directly to the heart. No one was made to look ridiculous without redemption, and no smarmy badmouthers were allowed. The spirit was always something to be elevated and stirred, not besmirched. It was a kinder, gentler time, certainly a more respectful, courteous one, and the characters acted accordingly. Even Willie, the family dog, was happy to see the mailman and didn't race around annoying the neighbors. Scenes were often introduced by the notes of a pipe organ whose musical tone, unfortunately, sounded more like a circus calliope. Yet neither corny music nor shaky cameras mattered once the action commenced. As a domestic comedy, *Mama*'s humor was gentle, restrained, always laughing with characters and their situations, not at them.

Every program opened the same way as Katrin reminisced while leafing through the pages of her diary/family album, passing over photographs and notes that sparked golden memories—"I remember my brother Nels…and my little sister Dagmar…and, of course, Papa. But most of all, I remember Mama." As portrayed with warmth and dignity by Peggy Wood, strict but always loving Mama was the lynchpin around whom all the family members and their actions revolved. Papa, played with endearing peasant nobility by Judson Laire, was a carpenter who always worked very hard to provide for his family.

A rare candid shot taken during a meal break on the set of Mama. *Seated, left to right, are Judson Laire (Papa Hansen, in dark shirt by camera), director Ralph Nelson, Robin Morgan (Dagmar), Peggy Wood (Mama), Rosemary Rice (Katrin), Ruth Gates (Aunt Jenny), and Dick Van Patten (Nels), standing unglamorously with plate and fork in hand. Others are part of the CBS production staff.*

In "Dagmar and the Girl Scouts," an episode commem-
orating the 43rd anniversary of the Girl Scouts of
America, broadcast March 11, 1956, Mama (Peggy
Wood) is saluted by her daughter Dagmar (Robin Morgan), a newly initiated Girl Scout of 1916. It is Mama
who tries to tell her daughter that the ideals of scouting
include much more than the accomplishment of crafts
and household tasks.

Each family member had his or her turn at being the main focus of an episode, near the end of which Mama would always appear to dispense some warm and supportive Norwegian-American advice which would be the glue to seal up the problem. Papa and Mama, with their lilting Scandinavian "accents," were always seen in authentic Norwegian folk costumes, and great care was taken to create a believable atmosphere. For instance, Papa pronounced his j's like y's, so "Jenny" always came out "Yenny." Though the three children were quite Americanized, they were never very far from their roots and never made fun of their immigrant parents. Mama and Papa were strong, wise parental models to whom the children turned with respect, and these caring, listening elders rewarded their children with compassionate, earthy wisdom which helped solve all youthful dilemmas. The key was the heart, the heart was the family, and on *Mama,* family love and loyalty could bridge any gap and resolve any pain.

KEEPING YOUR WORD

Nels and his girlfriend decide to take summer jobs—he at an all-boys camp, she down the road at an all-girls camp. It's a grand idea they agree, both will make some money, and on their time off have a chance to deepen their romance. At Camp Cattawampus, Nels is introduced to his young charges by the camp's stuffy owner/director. The precocious youngsters carry on constantly, and Nels quickly realizes his job is not so easy. Always late for his after-hours rendezvous with his girlfriend and exhausted much of the time, Nels decides he must leave his job. His girlfriend decides to do the same since they both can hardly find time for their romance. When told he must put aside his break time to drive a camper to a doctor because of a medical emergency, Nels at first refuses. He then relents when reminded by the director that it's part of his obligation to put the welfare of the sick child before his own needs. At this very moment, Mama and Papa make a surprise visit and listen to their son's dilemma. While Mama tells Nels to follow his heart, Papa is stern about Nels keeping his word once he has given it. Later another camper informs

Patty McCormack (Ingeborg) won the title role in Broadway's The Bad Seed, *and every Friday night she would race from the CBS studio across town to the 46th Street Theatre where they would hold the curtain for the little star. Here she receives flowers at the stage door from* Mama *costar Kevin Coughlin.*

Nels that the owner is a poor businessman because he lets those whose families have no money spend their summer at the camp for free. Nels then sees his girlfriend and tells her he won't be leaving his job as planned. She tells him she has also had a change of heart and has decided to stay in her job as well. The closing scene shows the camp owner enjoying a barbecue at the Hansens'. Nels and Papa exchange stories with the man, as Mama quietly smiles at them....

Mama played successfully to TV audiences because of its excellent warmhearted scripts, careful direction, fine ensemble acting, and the powerful presence of popular stage star Peggy Wood.* A New York brahmin, Miss Wood could trace her proud heritage back to the Revolutionary War. She was born in Brooklyn, and her father was a socialist and a writer for the *New York World*, while her independent-spirited mother had been employed as a telegrapher and was self-reliant and self-determining long before her marriage.

Miss Wood revealed in an 1956 interview, "Each week as I get into the role, I'm reminded of my own mother. She's the secret of my portrayal of Mama. Mama believes in herself and in her children, and in being able to transmit her faith, she makes them strong and secure. But it starts with her own security. This quality I try to bring out in Mama. The Hansens have a good life, the way the Woods did. Perhaps it comes of going to church together on a Sunday and of taking simple pleasures in one another as a family. Fun came from simple enjoyments like gathering around the piano in the front parlor and singing songs. Mothers didn't pontificate then, they didn't have to preach—all they did was set a pattern and children followed suit because there was so much love on both sides."

In words that still ring true, Miss Wood added, "I feel sorry for children today—they don't have enough space to grow up in, and they have to depend too much on material things instead of inner resources and family love. I think that *Mama,* in showing how things were in the old days, makes them want to get back to the more solid emotions that flourished then. From the letters I get, I can see that our story makes the older people nostalgic, and it gives a sort of wistfulness to the young folks. They feel they are missing something and know instinctively that what they're missing would be good for them."

PAPA GOES TO SCHOOL

Papa must go to a special school to study for his citizenship exam, but is reluctant and embarrassed and unwilling to admit that a man of his age should have a need to go back to school. Mama decides to go in Papa's place, and each evening teaches him what she herself has learned so that he may finally pass the test and become an American citizen....

The great authenticity of the program was due primarily to writer Frank Gabrielson and to director Ralph Nelson (who would later graduate to films such as *Lilies of the Field, Charly,* and *Requiem for a Heavyweight*). Wood remembered looking forward to each week's new script because each was "so beautifully written. We had a feeling of security in them because they were so right. Never maudlin, never sticky."

Both Gabrielson and Nelson were of Scandinavian descent which helped lend authority and credence to the scripts and direction. Wood recalled that if Nelson felt something in the script didn't ring true, he would say, "But we don't do things like that in this family." Wood recounted to author Max Wilk in his excellent book, *The Golden Age of Television* (Delacorte Press, 1976): "...we always wanted it to be absolutely right. I remember when Carol Irwin, our producer, first suggested to me that I might play *Mama,* I decided first I'd better find out exactly how the lady would have sounded. I went to the Norwegian Information Bureau, and I said, 'Tell me about this accent—I don't want to sound like a Swede, or a Finn, or a stage German.' The head of the bureau said, 'There is a sound to this accent—you go *up* at the end, you see? English is a falling cadence, but Norwegian goes up. It is a very sweet accent...lilting.' Once I had the song of it, I was fine."

PLAYMATES

Dagmar's little playmate, David, is a stutterer, and none of the boys at school will play with him. Discerning that David's mother pushes him hard to emulate his brilliant father long dead, Mama gently

---

*During the 1952 summer break, Peggy Wood headed a tour with the entire TV cast in a play based on the series, written by Frank Gabrielson and directed by Ralph Nelson.

The most famous episode from Mama, "The Night the Animals Talked," a holiday story shown each year during Christmas week. Left to right are Judson Laire (Papa), Rosemary Rice (Katrin), Dick Van Patten (Nels), Peggy Wood (Mama), and in front, Judy Sanford (Hedvig, Mama's niece).

persuades David's mother to ease up on the youngster. Once she does, the boy flawlessly recites the 23rd Psalm on the school's Visitors Day, elating his mother and winning the admiration and acceptance of his peers....

Mama was a very stable production because the sponsor, General Foods, didn't want to do anything to change the recipe in a good mix. Producer, writer, director, cast were immune to network meddling, because in those days the sponsor called the shots. Wisely, General Foods didn't interrupt the body of the show with its Maxwell House Coffee commercials, and *Mama* played a continuous twenty-six minutes with no middle break. "That gave us a chance to build the story from beginning to end," said Wood. "Once we had the audience involved, we didn't lose them. *Ever.*"

JEALOUS MAMA

An opera singer Papa knew back in Norway before he married Mama visits San Francisco and invites her old flame and his family backstage after her performance. Mama is clearly jealous of the singer's attentions to Papa. But Papa quickly notices that she is not a caring mother to her own child, and tells Mama of his disappointment with the woman. She, unlike Mama, is no longer the sweet girl he once knew a long time ago back in the old country....

The actors were a close-knit group and all referred to one another by their show names, even offstage. There was neither argument nor temperament on the set. Miss Wood said in 1955, "Papa and I agree that six years of growing up with the Hansen youngsters have kept us on our toes. We are coaches in French, music, and composition. Our teenagers, Nels and Katrin, have solicited opinions ranging from boy and girl friends to university courses and finances.

NELS THE DANCER

Nels, enamored of a visiting Southern belle, decides to take dancing lessons to impress her with his "sophistication," and accepts lessons from a girlfriend of his younger sister, Dagmar. After much practice, Nels discovers, too late to save face, that he's been taught to dance backwards just like a girl. Out of the embarrassment from this situation comes a newfound humility. When Nels (Dick Van Patten) took a real-life bride, Papa ushered, Dagmar was junior bridesmaid, and Mama and Katrin played support in the front pew.

Max Wilk was an intimate of Peggy Wood because of his association with *Mama* as scriptwriter for the series in its later years. He was actually a protégé of producer Carol Irwin, who hired him in 1952, he remembered in his book, with the admonition, "It isn't an easy show to write. We never go in for quick plots, with contrived twists and turns, and easy solutions. We're dealing with honest characters, and our audience knows them and identifies with them. We keep playing off their actual experiences—and that's why, I think, we are keeping our audience."

CHRISTMAS EPISODE

No doubt the best-remembered episode of *Mama* was the Christmas show, repeated annually, with powerful religious overtones, readily acceptable to mass audiences in those days. It contains a touching, beautiful scene wherein Papa tells little Dagmar how the animals were given the gift of speech only for a few hours each Christmas Eve, as a heavenly reward for their protection and devotion to the Christ child in the stable in Bethlehem. Later, with all the house asleep, Dagmar slips out the door and passes to the stable to await the wondrous moment.

Unfortunately for devotees of *Mama*, few episodes other than the last thirteen shot on film remain in existence. Hopefully, like Gleason's "Lost Honeymooners" episodes, someone will someday reclaim some old *Mama* kinescopes, then restore and make them available on videotape. Until then, we, like Katrin, will fondly remember *Mama*.

CAST LIST

FAMILY: The Hansens

MEMBERS:

"Mama" Marta Hansen . . . . **Peggy Wood**
"Papa" Lars Hansen . . . . **Judson Laire**
Nels . . . . **Dick Van Patten**
Katrin . . . . **Rosemary Rice**
Dagmar (1949) . . . . **Iris Mann**
Dagmar (1950–56) . . . . . . **Robin Morgan**
Dagmar (1956–57) . . . . . . **Toni Campbell**
Aunt Jenny . . . . **Ruth Gates**
Uncle Chris (1949–51) . . . . **Malcolm Keen**
Uncle Gunnar Gunnerson . . . . . **Carl Frank**
Aunt Trina Gunnerson . . . . **Alice Frost**
T. R. Ryan (1952–57) . . . . **Kevin Coughlin**
Ingeborg (1953–57) . . . **Patty McCormack**

TIMEFRAME: **1949–57**
NETWORK: **CBS**
ADDRESS: **Steiner Street, San Francisco**

▶

"America's favorite couple" Ozzie and Harriet Nelson bookend their TV and real-life sons, David and Rick. They represented the exemplary happy, healthy, postwar American family living the mythological middle-class White Anglo-Saxon Protestant dream life somewhere in friendly suburbia. Back in the 1950s, there was nothing deceitful about blatantly plugging a sponsor's product, which Ozzie and David eagerly proved.

Harriet doles out a glass of milk for Ozzie who's about to join the boys in their raid on the cookie jar. Note her nifty apron sporting old-time homilies, and check out Ricky's crew-cut hair with a couple of dabs of slick on it. The Nelson kitchen circa 1955.

"Hi, Mom."
"Hi, Dave."
"Hi, Pop."
"Hi, Dave."
"Hi, Pop."
"Hi, Rick."
"Hi, Mom."
"Hi, Rick."

Such was the typical opening to *The Adventures of Ozzie and Harriet,* wherein the stars were usually exchanging mundanities with "the boys," their two real-life sons, David and Ricky. The Nelsons family "adventures" supposedly repre-sented those of the typical postwar middle-class suburban White Anglo-Saxon Protestant healthy family aiming at normalcy during the second "Era of Good Feeling" in American history. Ozzie and Harriet Nelson, known to radio audiences as "America's favorite couple," brought their family comedy to television after eight successful seasons on radio in 1952, the same year Dwight Eisenhower was elected President.

Life for Ozzie and Harriet and their two growing boys was minimalist at best. Yet for fourteen years on ABC and in syndication, their small and fairly unrealistic "adventures" were beloved by most sitcom-adoring Americans. The genius of *The Adventures of Ozzie and Harriet* is that little of any great consequence ever happened to disturb all the somnambulistic bliss. Ozzie had no real job and always seemed to be hanging around their neat, traditionally-furnished house at 822 Sycamore Road, Hillsdale, Anytown, U.S.A., wearing his ever-present cardigan sweater (both boys later adopted this regulation relaxed uniform). There Ozzie puttered and patiently waited, either in the kitchen or the den, for the boys or Harriet to walk in and present some sleepy crisis which he would help to solve by bungling through the first twenty-two minutes before coming up with a happy resolution after the final commercial break.

The action which moved the comedy often began with the tiniest, bare-bones idea that was then expanded exponentially. A classic Ozzie and Harriet script weaving all four family members together demonstrates each character's strength, and a variation on this kind of situation was done again and again on the program over the years. Here are portions of a radio script called "Invitation to Dinner" which was broadcast on Sunday, February 20, 1949, a special day for the Nelsons because it was the first time the part of David was played by David Nelson, age twelve, and the part of Ricky was played by Ricky Nelson, age eight.

This time it's tea on the patio at Ozzie and Harriet's real house on Camino Palmero in Los Angeles (their TV home was modeled on this house). This photo was taken in 1949 during O & H's radio days and some three years before the TV show began. Since they weren't on TV, Ricky (then age nine) was more concerned with getting cookies from his brother David (twelve) than with his slightly open zipper.

HARRIET: What's wrong David? You've hardly said a word all morning.

DAVID: It's nothing, Mom.

HARRIET: There's something bothering you...What is it?

DAVID: It's nothing, really, Mom.

HARRIET: David...

OZZIE: Harriet, please. You say it's nothing, David, is that right?

DAVID: That's right, Pop.

OZZIE: All right, if it's nothing, it's nothing...We'll just forget it. (Sighs.) Let's see what's here in the paper.

DAVID: (Pause.) Well...it *is* something.

OZZIE: Oh...(Puts paper down.) I kinda thought you'd like to tell us about it. What seems to be the trouble?

DAVID: It's...nothing, Pop.

OZZIE: Look, David...We're not trying to pry into your personal affairs, but why don't you just tell us about it. Maybe we can help you...

DAVID: It's kinda silly, I guess...Grace An-

derson invited me to her party Friday night and I told her I'd come.

HARRIET: That sounds very nice.

DAVID: Yeah, but our team is supposed to play basketball Friday night...So I gotta tell her I can't make it.

RICKY: Is David a dope, Pop?

OZZIE: No, Ricky, read your comic book. In other words, David, you mean you forgot you have to play basketball and that's why you accepted her invitation?

DAVID: Oh, no...I remembered it.

OZZIE: You mean when you accepted Grace's invitation you knew you couldn't make it...that it was the same night as your basketball game?

DAVID: Yessir.

RICKY: *Now* is David a dope, Pop?

HARRIET: Ricky!...Then why did you accept it, David?

DAVID: Well, golly, Mom, she seemed so excited about the party...I just didn't have the heart to disappoint her.

OZZIE: I realize how you must have felt, David...but you're going to have to tell her sometime and now it'll be a bigger disappointment. You'll find it's much better to

tell people the truth right off…Otherwise you wind up in an embarrassing situation for everybody.

RICKY: Are they gonna have ice cream at the party?

DAVID: Oh sure…gallons of it…That's another thing, Pop. I'd feel awful silly if I turned down the party and then the basketball game was called off.

HARRIET: Do you think that's possible?

RICKY: They never called one off yet.

DAVID: Oh, Ricky, you keep quiet.

OZZIE: Do you think it may be called off, David?

DAVID: I don't know…There's always a chance…lots of things could happen.

OZZIE: Like what?

DAVID: Well…suppose the captain of the other team gets the measles.

OZZIE: That sounds to me like a pretty remote possibility.

DAVID: Maybe not, Pop…A couple of weeks ago, we were supposed to take an arithmetic test and the teacher got the appendicitis.

OZZIE: That was just a rare coincidence…I think the safest thing for you to do is call Grace on the phone and tell her you can't make it.

DAVID: Maybe I could go to the party first and then play basketball.

HARRIET: I think you'd be too full of ice cream to play much of a game.

RICKY: He could be the basketball.

DAVID: I guess I'll think it over.

OZZIE: It's your problem, David…but you know the old proverb…Never put off until tomorrow what you can do today … Procrastination is the thief of time…

◀

By 1957, Ricky was growing into Rick and had become a major teen idol, second only to Elvis in female adoration. Known primarily as an acoustic guitarist, Rick also enjoyed smacking the skins on occasion. Here he solos on conga to the delight of five worshipful, young, very fiftyish femmes. Note the American primitive painting above the mantel, and Ozzie's sporting ducks.

HARRIET: Oh…

OZZIE: Were you going to say something, Harriet?

HARRIET: Yes…you did go downtown and pay the gas bill yesterday? You said you would.

OZZIE: I'm glad you mentioned that, Harriet…Here is a perfect example of the point I'm trying to make, David. Your mother asked me to pay the gas bill yesterday, and instead of putting it off until tomorrow, I'm going down and pay it today.

In one of the show's early TV episodes, Ozzie plans a pleasant nineteenth-wedding-anniversary dinner for Harriet and himself at a romantic eatery sans the boys. Problem is, Ricky's having a teen party on the same night, and what will the neighbors think if Ozzie and Harriet don't remain at home and chaperone? With minor grumbling (no Nelson ever really got steaming angry on the show—have you ever heard of that fearsome, boiling Swedish temper?), Ozzie and Harriet agree to chaperone and remain in their bedroom reminiscing about the good ol' days while Ricky and friends boogie downstairs. Suddenly, both notice how loud the silence has gotten. When they have made their descent in darkness to the stairwell bottom, the lights flash on and Ozzie and Harriet are surrounded by all their friends who've turned out for this surprise anniversary party deftly arranged by tricky Ricky and David. A more saccharine ending could not have been. A friend remarked during the writing of this chapter that the Ozzie and Harriet show presented life "the way it should be." Ozzie couldn't have said it better himself.

So here was this simplistic, bungling yet somehow always graceful, well-written show (generally by Ozzie himself) tied together with a knot of Tinkerbelle dust. Yet all America was mesmerized, authors included, hoodwinked weekly and loving it because Ozzie and Harriet and the boys had no real anxiety in their lives, and maybe we too could sleepwalk through Hillsdale every week and never have to wake up to the real world either.

Teenage cruisers are what Dave and Ricky were back in the early 1950s, and one way to cut loose was to head for freeways in Dave's little MG sports convertible. Both boys went through the traditional Southern California "speed" rites of passage. Ricky was strong on motorcycles for a time and rode a Velocette.

In a later episode, Harriet, shopping in a department store, buys a couple of old but not rare doubloons. At home, meanwhile, the boys are trying to convince Ozzie to go fishing with them because he has a car and theirs isn't running. Ozzie turns them down until Harriet gets home and reminds him of his promise to rake and spade the backyard to prepare for her new garden. Suddenly Ozzie can't get himself and the boys to the lake fast enough for a lazy afternoon of fishing. Foxy Har-

riet, who always eventually gets her way without ever raising her voice, cleverly buries the just-purchased doubloons a little below the surface of the ground where she insists Ozzie must begin digging her new garden. Lo! What does Ozzie find? "Harriet! Look! Treasure!" Soon, with half the back-yard dug up but no more coins, Ozzie takes the two doubloons down to the very same coin department where Harriet purchased them and quickly discovers the ruse. He then decides to turn the tables on Harriet, buys two other doubloons, and "discovers" them back in the yard. Now Harriet is frantically digging for treasure till Ozzie confesses he planted them. A tender peck on the cheek follows, and all is right. Incidentally, tender cheek pecks are about as far as anything even remotely resembling sex ever got. Nobody on television in the 1950s had sex. How could they what with all those slippers, pajamas, girdles, nightgowns, and robes, and those obligatory separate beds as well?

The Wizard was Oz, an unlikely-looking magician, yet the man had his finger on the pulse of America's ideal home-life fantasies. Oswald Nelson, born March 20, 1906 and bred in Teaneck, New Jersey, of Swedish Presbyterian ancestry, was the country's youngest Eagle Scout at thirteen. A Rutgers University football quarterback, law school graduate-turned-very-successful-thirties-bandleader, he married his girl singer, Harriet Hilliard on October 8, 1935. Harriet went on to a sporadic film career beginning with the Astaire-Rogers *Follow the Fleet* and worked occasionally in more "B movies" after that until 1945.

A self-described conservative Republican, Ozzie was a driven perfectionist who translated his personal vision of the happy American family into our hearts and minds at a time when self-examination and subconscious interview was taboo, when God and Communist-fearing Americans drowned their darknesses in martinis and by cheering Mickey

The happy American family in the 1950s watched television together in the den just like Ozzie and Harriet and David and Ricky did in their traditionally furnished home. Here, Rick displays a bit of his teen individuality wearing blue jeans, but is redeemed by his white bucks and argyle socks.

A popular ongoing cast member and perfect slapstick foil for the dreamy-eyed Rick and somnolent David was the irrepressible Wally, played by Skip Young (1957–66). Wally was almost always instigating some harebrained scheme involving shapely coeds, from which Dave or Rick ended up rescuing him. Here, Rick and Wally are appropriately in the kitchen, Wally's favorite room in any house.

Mantle. On *The Adventures of Ozzie and Harriet,* Ozzie conceived, produced, directed, and was story editor and head writer, while Harriet supervised the boys' wardrobes and was responsible for most of the original set decoration. Ozzie involved himself in every aspect of the program. Nothing appeared on the show that didn't have Ozzie's personal stamp of approval. The Nelsons' was a seamless, self-contained world, laughably safe, "Comedy Lite." It seemed fairly certain if the Nelsons could weather their silly little family crises, perhaps so could the rest of us.

When *The Adventures of Ozzie and Harriet* had its first telecast, October 3, 1952, David was three weeks shy of his sixteenth birthday and Ricky was twelve. In real life, David was more outgoing and could be a bit of a mischief maker, while Ricky was quiet and tended to keep to himself. But on the show, David invariably played straight man to precocious Ricky's one-liners, much as Ozzie did to Harriet's fast retorts. With David always the voice of reason, Ricky could be counted on to enter the scene all skinny and crew-cut, with a twinkle in his eyes and mischief up his sleeve, and all America waited to be charmed. Rick's cuteness was heightened by his use of funny malapropisms which Ozzie and the writers cleverly chose to keep in the scripts. When he began on radio at age eight, he would pronounce "usual" as "unusural," and it always got a guaranteed laugh. Rick's favorite program was, of course, "The Lone Stranger" and he longed to become a "Club Scout" like his older brother. Rick's catchphrase on the show, as written by Don Nelson (Ozzie's younger brother), fit him perfectly—"I don't mess around, boy."

The program, with initial episodes budgeted at $14,000 each (not counting story cost and performers' salaries), was filmed at General Service Studios in Hollywood, which was a convenient ten-minute drive from the Nelson home—a Colonial-style shingled house, white with green shutters—located on a street named Camino Palmero. Ozzie was quick to adapt to the demands of creating for television. Most early programs were rehashings of radio scripts which helped Ozzie build up a backlog so he wouldn't have to feel rushed when shooting. He learned to cut corners by doubling up on shots. For instance, if Harriet was filmed walking downstairs for one episode, Ozzie would have her change her dress and repeat the action for use in some later show, never having to change camera position or lighting.

Said Ozzie, in his autobiography *Ozzie by Ozzie Nelson* (Prentice Hall, 1973): "The set we built on Stage 5 at General Service was an exact replica of the front of our home (in fact, we sometimes photographed a long shot in front of our house and then moved to the studio for the closer shots), but the interior, although similar in general layout and furnishings, was quite different from our own home. Throughout the fourteen years we filmed the show, however, we spent so much time on the set that the boys often said it was difficult to figure which was our real home."

Broadcast television was still in its infancy in the early 1950s, and telecast quality varied widely from program to program. The four networks (Dumont was still a contender back then) all agreed that *flat* photography—filming with brightly lit backgrounds to afford little contrast and to minimize shadows and dark areas—was the best way to go. The original film crew, like most other TV crews in the early years, came from low-budget movie studios like Republic and Allied Artists, notable for grinding out "B" pictures at notoriously rapid rates. The theory was that these technicians were used to grinding out "quickies" on short schedules and could therefore meet the demands for the dizzying speed that television required.

ABC hired Volcano Productions (the show was later produced by Stage 5 Productions) and associate producer Leo Pepin to produce the show. After several months, Ozzie, upset with the continuing poor broadcast *look* of the program, decided the filming was the problem. Ozzie hired William Mellor, an Oscar-winning cinematographer (for *A Place in the Sun)*, and guaranteed him forty weeks at $1,000 per ($250 above then union scale), and allowed Mellor to bring along his own gaffer (background lighting man). By the second season, Ozzie noted. "We were paying higher salaries than the major studios, had assembled a crew of the finest, most talented people in the industry, and our photography and overall production values were the equivalent of any 'A' motion picture."

Ozzie and Mellor ignored the "flat" lighting edict, but soon realized the problem lay not with the cinematography but with the transmission of the broadcast "picture" to the rest of the country. In the studio, a film projector was aimed at a white wall; a TV camera shot the projected image which was broadcast to a transmitter that then flashed it to sets in living rooms across the country. Ozzie found, much to his dismay, that a studio technician

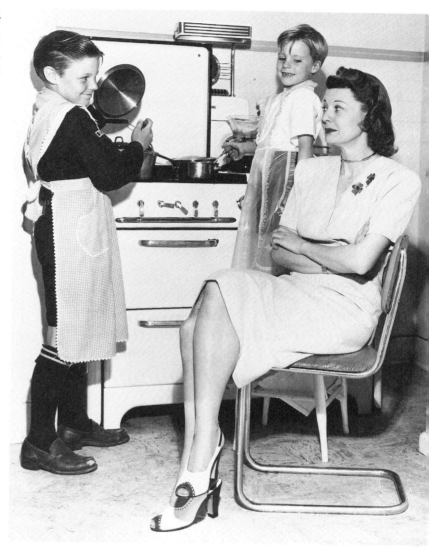

A publicity shot from the Nelsons' radio days. Both aproned boys do their best to give mom a break from slaving over a hot stove. David's a noble lad in his cub scout uniform replete with scuffed loafers, while Ricky does his cooking from atop a high stool, as the smiling, ever unperturbable Harriet looks on.

was adjusting the contrast of the picture according to his "own personal taste." By contrasting the image too sharply, he often obliterated some of the actors' faces. Ozzie and Leo Pepin devised ways to distract the errant union technician while their cohorts frantically adjusted the image being transmitted. Ozzie and Pepin kept on correcting the problem as best they could until technology caught up to them.

With eighteen Top Ten hits between 1957 and 1972, Rick Nelson needed no guitar with his name stamped on it to identify him. Rick was the first teen rock star "created" by television, when Ozzie cleverly used the show as a forum to carefully groom his son's popularity with young female viewers into an immense, for a time, musical career. Here, Rick and his combo perform on the show, circa 1959.

Perfectionist Ozzie continued to be involved in all aspects of the production including mixing the laughs and the music on the soundtrack. Crew members once gifted Ozzie with a framed plaque containing honorary membership cards in all the unions involved in creating the show. Within a short time, Ozzie had renegotiated the Nelsons' ten-year contract with ABC, and the family received almost $300,000 per year, with the boys earning $1,100 per week which went directly into trust funds.

No family show of the 1950s dared break ground concerning sex; however, Ozzie was particularly proud that he and Harriet were the first television couple to ever be shown sleeping together in a double bed. This "liberalism" never translated to the lifestyles of the boys, whose college campus antics were more reminiscent of Ozzie's raccoon coat days at Rutgers than of David's own fraternity at USC. David and Ricky never hung out at "the malt shop," but, like all young Southern Californians, preferred the local drive-in.

Within a few years, David was off to college to study law (just as Ozzie had done in real life), and by 1956, Rick had grown from a skinny, gangling youth into a teenage heartthrob. When Elvis Presley revolutionized early rock 'n' roll, Rick's interest in that music soared. Rick by then was playing drums, piano, and guitar, following in the musical footsteps of his onetime bandleader father.

Ozzie is arguably the father of the modern music video, having created the first "conceptual" music visualization to accompany Rick's singing of his biggest selling single, "Travelin' Man," in the spring of 1961. For a change, instead of having Rick and the band lip-synch the song in front of a group of screaming/swooning fans on the show, Ozzie headed into the editing suite and began superimposing images of Rick's face over some stock travelogue footage—all this twenty years before the rise of MTV.

"My dad loved all kinds of music, even rock 'n' roll," recalled David on the Disney Channel's cable TV tribute to the Nelsons in the mid-eighties. "I don't know if he ever knew the real reason Rick wanted to make a record." On the same program, Rick recounted the story of a date he had with a girl

Eric Hilliard Nelson, blue-eyed, blonde-haired, freckle-faced, and braces on his teeth, and all of twelve years old, circa 1952. Who would have suspected that within five years his fame and record sales would rival Elvis Presley.

who was carrying on about Elvis. "So I was taking her home…and Elvis's record came on the radio, and she did this whole thing about Elvis. I thought, 'I've got to say something,' so I said, 'Well, I'm going to make a record.' And she laughed, thought that was real funny. I thought, 'Well, I'm gonna make a record even if it's one record, and I'm going to hand it to her and say, 'Now laugh.'"

Rick re-tuned an old Fats Domino song called "I'm Walkin'" and Ozzie, no fool, witnessing the tremendous impact of rock 'n' roll on kids, wisely had Rick sing it at the end of a show. Within one week, "I'm Walkin'" had sold one million copies.

In a classic understatement, Rick later noted, "That's where the whole thing about the power of television comes in." For the next several years, Rick invariably would close an episode, with a song, whereby Ozzie assured the series of an ongoing audience of loyal young viewers. Rick

When she wasn't causing teenage "male" hearts to flutter as Thalia Menninger on The Many Loves of Dobie Gillis, *gorgeous Tuesday Weld was breaking hearts guest-starring on a host of TV shows during the late fifties and early sixties. Here, Weld's surrounded at a record "hop" by Harriet, David and Rick, in the episode "The Other Guy's Girl," broadcast April 8, 1959.*

went on to sell sixty million records and remains among the all-time record sellers. Until Elvis went into the Army, Rick was his strongest teen idol rival. Of course, Rick had the built-in advantage of a weekly TV series in which Ozzie would cleverly arrange to show groups of teenage girls swooning over his son, the rocker. In one episode, Ozzie parodied himself supposedly standing off-camera pressing his fingers to his cheeks and pushing up to create a grotesque-looking smile. This was a signal to Rick, onstage singing, all bedroom-eyed, doing his best imitation of Elvis's curled-lip sneer, and he can't be bothered to follow Ozzie's stage directions. Where Elvis was downright sexual and therefore dangerous, Rick was "dreamy" and "clean-cut" and decidedly not a threat to white Middle America. Within six weeks of the release of "I'm Walkin'," Rick's fan mail topped 6,000 letters per week, and within three months, he had 1,000 fan clubs across the country. The power of television, indeed.

By the late 1950s, both boys had grown into handsome young men. David had dropped out of USC and was pursuing a film-acting career while still appearing on the show as a happily married attorney (a career in law just as Ozzie would have pursued had not show biz beckoned). David's TV wife was, of course, played by his real-life wife, former *Playboy* Playmate, June Blair. As the show wound down in the 1960s, Rick joined Dave's law firm as his clerk, while Rick's real-life wife, the former Kristin Harmon—daughter of football great, Tom, and sister of athlete-turned-hunk/actor, Mark)—joined the cast as, of course, his TV spouse. (Who says nepotism doesn't work?)

By 1966, the Beach Boys and the Beatles had taken LSD, the Vietnam debacle was escalating, and the Eisenhower/Nixon days of innocence were all but gone. Cancelled by ABC at the end of the 1966 season after fourteen years, *The Adventures of Ozzie and Harriet* had enjoyed the most successful run for a family sitcom in television history. A record milestone which, likely, will never be broken. A sure testament to one man's powerful vision which helped shape, for better or worse, the vision of a whole generation of television viewers.

In 1987, David directed a special for the Disney Channel entitled, "A Brother Remembers." This warm reminiscence about the family and the show is an affectionate tribute by a brother mourning the loss of a brother and celebrating him through a legacy of images. David is quoted in Joel Selvin's *Ricky Nelson—Idol for a Generation,* saying: "In our family, there was no generation gap, and I think it's too bad, because I was a little old man at thirteen. I was polite, tried never to offend anyone, and I felt this great responsibility, because I wasn't just me, I was a quarter of a thing. Whatever I did, I felt the burden of three other people and all the crew who worked on the show. I wasn't a truck driver's son who could go out and bust people if he got mad."

Ozzie Nelson died in 1975. Harriet makes occasional guest appearances on TV series (one with her granddaughter Tracy on *The Father Dowling Mysteries*), and David directs and sometimes acts on television and in films.

THE TRAGEDY OF RICK NELSON

In the years since Rick Nelson's tragic death in a plane crash on New Year's Eve 1985, much has been rumored about his use of cocaine, alcohol, and other drugs to soothe his supposedly broken spirit. Born into show business royalty and a star early on, Rick, it's been suggested, was never prepared to cope with a life without consistent fan adulation, easy sexual conquests, and a domineering father who made all his important life decisions for him. In his book on Ricky, Joel Selvin asserts Rick couldn't live up to the "straight arrow" image of his father, and was troubled that he was never "taken seriously" as a musician, although he had had Top Ten hits every year from 1957 to 1963, more hits than Buddy Holly or the Everly Brothers. It is also stated in the book that Rick "hated" the TV show because it wasn't "cool." Much has been said about his rocky marriage to Kris Nelson and his estrangement from his four children, daughter Tracy, son Sam, and twins Gunnar and Matthew. Selvin says Rick rarely saw his children, and they were raised by housekeepers.

His family lived in Errol Flynn's former seven-bedroom Hollywood mansion. Rick's bedroom offered a spectacular panoramic view of the San Fernando Valley, yet according to author Selvin, he covered all the windows with tinfoil and newspaper to keep out the light and often slept all day. After his divorce, and in the last ten years of his life, Rick spent three hundred nights per year performing at venues which included county fairs and steak-and-lobster houses. The reason, according to Selvin, was his need to maintain $30,000 per month in alimony, child support, and for other expenses, which left him broke and $1 million in debt at the time of his death.

Details in the book suggest Kris was not an ideal mother, which prompted a custody fight for control of the children by her brother, Mark Harmon, and Mark's wife, Pam Dawber. Though much is made of the seamy side of Nelson's life based on scores of interviews with friends and associates—the Nelson family would not talk with Selvin, save David, who denies Rick ever took drugs—much praise is

By the 1960s, the boys had cruised out of teenagedom and were headed for more "toned down" adventures like adulthood and marriage. David had graduated from college and was a practicing attorney who hired his younger brother to be his law clerk. Ever obedient to Ozzie's unwritten rule to keep things in the family, David married former Playboy playmate June Blair (left) who, naturally played his wife on the show. When Rick married Kris Harmon, she also played herself on the series.

heaped on his music. Selvin, music critic for the San Francisco Chronicle, says, "His Stone Canyon Band was, without a doubt, the predecessor to the Eagles; it had a bit of Creedence Clearwater in it and even pre-Fleetwood Mac." Unquestionably, his best records rank with the best of the early California country rock scene. Happily, Rick's children are doing well. Tracy has worked pretty steadily as an actress, and costarred in two TV series, Square Pegs and The Father Dowling Mysteries, while Gunnar and Matthew have their own rock band, Nelson, and are enjoying immense record sales, much as their beloved father did at the beginning of his rock 'n' roll career.

CAST LIST

FAMILY: The Nelsons

MEMBERS:

Ozzie . . . . **Ozzie Nelson**
Harriet . . . . **Harriet Nelson**
David . . . . **David Nelson**
Eric "Ricky" . . . . **Rick Nelson**

SIGNIFICANT OTHERS:

"Thorny" Thornberry
  (1952–58) . . . . **Don Defore**
Darby (1955–61) . . . . **Parley Baer**
Joe Randolph (1956–66) . . . . . **Lyle Talbot**
Clara Randolph
  (1956–66) . . . . **Mary Jane Croft**
Wally (1957–66) . . . . **Skip Young**
Doc Williams (1954–65) . . . . . **Frank Cady**
Connie Edwards
  (1960–66) . . . . **Constance Harper**
Fred (1958–64) . . . . **James Stacy**
Ginger (1962–65) . . . . . **Charlene Salerno**
June (Mrs. David Nelson)
  (1961–66) . . . . **June Blair Nelson**
Kris (Mrs. Rick Nelson)
  (1964–66) . . . . . . **Kristin Harmon Nelson**

TIMEFRAME: **1952–66**
NETWORK: **ABC & CBS**
ADDRESS: **822 Sycamore Rd.**
                  Hillsdale, USA

435 episodes

Before making the leap from radio to television, media mastermind Ozzie decided Americans should be visually introduced to "radio's favorite family" via the big motion picture screen. It was a smart move indeed, as Here Come the Nelsons *was a big hit. The 1952 film also featured the talents of young, up-and-coming Rock Hudson.*

TV-3841-9

Perhaps the most famous picture of family togetherness from any family comedy/drama is this of patriarch Robert Young and his TV brood on Father Knows Best. The original press photo caption reads: "Though Thanksgiving Day fare be meager hamburgers, the Anderson family offers silent prayer in thanksgiving." This episode was broadcast November 21, 1954. Left to right are Lauren Chapin, Billy Gray, Robert Young, Jane Wyatt, and Elinor Donahue.

Life in the Anderson den is about a perplexed and paint-daubed father trying to explain the mysteries of football to his shoulder-padded, paint-stained son, while his youngest daughter is bedazzled by an old stuffed and mounted owl.

Some minor light-classical music chords herald there's something "important" about to happen, yet the television screen is filled only with a black and white still shot of a "typical" suburban home, trees in the front yard and a white picket fence harmoniously denoting the boundaries between the home and the whole world beyond it. Then we are inside the front door of this house and a neatly attired, pleasant looking man with graying hair is checking the time on his wristwatch. Now the soundtrack is filled with a brassy, happy theme that seems to shout, "How wonderful this world is and how happy the family this theme represents." An off-camera voice announces that this is *Father Knows Best* starring Robert Young, who now looks up into the camera smiling…Jane Wyatt, the camera pans to her hefting Young's briefcase into his hand, and after which he pulls his devoted wife to him and bends to kiss her. Yet just as his lips are about to touch hers...giggling spills from across the room and the screen fills with three happy, healthy, super clean children clutching the stair bannister. In descending order they are Lauren Chapin (Kathy "Kitten" Anderson, the youngest daughter), Billy Gray (James "Bud" Anderson Jr.) and Elinor Donahue (Betty "Princess" Anderson), smiling and just a bit embarrassed by the display of affection being shown by their father, Jim Anderson. This is, after all, the "I Like Ike" 1950s, the second era of good (not overtly sexual—that would come in the sixties) feeling.

Jim Anderson is not a secret drinker (although in real life Robert Young is a recovered alcoholic). "Princess" Betty is not a nymphomaniac, and Bud is not a closet gay. "Kitten" Kathy is not a drug addict (in real life, however, Lauren Chapin did suffer through years of drug addiction). Mother is certainly not hooked on diet pills and is not having an illicit affair with the milkman.

This is the good life—safe from war (but not the subliminal Cold War) and unhappiness. Jim Anderson (of Scottish descent, no doubt; the name means "son of Andrew"), and his family live on South Maple Street, Springfield, somewhere in the midwest. He is manager of the General Insurance Company (generally assuring everybody, including viewers, that everything is going to be okay at the end of twenty-six minutes). Jim is wise and calm, feisty and sometimes quick at the lip, manly but not macho, affectionate but not slobberingly sentimental, softly righteous but not pious and holier-than-thou, always ready and able to apologize truthfully but not a wimp; in short—pretty much all things to all people, and pretty darn good at doing just about anything including regularly cleaning up his act and everyone else's in each episode. A hell of a guy.

In the earliest press release for the show, a Robert Young biography dated September 16, 1954, there's a caricature of the five main characters—a smiling Young standing with arms crossed, while his wife and three children are all on their knees, eyes closed, and each with his hands clasped

This is a frozen moment from the famed opening sequence of Father Knows Best, *when Margaret hands her husband Jim his briefcase and he readies to kiss her before marching off to work. According to the original caption, Young is congratulating Jane Wyatt for winning her Best Actress Emmy Award for her thesping on the series.*

Slapstick comedic relief on the show was usually the domain of disarmingly precocious Lauren Chapin, then only eight. Kathy "Kitten" Anderson, "outer-space helmet and all, proves that even a space fledgling must pause for daydreams," according to the original photo caption In real life, Chapin would be first to admit that she acted like a space cadet during the immediate years after the show ended.

together as if in worshipful bliss of all-knowing Father. However, in the "reel life" of the TV show, Father is always well respected but certainly not worshipped. Much to the credit of Young and partner, Eugene B. Rodney, producer of the series, all the family members were written as finely chiseled characters who are three-dimensional (certainly in comparison to Ozzie and Harriet and just about all other sitcom families living a so-called average middle-American life in 1950s TV land). Jim and Margaret Anderson and their three children had *real* emotions and were unafraid to display them. Like most real-life parents, both had tempers and on occasion they lost their cool. Robert Young had a smooth, seamless quality to his acting and was absolutely believable in his role. The stories always revolved around his uncanny but always seemingly "normal" ability to make things right.

In an episode entitled "Margaret Learns to Drive," Bud is marveling at his parents' ability to get through their marriage always in a state of bliss. In the opening scene, setting up the premise why Mom needs to learn how to drive, we see the Andersons at their breakfast table but there's no morning toast or eggs. Father comes in, learns of the provisions shortage, and takes it all good-naturedly. The kids can't understand why he isn't annoyed. Bud reminds him of a neighbor's dad who is very testy in comparison.

BUD: You and Mom seem to have an understanding about everything.
FATHER: That's right, we do.
(Jim explains that the reason there were no eggs and bread is that Margaret had no one to drive her to the store.)
BUD: How come you never learned to drive, Mom?
MARGARET: Never had any reason to with two gallant men in the family.
KITTEN: Other kids' mothers drive around.
BUD: Everyone but Mom.
MARGARET: Alright, I'll drive. When do I get the ten easy lessons?
JIM: Honey, I've told you any number of times whenever you want to learn, I'll be glad to teach you.

Later that afternoon, Jim returns home in his usual cheerful mood and notices Bud looking very glum.

> BUD: She's going to have her first driving lesson today, and she sits there like it was nothing.
> MARGARET: First I have something more important to do.
> BUD: What?
> MARGARET: Kiss your father.
> JIM: Excuse me, Bud. (Jim and Margaret kiss).
> BUD: How can you two be so lovey-dovey after you've been married so long?
> JIM: With a woman like your mother, it's easy.

Of course, the driving lesson is a fiasco—Margaret doesn't really understand all the little doohickeys (even though it's a 1957 Ford with an automatic transmission). She backs up too fast, doesn't watch where she's going, etc. By the time they get home, Jim and Margaret are barely speaking. The kids come down and don't realize they have been fighting, but praise them for behaving like "mature, civilized people. We should give thanks to heaven each night that we have parents who don't bicker and quarrel. We realize how lucky we are." Jim and Margaret look embarrassed and ashamed (shame always played a part in this family, as some family member was always out of sync with the others and, by example, could be mildly "shamed" back into good behavior). Later that evening, Jim and Margaret are reading for sleep in their bedroom—with the requisite separate twin beds.

> JIM: What got into us, anyhow? We never jawed at each other like that before. How do you account for it? Is there some chemical change that takes place in a person as soon as they get in the seat of a car?
> MARGARET: Chemical, psychological or what. Something happened.
> JIM: You've never been as dumb as you were this afternoon.
> MARGARET: I'm not defending myself, dear.

Betty "Princess" Anderson half-heartedly struggles to keep eager Jerry Preston (Ron Ely, later TV's "Tarzan") from kissing her on their first date! *From the episode "Crisis Over a Kiss," broadcast February 16, 1959.*

Jim and Margaret celebrate twenty years of wedded bliss with a second wedding and a honeymoon which gets a misspelled send-off from the youngsters in the episode "Second Wedding," broadcast November 3, 1958.

The photo caption here read:"Elinor Donahue will be seen twice in a forty-eight hour period on two different programs on CBS-TV. At left, in her familiar role as Betty Anderson on Father Knows Best, 11/1/60, and at right as Miss Ellie on The Andy Griffith Show, 10/31/60."

But you've never been as impossible as you were this afternoon.

JIM: Maybe when the husband and wife change places in a car it upsets the cosmic balance of things.

MARGARET: You were probably just tired.

JIM: Well, that's probably the simple answer.

In the final scene, because father knows best, of course, Jim has hired an instructor from a professional driving school to give Margaret lessons. The children and Jim watch happily as she drives away.

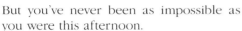

BETTY: Father, I don't understand this at all.

JIM: Well, Princess, I really don't understand it myself. It has something to do with chemistry or black magic. I don't know.

BETTY: But, father....

JIM: There are some things you can't teach the person closest to you. One of them is driving a car. Now, with a professional teacher, your mother will do just fine. Just take my word for it. It's better this way.

Jim, Bud, Betty, and Kathy all smile, then hear the sound of screeching tires and a crash. They turn to one another gazing in bewilderment. Fade to black and theme music.

So Robert Young, his directors, writers, and producers all understood, even back in 1957, that the world is a chaotic place especially when women are learning to drive in it. *Father Knows Best* showed problem-solving in less complex time. There were always respectful boundaries between family members, and the common expectation was that through mutual love and respect (though at times family members could look selfish and disrespectful, but not for too long) timely solutions could be found. It was a rare moment in the Anderson household that any member ever went to bed either angry or hungry. Margaret was every bit as capable as her knowing Jim, and though rarely out of her apron, was womanly wise and competent and never a second-class citizen. The children

43

could be self-centered and smug at times, but that was more representative of their ages rather than the times. When the show had its debut on October 3, 1954, Betty was seventeen, Bud was fourteen, and Kathy was nine.

The origins of the show are based on the true-life fathering experiences of Robert Young and partner Eugene B. Rodney. "Nearly every time Bob and I met," recalled Rodney, who first met Young in 1935 when they were working with Edward Small Productions, "he'd start the conversation with, 'That Barbara,' then as the years went on, 'That Betty,' then, finally, 'That Kathy.'

"When Bob and I got around to talking about a radio show for him, it seemed only natural that it jelled into a family series with a couple of girls and a boy. (Young remarked at the time: "The only way I could get a son was to have one written into the script.") Between the two of us, we kicked around enough truths and all-out bragging about our children to make a hundred scripts."

Young recalls that during his film studio days at Metro-Goldwyn-Mayer, "I was always telling people what Kathy [his youngest daughter, born 1945] had done, and it got so they'd ask me if I had any new Kathy stories. One day, I told Eugene that Kathy and I had an argument and that I tried to end it by telling her: 'Never you mind. Father knows best.'"

In 1946, the men became partners in Rodney-Young Enterprises and launched the radio version of *Father Knows Best* in the fall of 1949, with Ed James creating the characters and writing the scripts.* It was a very popular radio program and was commended many times by the national Parent-Teachers Association for its wholesomeness.

Rodney and Young began selecting a cast for the transition from radio to television in 1954. Jane Wyatt was Rodney's one and only choice for Margaret, and after some initial coaxing, she accepted. A total of fifty-eight boys were auditioned before sixteen-year-old Billy Gray became "Bud." Rodney thought Gray possessed the facial characteristics and coloring of his TV dad, and also had "a teenage

boy's abstraction, not flipness" and the ability to "say the gag lines—the Bud-isms—flat, able to resist a 'this-is-a-joke-see?' lilt." Pretty Elinor Donahue was seventeen, and all agreed she was perfect to play Betty, who was supposed to be "attractive, but not sophisticated," said Rodney. Casting Kathy, the youngest child, required sixty-eight auditions (including Young's own daughter, Kathy, upon whom the character was based) before nine-year-old Lauren Chapin won the role.

Seven writers contributed scripts at the beginning: Roswell Rogers, Dorothy Cooper, Phil Davis, and the team of Harry Clark, Sumner Long and Paul West, along with Ed James. Rogers and West also wrote the radio version's scripts for two years. After more than one hundred scripts, writer/originator Ed James had a falling out with Rodney and quit, before the program made the switch from radio to television. When the show hit the air, James began receiving a $250 royalty every time one of his scripted programs was broadcast, and his name appears in the credits of each of the 203 episodes and the two reunion shows.

Fathers abounded on the set: Young had four children, director Peter Tewksbury also had four, while producer Rodney had two. Ironically, all three "Anderson" children came from broken homes. The TV family quickly grew very close and in many ways acted like a real family. Donahue, Gray, and Chapin saw Young more regularly than their real fathers. The cast spent an average of fifty hours per week together at the Anderson "home." The home set was built for $40,000 and had two floors, a patio, driveway, and garage sprawling across Stage 10 at the Columbia Pictures studios. Screen Gems Inc., a subsidiary of Columbia, owned fifty percent of the program, while Rodney-Young Inc. owned the other half. Screen Gems financed the pilot film that won the first sponsor, Kent Cigarettes. The first season the show cost $265-per-hour to film, with Rodney running a very tight ship.

"There's nothing that'll grow ulcers faster than trying to do a show with children," Rodney remarked to the *Saturday Evening Post* in 1957. "For the same reason, I stay seventeen shows ahead of air dates [in those years they filmed between thirty-seven and forty episodes per season]. And the harmony on the set is planned. If you see a

*In the radio version, June Whitley was Margaret, Rhoda Williams was Betty, Ted Donaldson was Bud, and Norma Jean Nilsson was Kathy.

crabby electrician or grip man around, look close. He won't be here tomorrow."

Many scripts contained what Rodney called "built-in moral lessons." In one show, Betty told her father that her class had decided that selfishness motivates all human actions. Jim responded by telling her he thought the housepainter he had hired would not sacrifice his personal ideals concerning his craftsmanship. (How innocent those 1950s were.) To prove his point, Jim told the painter to use low-grade paint because he was going to sell the house—and was taken aback when the painter, disenchanted with Jim, pretended to agree. The man later lectured Margaret and the children on integrity, refusing to use cheaper paint, and scolded Jim. Jim accepted the man's admonition and happily shook his hand, gratified that his faith in man's basic integrity had been vindicated.

Part of creator/writer Ed James's objections to the TV version was his judgment that the show had too "much heartthrob and morals." Producer Rodney, on the other hand, openly wept while he would supervise the sound dubbing and insertion of the laugh tracks. "If I ever get a director so cynical," he bristled in 1957, "that he can't feel it deep in his heart when a little girl places a crippled sparrow in a nest and then goes upstairs to her room and prays to God that the sparrow lives—why, I fire him!"

The first sixty-two episodes were directed by William Russell, a big man who wept as easily as Rodney. Young says the cast used to gauge the effectiveness of any sentimental scene by looking at Russell after he yelled "Cut!" If the director's cheeks were covered with tears, they knew all was well. When Russell left for a higher-paying job, the cast turned to script girl Winnie Gibson as their sentiment barometer. The cast then began rating scripts in terms of "WCs," which stood for Winnie Cries."

The one real part of the set was the kitchen. There was only one bedroom, and it featured interchangeable papered walls which were made

▶

Margaret Anderson (Jane Wyatt), left, and her daughter Betty (Elinor Donahue) gang up on the head of the household, Jim (Robert Young), who looks on in astonishment as they swallow up his soda float, in the episode "Love and Learn" on Father Knows Best, *broadcast April 11, 1960.*

Does father always know best? Margaret isn't quite sure that Jim, with apron and rolled-up sleeves, is up to the task of brushing the kitchen cabinets while holding that sloppy looking paint can. This clearly looks like one of those tasks that father wasn't in a big hurry to get around to doing.

The immensely popular Father Knows Best *series spawned two reunion sequels almost two decades later. In this shot, Robert Young dons a Santa Claus outfit, while Jane Wyatt does the same sans whiskers in* Father Knows Best: Home for Christmas, *which was broadcast as part of NBC's "The Big Event" on Sunday, December 18, 1977.*

realizes the task of toting a heavy bundle of papers around on his bicycle and delivering them in a timely fashion to areas far from his neighborhood is more than he can handle. At first proud, Jim is quickly let down when Bud wants to "give up without really trying hard." Bud protests he can't complete his paper route, his tasks at home, and his homework and still be an effective human. He feigns illness, but Jim insists Bud must "keep his word." Finally, when Jim sees Bud dropping from sheer exhaustion and frustration on a rainy day, he decides *he* will deliver Bud's remaining papers for him. Quickly Jim learns how tough a task it really is to deliver soggy papers in the rain and to have to deal with an array of not-too-pleasant customers. (Jim, in the series, manages an inordinate time away from his insurance business.) Hours later, a soaking Jim knocks on the final door and asks the ornery owner to use the telephone to call Margaret to come and rescue him. Finally Margaret shows up in a yellow rain slicker and hat, looking like an angel of mercy. Jim is so thrilled his day of misery is at an end, he grabs his dear wife, they fall onto the wet grass, and he kisses her as passionately as he can under the impossible situation (and the wholesome constraints of 1950s television). When they get home, Jim apologizes to Bud for being overbearing and misunderstanding about the difficulties his son faced. This was one of the better episodes of the whole series as it exemplified the ideals of communication, affection, and loyalty in the family unit. It also gave Young an opportunity to get out of his usual "at home" characterizations. He gets wet, cold, and angry, and really displays his frustration in a sublimely human and un-1950s television way.

PRINCESS GOES TO COLLEGE

It's Betty's turn to be the outsider. Betty is graduating from high school and readying for college but hasn't made her final selection. Margaret and Jim excitedly recommend their alma mater and immediately plan a visit with Betty in tow. Throughout the drive to the school, they babble on about their fond college days. Once on

to look like whichever bedroom was called for in the script. The ritual every morning was that Bud's stand-in brewed a fresh pot of coffee for the cast. Everyone would chip in for coffee and a tray of fresh rolls. Lunches were kept in the Anderson refrigerator. If any script called for a meal, Rodney insisted that actual food be used.

In one of the earliest episodes, "Father Delivers the Paper Route," Young got an opportunity to relive some of his boyhood experiences. (As a youth, he actually sold and delivered papers for three years around the West Adams district of Los Angeles.) In this *FKB*, Bud ambitiously takes on his own paper route, both to earn his own money and to assert himself. No sooner does he start than he campus, Jim and Margaret rush about recalling their first meeting and the blossoming of their romance. In the meantime, Betty grows increasingly alienated from them and the school. When they introduce Betty to an old friend who is the school advisor, he wisely notes her withdrawn state and takes Margaret and Jim aside to explain that their daughter's feelings about the college are distinctly different from theirs. Brought back to reality by the chat, Jim apologizes to Betty for forgetting about her individuality and need to make her own choices based on her own feelings. In *Father Knows Best*, the lambs, both child and adult, may stray from home and good judgment, but never very far and never for very long.

ROBERT YOUNG

Born February 22, 1907, in Chicago, Robert Young is the son of an Irish immigrant carpenter father and Scots mother. One of five children, Young began working at eight as a helper in a grocery. The family settled in Los Angeles when he was ten. After high school, he held an assortment of jobs: truck driver, grease monkey, soda jerk, in the press room of the *Los Angeles Times,* bank teller, loan collector, and in a brokerage office until the stock market crash of 1929. At the urging of his former high school drama teacher, he began studying acting in earnest at the Pasadena Playhouse. Young broke into movies as an extra, but his mainstay was stage work. He won a screen test and then an MGM contract in 1931. He received his first credit on loan out to 20th Century-Fox that year for *The Black Camel,* a Charlie Chan film. His first important role was as the son of Helen Hayes in *The Sin Of Madelon Claudet* (also 1931). He's since made well over one hundred films and television movies. Young's favorite role came in 1945 when he costarred with Dorothy McGuire in the romantic drama *The Enchanted Cottage.*

Young began a parallel career in radio in 1936, which led finally to the radio version of *Father Knows Best* in 1949 and lasting five years. During that time, he was active in the radio portion of a national campaign to reduce highway accidents

A dapper Robert Younger in the early 1950s looking quite the handsome movie star. A movie star from the early 1930s on, yet mostly in "B" feature films as a reliable if unglamorous leading man (MGM mogul Louis B. Mayer once groused that Young "has no sex appeal" and that's why he usually didn't get the girl). What Young may have lacked in sex appeal he made up for in endurance. Young became a "A" star in television with two immensely popular series, Father Knows Best (1954–60) and Marcus Welby, M.D. (1969–76).

among teenage drivers, and he spoke at high schools and to civic groups around the country. As a result, there were five million members of the Robert Young Good Drivers Club in 1954. Young had a very personal reason for his participation in the safe driving campaign; his father had been killed by a drunken teenage driver.

Young has been married to his high school sweetheart, Betty Henderson, since 1933. It is Hollywood's most enduring marriage. Young fathered four girls: Carol, Barbara, Betty Lou, and Kathy. After the birth of Kathy, Young received a telegram from famed comic Eddie Cantor, the father of five girls; it read: "Copycat."

Although Young began his career as the perennial "Tennis anyone?" youthful fop, he quickly earned a reputation as a solid, reliable "good guy" leading man, which obviously helped carry him over into his "everybody's dad" Jim Anderson, and later Marcus Welby, M.D., characterizations. Yet, unknown to his public, Young was filled with self-doubt and anxiety, plaguing him with constant headaches and leading to a three-decade bout with alcoholism. "For over thirty years, I lived almost every waking hour filled with fear. Fear of many things—the unknown, of some expected calamity around the corner that never comes. A feeling that this stardom I was lucky enough to attain would not last, that I was not worthy, that I didn't deserve it." To quiet the pain, to ease the fear, Young admitted in 1971, "I drank, and I drank a lot." It took four long years, but Young, with the help of Alcoholics Anonymous, brought his drinking problem under check.*

Ironically, on *Father Knows Best,* neither Jim nor Margaret Anderson smoked or drank. "We never wanted to call attention to it," said Young in 1956. "To make a point of it would be moralizing, and that's the last thing we want to do." Young always considered the show to be entertainment and has never cared for the criticism it's received over the years for not being realistic. "So what's realistic? Drugs and such? Had the producers chosen to portray tragedy as well as comedy we would have been doing a disservice to our viewers," Young said in 1977. "Would it have pleased people if we'd had daughter Kathy contract multiple sclerosis, for instance? What would have been the point? It would have been like taking a beautiful painting and obliterating it with black paint—and that really would have turned the audience off. We never intended the series to be more than a weekly half-hour of fun and entertainment. We never meant to imply that life was a bowl of cherries, or that the Andersons were the typical American household—and yet we are constantly accused of not showing the family in a realistic light."

Realistic or not, *Father Knows Best* remains immensely popular to this day, constantly being

rerun the world over. The show terminated production mainly because Young felt burned out with the character and the situation after six seasons and 203 episodes. Shortly after the show's premiere, ironically, there was doubt it could make it to a second season. In fact, CBS—which had had the misguided wisdom to premiere the program at ten o'clock on Sunday nights—cancelled it after its first twenty-six weeks. (Could it have been that its sponsor, Kent Cigarettes, didn't appreciate Jim and Margaret's non-smoking approach to parenting?) The program's promise and popularity were not lost on the powers at NBC, which picked up the show and smartly began playing it Wednesday nights at 8:30 when the entire family could enjoy it. Upon its initial cancellation, public outcry caused *FKB* to become one of the first programs in network television history ever to be resurrected. In its final season, *FKB* ranked sixth overall in the ratings, its highest numbers ever during its six-year run. Young, still owner of fifty percent of the rights to the show, today is a millionaire many times over, and continues to collect residuals from *FKB,* already over thirty years in syndication.*

JANE WYATT

"I just cannot accept the complaint that the part I played in *Father Knows Best* doomed women in television," said Jane Wyatt in 1975. "The character was an awareness the times in the mid-1950s. There was no women's liberation movement and mothers were still serving their families in traditional ways. What I did in 1955 did not hurt Mary Tyler Moore, Carol Burnett, or Angie Dickinson. I think women are more important than ever in television today."

Her patrician good looks remain, and another generation of TV viewers know her as Mr. Spock's extraterrestrial mother from reruns of *Star Trek.* But Margaret Anderson is her most identifiable role, earning her three Emmys. In fact, she holds a television record for three consecutive wins: 1957, 1958, 1959, for Best Leading Actress in a Comedy.

She was born into wealth and privilege on August 12, 1912, in Campgaw, N.J. Her father was Wall Street financier Christopher Billop Wyatt, and her mother, Euphemia Van Rensselaer Waddington,

*Sadly, Young's depression problems deepened so that in early 1991, after several years of deteriorating health for both himself and Betty, he tried to take his own life. His dark efforts failed and Young began the process of recovery and recuperation.

*There subsequently were two ninety-minute reunion shows, both in 1977: *The Father Knows Best Reunion* and *Father Knows Best: Home for Christmas.*

The patrician good looks, upper-class accent and sensibility of Jane Wyatt made her the perfect wife, WASPy counterpart to the affable, bit more earthy Robert Young on Father Knows Best. *This photo proves that Margaret Anderson was the originator of wearing housewife pearls long before June Cleaver came on the TV scene.*

for thirty-five years drama critic of *Catholic World.* Both were listed in the New York Social Register. Jane's family has been in America since colonial days, her mother being one of the Colonial Dames of America. Of English-Dutch descent, Wyatt is a practicing Catholic, although on her father's side there is a long line of Episcopalian priests. She remembers growing up having "two cars and two chauffeurs." The family fortune was wiped out in the 1929 stock market crash, and when her father died in 1931, Mrs. Wyatt opened their regal Gramercy Park home to boarders. Jane attended New York's exclusive Miss Chapin's School and spent two years at Barnard College. "I was taken out of the Social Register when I became an actress, but I got back in when I married Edgar Bethune Ward." That was in 1935, one year after she made her film debut in *One More River.* Jane had two sons, Christopher (born 1937) and Michael (born 1942) with her investment broker husband.

Wyatt's most famous film role came in 1937, in *Lost Horizon,* playing the mysterious love interest of Ronald Colman. Her first love is the stage, and she appeared on Broadway with the likes of Charles Laughton and Lillian Gish. She enjoyed her years on *FKB,* but admits it was exhausting. "It was seven in the morning till seven at night for six years with only tiny hiatuses for your children. The sixth year was very hard. By then we had the third Anderson child graduating from school, and it was so dull by that time. Later on, we got into more sets and characters, and the cost skyrocketed. But we tried to preserve the tradition that every show had something to say. The children were complicated personally, not just kids. We weren't just five Pollyannas."

Wyatt still does occasional TV and film roles, such as the 1989 *Amityville: The Evil Escapes* (the fourth in the series). Wyatt's best words on *FKB* were uttered during a 1966 interview with our father when she remarked: "I did *Father Knows Best* all those years and it proved that father knows best, and mother puts him up to it."

ELINOR DONAHUE

She was born Mary Elinor Donahue in Tacoma,

Washington, on April 19, 1937, and is of Irish-French descent. She has a sister, twenty-one years her senior, and a brother eighteen years older. Her mother, a one-time theatrical costumer, separated from her father when Elinor was five. She's worked steadily in show business since age two, beginning in vaudeville, was a child actress in films, and admits she missed her childhood and didn't get around to having one until she was well into her second marriage. She had a brief marriage to *Father Knows Best* sound man, Dick Smith, whom she wed in May 1956. Her first son, Brian, was born in 1957, and she was divorced by 1958. "We were two very lonely people," she said of her early marriage. The producers kept her marriage and the birth of her son (which happened while the show was on hiatus) quiet. "They were very protective of me."

Donahue met her second husband also on the set of *FKB.* Harry Ackerman, twenty-five years her senior, was executive vice president of Screen Gems when they wed in April 1961. They have three sons together and were married for nearly thirty years until his death in February 1991.

Donahue has worked steadily since her *FKB* days in seven different series and even did a stint as an evil nurse on the daytime soap, *Days Of Our Lives* (1984–85). Most recently, with graying hair, in a wardrobe solely of pajamas and bathrobe, she played Bob Elliott's slightly off-center wife on *Get a Life,* the Fox sitcom. "My goal is to be like Jane Wyatt," says Donahue. "Jane has aged along with her roles, and that's what I'd like to do."

BILLY GRAY

"I'm so ashamed," said Billy Gray, in 1977, of his participation and role on *Father Knows Best.* "I'm ashamed I had any part of it. People felt warmly about the show and that show did everybody a disservice. Hundreds of kids—hundreds—have come up to me and said, 'I really got raked over the coals because of you. My mother keeps asking me why I wasn't like Bud.' I feel responsible to some degree for that.

"I felt that the show purported to be real life, and it wasn't. I regret that it was ever presented as a

All the regulars were reunited for two 1977 specials: The Father Knows Best Reunion *and* Father Knows Best: Home for Christmas, *from which this photo is taken. The now grown "Princess," "Bud," and "Kitten" join Margaret and Jim around the tree to open their presents.*

model to live by. Consider some of the things that the show taught people: Girls were always trained to use their feminine wiles to pretend to be helpless to attract men. The show contributed a lot to the problems between men and women that we see today."

Gray's anger isn't only confined to the show and what he felt it stood for; he also felt betrayed by his fellow cast members. In 1961, the year after the show left the air, Gray was arrested in Hollywood for possession of marijuana, and his subsequent conviction ruined his career, he claimed. "Today," he recalled in 1981, "that same incident would have been treated like a parking violation. I served forty-five days at the Wayside Honor Ranch, the same place that Robert Mitchum went when he got busted for marijuana possession in the late 1940s. In fact, my job at the ranch was to hand out athletic equipment which had been donated by Mitchum."

There's irony also in the fact that the show keeps Gray alive to this day. "I was more or less set for life," said Gray (born 1938). "I haven't had to work." He continues to live off of the residuals he receives whenever *FKB* airs the world over, and what he earns from Class A (500 cc) motorcycle racing. Gray has been frank about his experimenting with drugs since his early days, and about his two divorces. Regardless of his resentments toward the show, Gray is still in touch with the other cast members, and they communicate with each other on a fairly regular basis. They've appeared together on *FKB* television tributes—although Robert Young is usually taped separately. Yet his negative feelings about the program persist. "I think we were all well motivated but what we did was run a hoax. We weren't trying to, but that is what it was. Just a hoax."

LAUREN CHAPIN

Lauren Chapin (born May 23, 1945) came from a broken home and saw more stability on the set of *Father Knows Best* than she ever did in real life. She even addressed Robert Young as "Daddy" when the cameras stopped filming. The six-and-one-half best years of her life ended when the series folded in

1960. From ages nine through fifteen, "Kitten" had indeed been treated like a princess. She then suffered the terrible downside that many child stars faced when they "grow up"—she couldn't get any work as she was hopelessly typecast as Kathy Anderson. Everything had always been done for her—there were accountants, lawyers, agents, and her mother as her personal manager. Now she was on her own with few social skills. Lauren went back to high school but had a hard time adjusting. She later claimed her mother tried to keep her in the character of "Kathy" and tried to suppress her personality. Of course, she rebelled. She ran away from home and eloped, at age sixteen, with a school classmate she barely knew. During this time, she began doing drugs. "I started when I was sixteen and was chubby and went to the doctor and said, 'Would you please give me something to help me lose weight?' So he gave me benzedrine, or speed. Then when I was eighteen I ran into a man older than me who said, 'Let's get high.' He was a drug pusher. So I started using with him. I stayed with him almost four years...I really almost died."

When she turned eighteen, Lauren was entitled to monies held in trust for her from her *FKB* earnings. Her mother sued her trying to gain control of $180,000. Lauren countersued, claiming her mother forced her to sign over all her residual payments. Lauren's mother spent most of her daughter's earnings and eventually committed suicide. Lauren suffered eight miscarriages and seven years of heroin addiction. "I floated in the real seedy side of life from fourteen to twenty-six, caught up in the free-sex, free-drugs, free-love society," she told the New York *Daily News* in 1990. Lauren spent three years in the California Institute for Women as her sentence for attempted forgery. While incarcerated, she entered a drug rehabilitation program and had an affair with another inmate. She became pregnant with her son, Matt, born in 1973. Five years later, Lauren had a second child out of wedlock, her daughter, Summer. "I slept with many, many people trying to find love," Chapin admitted, "and the more people I slept with the less self-esteem I had."

Once released from jail, Chapin was turned by friends toward religious life, and she became a

The original cast of Father Knows Best *gathers together seventeen years after the final broadcast for the* The Father Knows Best Reunion *which aired on NBC on May 15, 1977. Top, Elinor Donahue (left), Robert Young, Jane Wyatt. Bottom, Lauren Chapin and Billy Gray.*

born-again Christian, at a Pentecostal service, and began a ministry traveling the gospel circuit. "All my life I've wanted to be loved," she said, "and God's love is the most complete love...what I was looking for."

Chapin stays in touch with Gray and Elinor Donahue, but hasn't seen her "mother" and "fa-

ther" in many years. As of 1990, Chapin was living in Killeen, Texas, engaged to a firefighter at work as a high school science teacher, and enjoying praise for her autobiography titled *Father Does Know Best.*

A rare still from the premiere episode of Father Knows Best, *broadcast Sunday, October 3, 1954. Striped-suited Jim Anderson gives some fatherly advice to son, Bud (Billy Gray), and a generation of television viewers forever changed their vision of the "average" American family.*

CAST LIST

FAMILY: The Andersons

MEMBERS:

Jim Anderson . . . . **Robert Young**
Margaret Anderson . . . . **Jane Wyatt**
Betty Anderson
  (Princess) . . . . **Elinor Donahue**
James Anderson, Jr. (Bud) . . . . **Billy Gray**
Kathy Anderson (Kitten) . . **Lauren Chapin**

SIGNIFICANT OTHERS:

Miss Thomas . . . . **Sarah Selby**

Dotty Snow (1954–57) . . . . . **Yvonne Lime**
Kippy Watkins (1954–59) . . . **Paul Wallace**
Claude Messner (1954–59)　**Jimmy Bates**
Ed Davis (1955–59) . . . . **Robert Foulk**
Myrtle Davis (1955–59) . . . . **Vivi Janis**
Doyle Hobbs (1957–58) . . . . **Roger Smith**
Joyce Kendall (1957–58) . . **Roberta Shore**

TIMEFRAME: **1954–63**
NETWORK: **CBS (1954–55, 1958–62),**
　　　　　(1960–62 prime-time reruns)
　　　　　NBC (1955–58),
　　　　　ABC (1962–63) (prime-time
　　　　　reruns)
ADDRESS: **607 South Maple St.**
　　　　　Springfield, USA

203 episodes

GREAT PERFORMANCES

Emmy Winners

Robert Young

Best Continuing Performance by an Actor
in a Leading Role in a Dramatic or
Comedy Series

1956, 1957

Jane Wyatt

Best Continuing Performance by an
Actress in a Leading Role in a Dramatic or
Comedy Series

1957, 1958–59, 1959–60

Peter Tewksbury

Best Director for a Single Program of a
Comedy Series: "Medal for Margaret"

1959

"Father Knows Best"

Sylvania Award for Outstanding Family
Entertainment

1954

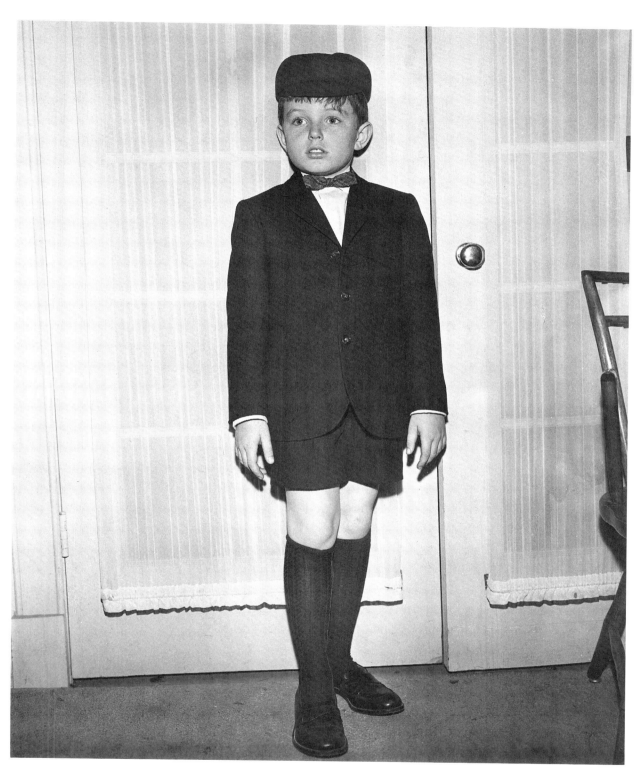

And here he is, the one and only Beaver Cleaver—cap, bow tie, knee socks, shorts, and that endearingly bewildered look as if a flying saucer had deposited him from another galaxy, and he's saying to us all: "Gee, what am I supposed to do now?" This episode, "Beaver's Short Pants," was broadcast December 13, 1957.

Caught in the act of being themselves, Wally and Beaver (Tony Dow and Jerry Mathers) take a popcorn break between camera set-ups on the set of Leave It to Beaver, *in this backstage candid, circa 1958.*

Let's all face the truth unflinchingly—The Beaver was a jerk. But what nice, white middle-class kid growing up in fifties American suburbia, with astonishingly understanding, level-headed, somewhat straitlaced parents like Ward and June Cleaver, and a loyal, protective, older "neat" brother like Wally, wouldn't be a jerk in the face of so much unreality? How easy it is to look back now on *Leave It to Beaver*—an exceptional show in that it was the first sitcom to deal with life from a kid's point of view—and condemn it for being so unreal. Back in 1957, when the series had its debut, every young viewer looked at Beaver and instantly identified with his awkward, naïve "Gee, what's gonna happen to me now?" innocent ways. Beaver was squeaky clean because we all knew June was there to make him and Wally take their baths every night, and Ward was always near enough to wag a finger at the boys reminding them to scrub behind their ears; because life any other way just wasn't acceptable. And although other less fortunate kids were to be tolerated and understood if they didn't scrub behind their ears, have good table manners or at least names like Lumpy and Whitey, they wouldn't be found for long in the Cleaver household.

Beaver's house had a white picket fence, and Ward, an accountant by profession, was usually around to dispense homilies and advice which, frankly, Wally and Beaver usually ignored. June, like a good TV sitcom mom of the time, spent most of hers in the kitchen. The suspicion is that when she wasn't cooking or sitting in the den worrying about when Beaver was going to get home, she was probably ironing like the dickens because none of her brood ever wore anything that wasn't perfectly cleaned and pressed. Did you ever notice how June *always* wore a pearl necklace? (Ex-model Barbara Billingsley wore them as a distraction from her long, but thin neck). It was also pretty natural for Ward to be a bit pious and pontifical, because the actor who played him, Hugh Beaumont, was in real life a longtime Methodist lay minister (referred to in his 1957 CBS publicity biography as a "licensed preacher").

The Cleavers lived at 211 Pine Street, Mayfield, U.S.A., and were the creations of Bob Mosher and Joe Connelly, formerly of the J. Walter Thompson advertising agency, who had moved into radio and TV scriptwriting. The team's idea was to create a family comedy television series about the lives of kids and their parents, but done from the kid's point of view. They wanted the show to be "clean and honest," portraying the mother and father not as caterwauling dolts or bumbling fools, but as frequently erring humans. The two boys would be represented as just regular kids—not as in many other family comedy series of the times, which featured comic versions of children who were either super-precocious and bratty, able to figure out every one of Dad's preposterous dilemmas, or mini-adult wiseacres or churlish numbskulls—kids who had everyday "Gee, I lost my new watch" and "How am I gonna tell Dad about those two Ds on my report card?" problems.

Both Mosher and Connelly used their own child-hood days and then-present families (Mosher had two kids, Connelly six) for script inspirations. Beaver himself was inspired by Connelly's eight-year-old son, Ricky. Besides, Beaver was a peppy, catchy name representative of a happy, open-faced youthful creature. At eight, Jerry Mathers was already a show business professional replete with toothy grin, a relaxed natural acting ability, and just an edge of mischief like the Beaver.

JUNE: Beaver, your father and I both want you to know if you ever have a problem, we want you to come and talk it over with us.
WARD: If anything's ever bothering you, don't keep it to yourself. You come to us with it, and be assured that we'll understand.
BEAVER: Gee, Dad, it sounds so neat I wish I was in trouble right now.

Mathers was born in Sioux City, Iowa, on June 2, 1948, and grew up in Los Angeles. A local department store clerk convinced his mother to try her one-year-old out for a "beautiful baby" calendar. At almost three, Jerry was chosen by Broadway comedian Ed Wynn, who then had his own TV show, as the youngest cast member. Innovative band leader Spike Jones saw Jerry and hired him to be his TV

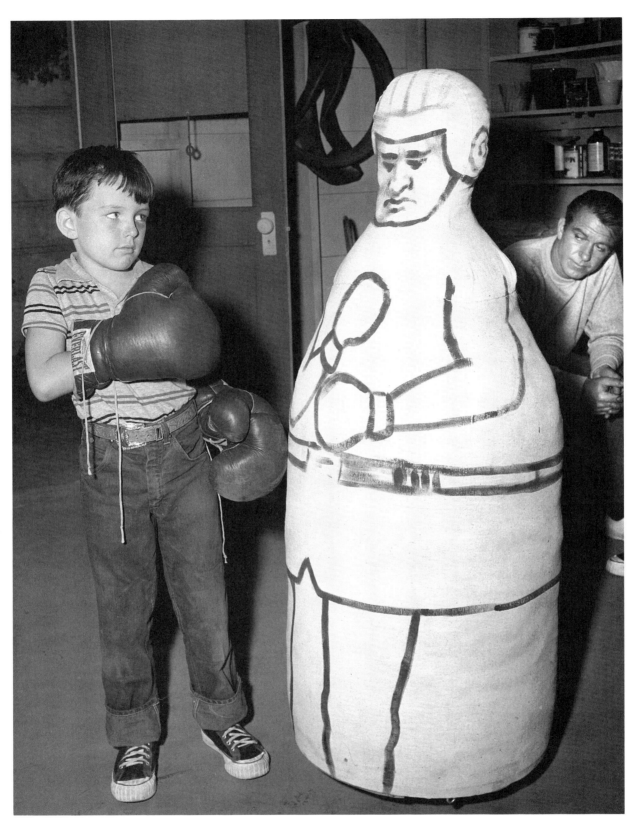

A guy's gotta learn how to defend himself, so Beaver asked Ward for boxing lessons to avenge a black eye given to him by some "creepy" kid in school. Here the Beaver pummels a dummy while Ward "supervises" from a safe distance in the episode "The Black Eye," broadcast October 18, 1957.

show's New Year's baby. By age five, Jerry played in his first movie, *This Is My Love*, with Dan Duryea and Linda Darnell. In 1954, Jerry got his big break when he was cast as Shirley MacLaine's son in Hitchcock's *The Trouble With Harry*. He followed that with a role in *The Seven Little Foys*, with Bob Hope, and many TV guest appearances. While auditioning for Mosher and Connelly for the role of Beaver, Mathers was spied by the writers impatiently fidgeting in his chair. When asked what the matter was, Jerry replied, "I'm gonna be late for my cub scout meeting." Mosher and Connelly loved the spontaneity of his answer and gave him the role. By 1958, Mathers was reportedly earning $500 per week.

> WALLY: You know what you are, Beaver? You're an optimist.
> BEAVER: What's that?
> WALLY: Well, that's the kinda guy, if he fell off a cliff, all the way down he'd be saying, "Everything's gonna be okay."

There were clear dividing lines on *Leave It to Beaver* which left little room for confusion. Back in 1957, and for the duration of the program, things were pretty simple: Boys were boys, got dirty and hated to wash up, and always felt "icky" (uncomfortable) around girls at least until they got to be Wally's age (even then, teenage girls could be pretty "confusin'"); Moms were always perfectly coiffed, wore earrings and pearls to wash dishes; Dads wore business suits or cardigans, sports shirts and chinos, and wouldn't be caught dead in jeans; girls were mostly perfect little angels who got great grades in all school subjects including deportment, but could be, you know, "funny" sometimes....

> BEAVER: There's something funny about this girl.
> WARD: Funny?
> BEAVER: Well, not funny, but it's kind of hard to explain. Sometimes when I'd look at her, I'd feel real good, and other times I'd feel like I was gonna get sick right to my stomach. But I guess you wouldn't understand.
> WARD: I think I do, Beaver.
> BEAVER: (A momentary pause) About girls, Dad—

> WARD: Yes?
> BEAVER: Does it ever get better?
> WARD: I wish I could say so, son, but it gets an awful lot worse before it gets better.

Beaver was a chuckling kind of show; you wouldn't double over laughing at what went on, as you might at some of the burlesque-type pratfalls on *The Honeymooners*. You'd perhaps chuckle or smile in warm recognition of the sweet humanity of the attempts of Ward and June or Beaver or Wally at problem solving.

If the Cleavers were fairly bland WASPS, and the boys were a bit on the dull side, their friends were not. The Cleavers were most helpfully surrounded by colorful character players who added some real spice to the show. Beaver's best buddy was tubby Larry Mondello, a walking candy store of a kid, constantly munching or looking for something to stuff in his mouth. Carrot-topped, freckle-faced, and whiny, Larry always looked hungry and unhappy, maybe because there was never enough snacks for him or because he had perpetual indigestion.

> BEAVER: Larry, how come you eat your cake first?
> LARRY: If I eat the sandwiches first, I might not have room for the cake.

Beaver's other pals were Whitey Whitney and Gilbert Bates. Whitey was pasty-faced with a shock of white-blond hair and a high-pitched voice. His real name was Hubert...'nuff said. Gilbert Bates was an instigator, and Beaver was usually dumb enough to go along with the wild schemes and woolly stories his pal was always cooking up. While Beaver was constantly wrestling with his conscience, Gilbert was way ahead of him in that he hardly had any at all.

The most beloved of Beaver and Wally's pals was the obnoxious, two-faced Eddie Haskell, an out-and-out adolescent creep, always ready to sell out his friends and to lie so long as it forwards Edward Clark Haskell's number one concern—himself. Eddie's trademarks are his oily politeness to all adults and his unbridled, smart-alecky tongue lashings to all his "friends," especially the Beaver,

The first family photo from the premiere episode of Leave It to Beaver *broadcast on October 4, 1957. Top, Barbara Billingsley (June Cleaver), Hugh Beaumont (Ward Cleaver). Bottom, left, Jerry Mathers (Beaver Cleaver); right, Tony Dow (Wally Cleaver). The original CBS-TV photo caption described Mathers and Dow as "their apple-pie-normal little boys, Beaver and Wally."*

whom he calls "Squirt" or "Creep." "Hi ya, Beaver—you gnaw down any trees today? Heh, heh, heh." We all hated Eddie, but couldn't wait for him to come through the door, knowing that the real fun part of the program was about to begin.

He wasn't above sassing June.

EDDIE: Mrs. Cleaver, I don't like to carry tales, but I just saw little Theodore going down the street. I believe he had some of Mr. Cleaver's gardening tools hidden in his wagon.
JUNE: Yes, we know, Eddie. He and Gilbert have a job cutting lawns.
EDDIE: Oh, I'm glad to hear it's a worthwhile project, Mrs. Cleaver. I know you would appreciate me letting you know if Theodore was engaged in some sort of mischief.

But most of his barbs were saved for "The Beav."

EDDIE: Hey, I hear they got you in solitary confinement. What'd you do, spill jam on your bib again?
BEAVER: No, I stayed out late, so I'm not allowed out on school nights.
EDDIE: Hey, that's rough. If that ever happened to me, eight or nine girls would kill themselves.

As the years passed and the boys grew, the focus of the program was less on Beaver's adventures with pet frogs, paint-stained clothing, and "creepy" girls. By the sixties, Wally had turned into a teenage hunk, and Beaver had finally taken off his everpresent baseball cap. In an episode that emphasized these changes, Wally got a date with the pretty new girl in town who, unfortunately, had to baby-sit for her little sister the night of their date. Figuring to take Beaver along to date the little sister, Wally thinks he'll have to trick his kid brother into it. To his amazement, his cracking-voiced sibling accepts and speechifies on how grown up he really is. But the night of the date, the little sister gets cold feet and cancels, much to Beaver's secret relief. Wally again tried to rectify

Even a neighbor's little dog expresses dislike for the "perfume" which Beaver and Wally attempt to sell in an effort to earn money for a movie projector, in "The Perfume Salesman," broadcast December 27, 1957.

the situation by putting Beaver on the telephone with the little sister, who admits to Beaver she won't go on the date because she's scared. Happily, Beaver admits his fear too, and they both agree to try again sometime in the future. Beaver then announces to Ward, June, and Wally that the girl won't go, and sniffs to his brother, "Next time find me a girl who knows the score."

By September of 1963, Tony Dow was eighteen, and Jerry Mathers was fifteen, and time for the Beaver had run out, after 234 episodes. Although the program never ranked in the top twenty-five shows in the ratings, *Leave It to Beaver* was a far greater success to both CBS and ABC than either network had at first suspected. Yet now, three decades later, the images of Beaver and Wally, June and Ward, Eddie Haskell and all the rest glow warm and remain fresh, as if it were yesterday.

JERRY MATHERS

Gerald Patrick Mathers attended high school and formed a rock band with former Beaver cast-mate, Richard Correll. Mathers played guitar and sang while Correll played drums, and, as "Beaver and the Trappers," recorded a single, "Happiness Is." After college, Mathers spent six years in the Air National Guard stateside during Vietnam. A recurring rumor during those years was that the Beaver had been killed in action in the war, and this was greatly fueled one evening in the 1960s when actress Shelley Winters mentioned his "death" on "The Tonight Show." Mathers's philosophy studies had taught him to be a "pragmatist" (he got an undergraduate degree from Berkeley), and he took jobs working in banking and real estate. He also did a brief stint as a radio disc jockey for a popular weekend show in Anaheim, California, called "Jerry Mathers Gathers Rock 'n' Roll for the Mind, Body, and Soul." Occasionally, he takes TV roles, and spent one season (twenty-six episodes) with *Still the Beaver* on the Disney Channel, with Dow, Billingsley, and Osmond (Hugh Beaumont had died). Ultimately, viewers didn't buy the Beaver grown up with his own kids and marriage troubles. The same cast repeated the ritual in seventy-four episodes of *The New Leave It to Beaver* for Superstation WTBS, beginning in 1987. Mathers is active

Beaver makes the supreme sacrifice to help his older brother, Wally, make up with a girlfriend by gift wrapping his pet toad, Herbie, and sending it to the young lady in his brother's name, in "Wally's Girl Trouble," broadcast on November 29, 1957.

The first CBS press photo of Wally and the Beaver. "Mathers, eight years old, and Dow, twelve, play the parts of Beaver and Wally Cleaver, two lovable but unpredictable brothers who keep things moving at a hilarious and lively pace on Leave It to Beaver, *a new domestic comedy series."*

It's the first Christmas on TV for Beaver and Wally and June and Ward. Jerry Mathers's feet aren't the only undressed items on the set—look at that bare linoleum floor, and to the left of the mantel at the bottom, the wallpapering didn't get finished. But June's got her pearls, and Ward's got a hairy chest, and all looks well with the Cleavers.

on the promotional circuit speaking at colleges and media events around the country. He, wife Rhonda, and their three children presently live in southern California.

TONY DOW

TV's once-and-always Wally Cleaver believes the show still works after all these years because "the characters are established and everyone likes them." Dow acknowledges the care the creators of the show back then took to make it work. "The producers were very conscious that we actors should remain as 'normal' as possible," he says. "The directors and writers wanted us to be the kids next door. The writers even requested that our parents not let us watch the show because they didn't want us to become affected. Everyone was concerned with our well-being, our state of mind. They didn't want us to turn into monsters."

Tony Dow was born April 13, 1945, in Hollywood. His mother, Muriel Montrose Dow, was a former "bathing beauty" in silent films for comedy producer Mack Sennett. His father, John Dow, Jr., was an industrial designer/builder. Blond-haired, blue-eyed Tony was cast in two unsold television pilots before winning the role of Wally, beating out 270 other youngsters for the part.

Always a superb all-around athlete, Dow played center on the Los Angeles Athletic Club's volleyball team which won the statewide championship in 1963. He also held the LAAC championship in handball, singles and doubles, plus the club records for water-skiing endurance and the trampoline. He still surfs, but back in the late fifties and early sixties, body and board surfing, water-skiing, skin diving, and high diving took up most of his spare time. When playing sports indoors, Dow preferred gymnastics, especially tumbling.

At his peak of popularity, Dow received 1,000 fan letters per week, and a dozen marriage proposals. One month before his eighteenth birthday, Dow gifted himself his first car, a 1962 blue-gray Cor-

Blond, blue-eyed Tony Dow, circa 1960—girls love him, mothers trust him, and fathers think he's a really good kid. As older brothers go, Wally was a pretty good guy who could explain "stuff" to the Beaver, and even interpret Beaver's behavior to oft confused Ward and June.

◀

Snake-eyed Eddie Haskell (right), the ultimate creepazoid. Would Eddie let some girl get between his friendship with loyal-but-wary Wally? You bet he would, as long as there was "somethin' in it for me"—one of Eddie choice typical lines. In this episode, "Eddie's Girl," is lovely Caroline Cunningham who, when introduced to Wally, quickly forgets about Eddie and has Wally escort her to the dance.

vette, which was promptly stolen. At age twenty, tragedy struck when Dow, after making a personal appearance in Asheville, N.C., accidentally struck and killed an eighteen-year-old boy walking across a highway. Dow was cleared of any wrongdoing. At twenty-one, he received $41,650 in bonds and bought himself a fifty-four-foot sailboat and a cabin retreat on Catalina Island, where he kept two pets, Oliver, an otter, and Miles Francis Dow, S.P., for Stupid Penquin.

In 1965, Dow began playing Chet on the ABC daytime soap opera, *Never Too Young.* In 1974, he joined the cast of *General Hospital* and made occasional appearances on shows like *Mod Squad* and *Emergency.* Married for a while in the seventies, he became the father of young Christopher and filled in his time between acting jobs painting and sculpting on commission (he studied art and psychology at UCLA), ran a construction firm, and did a three-year stint with the National Guard. With Jerry Mathers, he toured the country in plays like *Boeing, Boeing* and a comedy written for them called *So Long, Stanley.* At the height of his *Beaver* popularity, Dow received constant offers to become a rock star but always declined. "I tell them I can't sing, but they all say it doesn't matter."

BARBARA BILLINGSLEY

Born Barbara Lillian Combes on December 22, 1922, in Los Angeles. She has blond-gray hair and blue eyes, stands five-feet-five-and-one-half inches tall. After one year at Los Angeles Junior College, she landed a role in *Straw Hat,* a revue that made it to Broadway but closed after five days. She then "decided New York was more fun than college," took an apartment on West 57th Street, and went to work as a $60-per-week fashion model. Barbara Combes married Glenn Billingsley, nephew of Stork Club owner Sherman, in 1941. They had two sons, Glenn and Drew, then divorced in 1947. In the mid-forties she "played Tom Conway's wife in more

It was all smiles when television Superstation WTBS ordered seventy-four new episodes of The New Leave It to Beaver *in April 1986, from MCA studios. Here, Jerry Mathers (right) presents a Mayfield High School sweater to WTBS chairman Ted Turner while MCA President Sidney Sheinberg (left), Tony Dow, and Barbara Billingsley look on.*

"B" picture detective stories than I care to count up." Billingsley made more films in the fifties, including *The Bad and the Beautiful*, and appeared in over one hundred "live" and filmed TV shows. In 1953, she married prominent television director Roy Kellino (James Mason's brother-in-law), who died in 1956. In 1955, she played another mom role on *Professional Father* a TV sitcom that lasted half a season. In 1960, she married a physician, William Mortensen, a widower with two children. After *Leave It to Beaver* ended, she and Mortensen traveled around the world on a freighter. Aside from the two series, *Still the Beaver* and *The New Leave It to Beaver,* she does movie and TV cameos, her most memorable being in *Airplane* (1980), talking "jive" with two black brothers aboard the plane. Her hilarious dialogue included perfect renditions of "Cut me some slack, Jack" and "Jus' hang loose, blood." She was also a judge on *Dance Fever* and played an ax murderess on *Mork and Mindy.* She lives in Malibu, California.

HUGH BEAUMONT

Actor/author/businessman/preacher Hugh Beaumont was born February 16, 1909, in Lawrence, Kansas. His father "promoted everything from wrestling matches to independent banks." As a result, Beaumont received his early education all over the southern half of the U.S. while his family traveled from place to place. When he was in his early teens, his parents settled long enough in Chattanooga for Hugh to attend Baylor Military Academy and the University of Chattanooga. Moving to Los Angeles, he finished his education at USC, with a major in religion and minor in social studies, and received athletic letters in football, basketball, track, and swimming. He also received his license allowing him to practice as a Methodist minister. In the mid-1940s, he served for four years as pastor of the Vincent Methodist Church in a ghetto neighborhood of Los Angeles. While he was still in college, the acting bug bit, and he joined a local theatrical group. His career was almost over before it started when, while playing the villain in *Ten Nights in a Barroom,* he acted with such conviction that the incensed audience began hur-

Beaver and Wally got Ward to help build them a "real racin' car" out of old boxes and wheels and a one cylinder motor, in "The State Versus Beaver." Of course, Beaver gets a ticket for driving without a license, but the judge lets him go when he starts crying, and leaves it up to Beaver and Wally to tell their dad.

ling glassware. For several years he juggled acting assignments, graduate school, and ministerial work, and meanwhile, in 1941, he married Kathryn Hohn, an aspiring starlet and a minister's daughter from Crookston, Minnesota. Beaumont was broke and out of work at the time of his marriage, but his wife had minor parts in a number of "B" pictures, although she gave up her career after the birth of their first child, Hunter.

Beaumont was featured in twenty-five movies including the lead in a series of Michael Shayne films. By 1949, two more children, Mark and Kristy, had been born, and the Beaumonts bought a twenty-five-year-old ranch house in North Hollywood. By the early fifties, Beaumont was appearing on and writing for TV. With money from his role as

Ward Cleaver, Beaumont purchased ninety-three acres and a cottage in Itasca County, Minnesota, as a family refuge from Hollywood. In his spare time, Beaumont wrote and sold articles to *Ladies' Home Journal* and *Saturday Evening Post*. He claimed he had more literary success when his fictional characters were ministers. When *Leave It to Beaver* ended, Beaumont did guest shots on *The Virginian, Mannix, Petticoat Junction*, and other TV programs, but in 1972 he suffered a stroke that left him partially paralyzed, and he retreated to his tree farm in Minnesota, which produced ten thousand Christmas trees every year. While visiting his son Hunter, a college psychology professor in Munich, West Germany, Beaumont had a heart attack and died, on May 5, 1982.

KEN OSMOND

Wiseguy Eddie Haskell grew up to become a real-life Los Angeles motorcycle policeman, and is the very opposite of the "me-first" *Leave It to Beaver* creep he portrayed. While pursuing the gun-toting driver of a stolen cab down a Los Angeles street, Officer Ken Osmond was shot four times by the felon, but survived because of his body armor, his belt buckle, and his partner.

Tony Dow recalled a surprise meeting with Ken Osmond a few years back. "He once stopped me for speeding on the freeway. You should have seen his face when he found out it was me."

For years, Osmond also suffered the indignity of rumors that he was "really" notorious porno star, John "Johnny Wadd" Holmes. (In the 1970s, several X-rated films reportedly featured "John Holmes who played Little Eddie Haskel [sic].") On occasion, Osmond moonlighted with acting jobs, such as appearing as shop teacher Freddie Paskell on *Happy Days*, and returned as the adult Eddie on *The New Leave It to Beaver* in the late eighties. He lives with his wife and two sons in a suburb of Los Angeles.

WHERE ARE THEY NOW?

Frank Bank (Lumpy) is a successful municipal bonds salesman in Palm Springs, California.

Robert "Rusty" Stevens (Larry) lives in New Jersey with his wife and is an insurance salesman.

Steven Talbot (Gilbert) is a distinguished documentary filmmaker who won a Peabody award for his 1980 film, *Broken Arrow.*

Richard Correll (Richard), after working with Mathers in their rock group, majored in cinema at USC and entered into the production end of television.

Richard Deacon (Mr. Rutherford) was the only actor in television to have continuing roles simultaneously in two classic sitcoms—*Beaver* and *The Dick Van Dyke Show*, in which he played the obnoxious Mel Cooley. Deacon died in 1985.

BEAVER SECRETS

• To reflect more accurately the world of the child, many scenes were shot from Beaver's eye level.

• Tony Dow and Hugh Beaumont weren't in the original series pilot film.

• *Leave It to Beaver* featured a thunderous milestone, the first toilet ever shown on television!

• June's maiden name was Bronson.

• The Cleavers' first house was located at 485 Maple Drive.

• Writers Mosher and Connelly's major credit before creating *Leave It to Beaver*—they penned over 1,500 *Amos 'n' Andy* television and radio scripts.

• The original show title of the pilot was *Wally and Beaver.*

• Yes, there was always a "canned" laugh track accompanying each episode.

• After *Leave It to Beaver*, Mosher and Connelly created a comedy/horror spoof of *Beaver*, even reworking several old episodes, and called it— that's right—*The Munsters.*

• Mathers received residuals only for the first seven airings of the programs once the series went into reruns, and none of the cast has received a dime since, yet *Beaver* is still in worldwide syndication.

In one of the last episodes of the final season, "Wally's Practical Joke" (1963), Wally takes revenge against Lumpy who's smoke-bombed his car engine. Wally and Eddie Haskell chain Lumpy's car axle to a tree and when Lumpy attempts to drive off his axle tears away from the rear of his car. The two get found out and must repair the car as punishment. In this shot, Wally's just about finished making repairs and has the grime all over himself to show for it.

CAST LIST

FAMILY: The Cleavers

MEMBERS:

Beaver (Theodore) Cleaver   **Jerry Mathers**
June Cleaver . . . . **Barbara Billingsley**
Ward Cleaver . . . . **Hugh Beaumont**
Wally Cleaver . . . . **Tony Dow**

SIGNIFICANT OTHERS:

Eddie Haskell . . . . **Ken Osmond**
Miss Canfield (1957–58)   **Diane Brewster**
Miss Landers (1958–62) . . . . **Sue Randall**
Larry Mondello (1958–60)   **Rusty Stevens**
Whitey Whitney . . . . **Stanley Fafara**
Clarence "Lumpy" Rutherford
   (1958–63) . . . . **Frank Bank**
Mr. Fred Rutherford . . . . . **Richard Deacon**
Gilbert Bates (1959–63) . . **Stephen Talbot**
Richard (1960–61) . . . . **Richard Correll**

THEME SONG: Michael Johnson,
                  Melvyn Lenard
TIMEFRAME: 1957–63
NETWORK: CBS (1957–58),
                 ABC (1958–63)
ADDRESS: 211 Pine St.
                 Mayfield, USA

234 episodes

Looks like the Beaver is not so sure if he likes the news that older brother Wally may be headed for boarding school, in this visit with the Cleavers broadcast June 11, 1958. Gee, what's a fella gonna do without his older brother to knock around with? June and Ward Cleaver always had a solution by episode end, but not before a "serious talk" with the Beaver. From left to right: Jerry Mathers, Barbara Billingsley, and Hugh Beaumont.

THE DONNA REED SHOW

The picture perfect all-American fantasy family of series television, the Stones. Left to right, Donna Reed (Donna Stone), Paul Petersen (Jeff Stone), Carl Betz (Dr. Alex Stone) and Shelley Fabares (Mary Stone). This is how they all looked at the happy beginning of their second season on ABC on October 1, 1959.

Donna Reed and Carol Betz, in character as Donna
and Dr. Alex Stone, cuddle twins Judy and Susie Mintz,
three-months-olds who made their TV debut in the
episode "The First Child" broadcast on October 15, 1959.
The story concerned overanxious parents of a newborn
child and Dr. Alex's dilemma because he can't keep up
with their constant nervous phone calls.

*It's tough trying to scam your way out of a day from
school when your dad's a doctor and knows how to
read a thermometer. But young Jeff wouldn't be all-boy if
he didn't try. The episode is "Flowers for the Teacher,"
broadcast November 12, 1959.*

If there was a patent for TV fluff, *The Donna Reed Show* owned it. This program was about as far from real life as it was possible to get. The Stones of Hilldale, Middle America, U.S.A., were a dream family of cookie-cutter figures who were all sugar, no spice, and a hundred percent saccharine. Living in their own tidy world, each member was a vision of squeaky clean perfection.

First, there was Donna Reed herself as Donna Stone, apple-pie-perfect American mom, the ideal apron-clad housewife hovering over a household brimming with naïveté and cheerful idiocy. Her personality had the depth of a very sincere pinprick. Donna Stone had three basic emotions: pleasant, pleasant, and pleasant. She was pretty, pert, perky, and eager to please, never ever suffered from PMS, and never ever experienced, created, or was responsible for *any* passion. This was upper middle-class American life in its blandest fantasy form. Donna's traditionally furnished home (the outdoor patio built on the studio set was an exact replica of one Donna Reed had at her Beverly Hills home) was spotless, and so were her husband and kids. Burning the roast or having a particularly hard time getting the oven clean was the closest she'd ever come to having a reason to even think about becoming hysterical. Donna was always the voice of reason, because nothing ever happened in her household that was even vaguely unreasonable.

Carl Betz played Alex Stone, her handsome pediatrician husband. He was Donna's perfect foil, always ready just off-camera to spring though the door with "Honey, I'm home" and always conveniently "around" to listen to the newest "reasonable" crisis and give his instant "diagnosis" of how to solve it before disappearing back into the ether. How convenient that his doctor's office happened to be located in another wing of their expansive colonial-style house. No doubt dealing with all those cute, pesky little kids all day long kept him so childlike. Dr. Stone was less a father figure to his own children and more a trying-to-be-earnest pal. Of course, his kids didn't need much coaching, because they too were pretty darn near perfect.

Jeff Stone's (Paul Petersen) biggest imperfection was probably the gap between his two front teeth. That gap could make it easy to whistle well and,

Shelley Fabares as Mary Stone single-handedly caused a national fad for ponytail hairdos that teenage girls everywhere imitated for years during The Donna Reed Show's *run.*

heaven forbid, when no one was watching, to spit through! His toothy grin belied a toothy personality. When Jeff wasn't grinning, he was frowning, but not for long, because if he had a problem, good ol' Mom was always nearby to solve it. Being the sensible 1950s housewife, Donna would always first consult her husband for a solution to this week's family crisis, and Dr. Alex would happily oblige, wag a finger or two, and bumble up some reasonable solution. Donna would then get that serious little knit-eyebrows look (as if she was really puzzling and thinking hard or perhaps…no, it's not possible…worrying!) and go off and solve it *her* way just like she did every episode.

Shelley Fabares as Mary Stone was as near perfect as Mom, but could be forgiven her little bursts of temperament because she was, after all, a "teenager." Mary was also the picture perfect little 1950s virgin who wore white gloves on a date. The closest any boy ever got to Mary's breasts was when pinning a corsage on her dress. Mary wasn't above sometimes being a little bitchy so long as a good moral could follow by episode's end, always personally delivered by her saintly mother.

Paul Petersen and Shelley Fabares, sans makeup, in the recording studio. Though neither was a singer, the show's producer, Tony Owen (real life husband of Donna Reed), wanted them to cash in on their immense teen popularity a la Ricky Nelson. Both kids had hits, but Fabares's "Johnny Angel" rocketed up the charts and sold over one million singles. Only under Owen's threat not to renew her contract with the show did Fabares acquiesce and record the song.

MARY'S LITTLE SCHEME

Mary schemes to get two star football players to take her to the junior prom. Meanwhile, awkward shy boy Charlie, who has a hopeless crush on Mary, puppy-dogs her everywhere, while she continually mistreats and takes advantage of him, running him on endless silly errands for her. While talking with Charlie in the school hall, Mary sees her two footballers and gets rid of Charlie.

MARY: Charlie, would you run down to the bookstore and get me an eraser?
CHARLIE: Sure! Oh, which kind?
MARY: Any kind, just hurry!

Mary then pits one footballer against the other in her scheme to get her favorite to ask her so she can turn down the other. Each boy asks her her plans for the prom, then they fight one another. At home, Mary sees Charlie coming in to look for her.

MARY: Mother, that's Charlie, and I've been dodging him all day. Please get rid of him.
DONNA: Darling, that's not nice.

Donna gives a pep talk to Charlie, telling him not to let Mary manipulate and disrespect him.

DONNA: Let me give you some advice about the female of the species. Watch out! The female can be a sweet but loving creature, but you must be firm with her. If you're a shrinking violet, she'll be a lawnmower.

She teaches Charlie to say "no" to Mary. Meanwhile the two footballers figure out they've been conned by Mary and decide to turn the table on her. They both call her from the same phone, and each cancels out on taking her to the prom. Mary is devastated, but Mom is there to pick up the pieces.

DONNA (with violin music whimpering in the background): Mary, you played a dangerous game and you lost.

Mary counters that she'll get Charlie to take her. Donna says not to count on Charlie.

DONNA (more violins): You have to learn to use your womanly powers gently and with kindness. When you handle yourself, use your head. When you handle others, use your heart.

The new, assertive Charlie shows up in time to save Mary and take her to the prom.

MARY (still more violins): Oh, Charlie, I've been horrible.

Charlie demands obedience to his wishes before giving in and taking Mary to the prom.

CHARLIE: Where do you want to go for hamburgers after the dance, Mary?
MARY: The malt shop, Charlie.
CHARLIE: No, Mary. I want to go to the canteen.
MARY: Whatever you say, Charlie.

Donna and Dr. Alex smile proudly as the sweet kids head for the dance.

After Shelly Fabares departed the show in 1963, Paul Petersen's real-life sister, Patty (left), replaced her portraying Trisha, an orphan who followed the Stones home one day, and was, naturally, adopted by the happy family.

The Stones weren't just Velveeta Cheese bland, they were like, well, stoned. The ever present smiles, the unruffled clothing, the constant bird-like cheeriness...these were the "Stepford Wives" type of ingredients that Donna Reed and her coproducer husband, Tony Owen, and their writers thought would make the perfect vehicle for her as her film career was on the wane in the late fifties.

Reed was born Donna Belle Mullenger on January 27, 1921, in Denison, Iowa (population: 4,000). Of German/Irish ancestry, Donna's parents were sturdy farmers, and their resourceful daughter grew up to be a hearty all-American farm girl who could bake bread, milk cows, and drive a tractor. Reed had moved to Los Angeles and was studying stenography at L.A. City College, where she was named campus queen, the same title she won in high school. Her sweet but strong farm girl personality, which radiated a fresh innocence, and her all-American good looks (five-feet-four, 115 pounds, hazel eyes and brown hair with red highlights) were not lost on studio scouts who saw her picture

The picture-perfect all-American mom, Donna Reed was the envy of apron-wearers across the nation. In real life, Reed was a canny businesswoman who parlayed her picture-perfectness into a successful eight-year run on TV. Although she not-so-privately griped about not having enough time to spend with her own growing family, the millions she made from the sale of rights to the program were the perfect balm for her upset.

as new campus queen in the *Los Angeles Times.* Three studios offered her screen tests. She turned them all down because she had not yet received her diploma as a qualified stenographer. Following graduation, she made an MGM screen test with another young up-and-comer, Van Heflin, and both were signed to $75-per-week studio contracts.

Reed labored for several years as "B" picture ingenue before moving up from starlet to star on loan-out to play James Stewart's small-town girlfriend/wife Mary in *It's a Wonderful Life.* Ambitious and highly motivated, Reed went about her acting career with the same determination that ruled her business and private lives. "I work at what I desire logically and systematically," she said in 1955, "waiting for the break."

In her private life, Reed married studio makeup man William Tuttle in 1943. They divorced in 1945, the same year she wed Tony Owen, an agent/producer fourteen years her senior. Of these marriages, Reed said in 1985, "one lasted twenty-five minutes, and one lasted twenty-five years." Her union with Owen produced four children: Penny Jane, Anthony, Jr., Timothy, and Mary Anne. The two eldest children were adopted.

Reed's movie career peaked with her greatest film triumph: winning the Best Supporting Actress Oscar for playing Lorene, a prostitute, in *From Here to Eternity* (1953). Donna Reed, a prostitute! Yet clever director Fred Zinnemann's casting worked. Lorene, the Honolulu hooker-with-a-heart she played, really showed the dark side of an essentially good small-town girl. In fact, Lorene recites lines that were somewhat prophetic, weirdly played out years later on Reed's TV program. She tells her G. I. lover, Montgomery Clift, that she won't marry him because he's not good enough for her. All she wants is enough money so she can go back to her hometown "and marry the proper husband. I'll be the proper wife and raise the proper children, and I'll be safe."

"The Oscar," Reed remarked in 1985, "did *not* help my career. I was a very *old* actress, remember. I was thirty-three, the age of Jessica Lange. I could see the handwriting on the wall. That's when I decided to take control of my career." Reed had already formed her own production company, Todon Productions, with her husband. "We knew I

Big sister Mary knows her little brother, Jeff, can be "such a brat!" and deserving of a good twist of the ear. But lo! is it possible that Mary's behavior could unleash such an uncharacteristic response from her mother? Yes, we have the photographic truth—Donna Stone is actually frowning *and Dr. Alex is* not *smiling. This photo has probably been faked.*

couldn't play a lawyer or any other professional, because no one then would accept a woman in that role. Secretaries and teachers had been done to death. [*Our Miss Brooks,* starring Eve Arden, and *The Ann Sothern Show* were 1950s TV sitcoms both starring former movie queens as teacher and secretary, respectively.] So I ended up being a mother."

The Donna Reed Show premiered on September 24, 1958, on ABC and got off to a very shaky start. This tame sitcom had the misfortune to air opposite *The Millionaire* on CBS and *Milton Berle on the Kraft Music Hall* on NBC. "We thought we'd had it after the first few weeks," the star recalled in 1960. "Berle was like a steamroller, and it was murder!" The critics were none too kind either. "They thought Donna was 'too nice' and 'too soft,'" recalled Owen. One of the severest critics was acerbic New York talk show host David Susskind, who sneered that "they ought to call it 'The Madonna Reed Show,'" and also called the program "pure drivel." Reed later shot back, "Mr. Susskind is sick, insecure." Yet she later admitted, "The critics were right. The first episodes didn't jell. We were stiff, and there weren't many laughs." According to the Trendex ratings system, Berle's

America's favorite little Virgin Princess, Mary Stone, demure, feminine, and sweet-natured like her TV super Mom. In real life, Shelley Fabares, was a shy, strictly raised devout Catholic, who was also very close to her TV mother, Donna Reed.

It would be years before Reed, who was part owner of her show and had creative control over its content, would find herself sufficiently radicalized to begin openly criticizing the program for its mindless unreality. These criticisms took place after she and Owen had tucked away millions from the show. (Reed reportedly walked away from the series some $7 million richer.)

Around the Screen Gems studio set, Todon employees let it be known that Reed displayed a "whim of iron" to ensure the program conformed to her perfectionist ideals. It was no secret that she warred with her directors. Reed remarked to *TV Guide* in 1964: "They're terrible. Directors seem to hate women—make them look as though they'd never seen a comb, and give them roles of unwed mothers and tramps. There's nothing left for families but Walt Disney and Doris Day. Doris never says 'yes' until the fellow marries her."

William Dozier, then Screen Gems production head, remembered Reed as a canny businesswoman: "Every year since the fourth season Donna has wanted to quit. Both of us know it was a game. She wanted to be coaxed. She wanted more money. She's a woman. We'd settle it, then await the end of the next season when the music would start…and we'd all waltz around again."

Never a ratings blockbuster, the show nonetheless sustained eight seasons by capturing an audience who bought into the Donna Stone fantasy and remained loyal. According to the Nielsen ratings, *The Donna Reed Show*, placed only once among the top twenty-five programs, during the 1963–64 season, when it hit #16.

The following item was taken from a 1959 ABC press release: "On the set at Screen Gems, Donna Reed's dressing room door is adorned with a sign that says, 'Beware of Tiger' and with it is a picture of a fluffy kitten. Donna, star of the ABC-TV program, 'The Donna Reed Show,' took to this decoration on her door with good-natured amusement. No one in the cast or crew admits putting it there, but all readily agree that to work with Donna is 'purr-fect.'"

debut show on October 8, 1958, clobbered the opposition. At 9:00 P.M., 31.2 percent of the nation's television sets were tuned to Berle, while *The Donna Reed Show* grabbed only 10.9 percent. The following week it dropped by four points!

Despite its poor ratings, both ABC and the program's sponsor, Campbell Soup, decided to stick by the fledgling show and give it a chance to grow in popularity and, hopefully, in ratings. The following season, ABC wisely switched the show's time slot from Wednesday night at nine to Thursday at eight, and *The Donna Reed Show* slowly began to build from there. As its audience grew, the grueling pace of shooting thirty-nine episodes per season began impacting on Reed's personal life. She fretted about not spending enough time with her four children, and stated in 1960: "I don't know how much longer I can cut myself up between the show and the children. But one thing is certain— the children come first, absolutely." Everywhere but in Hollywood. Children or no, Reed managed another six seasons before the series moved to the great syndication market in the sky.

JEFF GOES CAMPING

Jeff is annoying his sister and her friend. Mary complains to "Mother," who calls Jeff to task.

DONNA: Jeff, will you stop annoying those girls.
JEFF: Well, what's there to do, you won't let me have the air rifle.

This is the preamble to a show on how bored white-bread boys cause grief to their parents. Jeff doesn't know what to do with himself, and even when his equally bored buddy, Ricky, shows up at the door, his presence spells no relief.

DONNA: Ricky is here. Wants you to play with him.
JEFF: Mom, guys don't play.
DONNA: What do you do then?
JEFF: I don't know. Hack around.

Jeff complains that Ricky never wants to do anything that he wants to do, so Donna recommends Jeff do what Ricky wants for a change.

JEFF: Well, who wants to do that! (Nevertheless, Jeff invites Ricky inside.)
JEFF: Come on in. If you want to.
RICKY: What's so special about inside?

They bicker, then finally agree to go out back. Both boys then argue the merits of their father's heroic accomplishments in World War II. Ricky then brags his Dad is going to take him camping and hunting. Jeff, clearly jealous, tries to wheedle an invite from Ricky to tag along on his friend's trip. When turned down by Ricky, Jeff makes up a story that his father is going to take him on a hunting trip, then throws Ricky out of his backyard.

Unfortunately for Jeff, Dr. Stone is away for the weekend and can't take him on the hunting trip, so Donna volunteers. This solution is barely tolerable to Jeff, but when Mom says they'll camp at the local park and take his sister and her girlfriend along, Jeff throws a temper tantrum. Mary's none too pleased with the idea either.

MARY: But Babs and I had plans.
DONNA: To do what?.
MARY: We were going to work on our tans.
DONNA: There's no reason you can't work on them separately.
MARY: It's just not the same.

After a shaky first season, ABC held the faith and returned The Donna Reed Show *to the airwaves, and changed its time slot from Wednesday at 9:00 P.M. to Thursdays at 8:00 P.M., and the ratings began to climb. Here, with Carl Betz smiling over her left shoulder, is the star in a still dated August 1959.*

DONNA: Well, Mary, a tan is a tan.
MARY: What fun is getting a tan with Jeff? I can think of nothing worse than being cooped up in the great outdoors with Jeff.
JEFF: Camping is supposed to be for guys. She and Babs will gang up on me and tell me to get lost. This was supposed to be *my* trip. Now I gotta go with a harem.

Jeff and Mary make faces at each other, but neither will back out of the trip because they don't want to disappoint their mother. Just then, Ricky and his father show up and announce they are going on a camping trip, but only to the park, just like Jeff. Both boys have lied to each other and go outside to settle their differences. Ricky's father admits he was only taking his son because Ricky was jealous of Jeff's supposed trip with Dr. Stone. The boys return and now say they want to go to the movies, anyway. Obviously, the movies are the best antidote to boredom in suburban Hillsdale (drugs and sex haven't been heard of yet).

In 1959, Reed was nominated for an Emmy Award for Best Actress in a Leading Role in a Comedy Series, and also received a citation from the American Mothers Committee for her show's "outstanding portrayal of family life." So much for reality in 1959. Jane Wyatt won the Emmy that year for her far more realistic portrayal of an upper middle-class WASP suburban housewife in *Father Knows Best* on CBS. (When *The Donna Reed Show* was broadcast in West Germany it was retitled *Mama Knows Best*.)

In 1962, to keep Reed happy, Screen Gems cut production from thirty-nine to thirty-four episodes per season, at the same time raising her salary to a point where she earned more from thirty-four episodes than she had from shooting thirty-nine. Schedules were arranged so Donna wouldn't have to be in either the first or the last scenes filmed each day. A hike in the sale price of the series increased capital gains to Todon Productions, which owned all the program's negatives, and paid out twenty-five percent each to Screen Gems and ABC.

As the seasons passed, and Reed's bank account grew fatter, she became more openly critical of TV programming and women's roles in it, sounding more feminist in her comments. "We have proved on our show," she remarked in 1964, "that the public really does want to see a healthy woman, not a girl, not a neurotic, not a sexpot. We proved you don't have to have an astonishing bosom. The public doesn't give a damn about such things. On my show, I wear one kind of bra, and it's not too small, and it's not stuffed with cotton, and I'm not pushed up, pushed out, squeezed in, out, or sideways. I simply wear a bra that fits. Forty movies I was in, and all I remember is, 'What kind of bra will you be wearing, honey?' That was always the area of decision—from the neck to the navel."

Donna Reed never did burn her bra in public, but after leaving the show, she became a vociferous critic of the war in Vietnam. By 1971, she had become co-chairman of AMP (Another Mother for Peace). In 1968, she had turned from being a lifelong conservative Republican to supporting presidential peace candidate Eugene McCarthy. By then, her eldest son, Tony, was busy fighting the draft as a conscientious objector. By the early

seventies, Reed was remarking of her halcyon TV days, "I don't miss that life because I don't think those years were very important."

By 1971, Reed had divorced Tony Owen. In 1974, she married Grover Asmus, a retired Army colonel who had been a senior aide to General Omar Bradley and, ironically, had served in Vietnam. For years, she traveled with her husband following his new career as a petroleum engineer. In 1979, Reed commented: "As most actresses over forty know, television is a vast wasteland for women. It's a golden age for men between forty and sixty. I don't know why it isn't for women."

In 1984, Reed, then sixty-three, was called in by the producers of mega-soap *Dallas* to replace Barbara Bel Geddes as Ewing family matriarch, Miss Ellie, because of Bel Geddes's pending heart surgery. By spring 1985, Bel Geddes had recovered sufficiently to return to the show. The production company, Lorimar, fired Reed and did not consult her on the wording of the press release making the announcement, a common studio courtesy. Humiliated, Reed sued Lorimar claiming she was owed a tidy sum based on her four-year contract with the show. Reed settled out of court for $1 million later in 1985.

In December 1985, while undergoing treatment for an ulcer, Reed found out she was suffering from pancreatic cancer. She died January 14, 1986, just thirteen days before her sixty-fifth birthday.

SHELLEY FABARES

When smiling and standing next to her TV mom, Shelley had an almost uncanny resemblance to Donna Reed. They were the same height, five-feet-four, and had a similar coloring. She was hired by Reed because the star found her to be the embodiment of a "happy, healthy, all-American teenager."

She was born Michele Fabares (Fah-bear-aye. French origin. Original name, Abares) on January 19, 1944. Her aunt is comedienne Nanette Fabray. Shelley's slim figure and fresh good looks carried her into an early, successful modeling career. Said her lifelong friend, actress Annette Funicello, who met Shelley when they were both Mouseketeers on *The Walt Disney Show*, "Shelley was the most popular child model on the West Coast."

When Shelley left The Donna Reed Show *after the 1963 season, she wanted to try new roles and alter her image. "I'm growing up, I'm becoming a woman," she said in 1963. As evidenced by this photo, the fact that Shelley had turned into a shapely knockout in a bikini was not lost on the Hollywood film studios which quickly hired her to costar in several surf-and-sand flicks. Shelley holds the distinction of playing leading lady to Elvis Presley three times in* Girl Happy, Spinout *and* Clambake.

Remarks Shelley made to our father, Paul Denis, when he interviewed her in Hollywood in 1961, portrayed "an innocent and naïve girl who was very sweet," he remembered. "The most important thing is to marry and have children," Shelley had insisted. "After marriage, then it will be up to my husband whether to continue my career."

Though raised a devout Catholic, Shelley married record producer/songwriter Lou Adler in a civil ceremony in 1964 (Adler is Jewish). As with so many Hollywood marriages, it didn't last, and within three years they had separated. Fabares refused to comment about her marriage, other than to say, "I'm a very private, quiet, and cautious person." (Today she is married to Mike Farrell of *M*A*S*H*.)

Fabares holds the distinction of having costarred with Elvis Presley in three films—*Girl Happy, Spinout, Clambake*—more than any other actress. When film work diminished, she returned to TV and has worked steadily ever since costarring in sitcoms: *The Brian Keith Show* (1972–74), *The Practice* (1976–77), *Mary Hartman, Mary Hartman* (1977–78), *Highcliffe Manor* (1979), *One Day at a Time* (1981–84). As of 1991, Fabares was working in her sixth sitcom series, *Coach.* Her ties to *The Donna Reed Show* remain strong. In 1988, Fabares was visiting high schools and colleges in Iowa to give out details about the annual Donna Reed Scholarships Workshops in Denison. "I love to do this," said Fabares. "Even though she passed away two years ago, Donna remains one of the most important people in my life."

PAUL PETERSEN

"I contend that famous youngsters...in the entertainment industry don't have careers," said Paul Petersen in 1978. "They have sentences." Like many a child star before him, Petersen spent years "recovering" from the effects of early childhood fame. He figures that by age twenty-four, he had squandered $1 million by living wildly. He grew a beard, mustache, and long hair and survived, virtually, by "eating hors d'oeuvres" at parties he was still invited to. "I was the resident corpse in Hollywood...the walking dead. I was the kind of guy parents pointed out to their kids and said, 'Don't turn out like him.'"

A delightfully youthful and toothy Paul Petersen as he appeared on the November 26, 1959 episode of The Donna Reed Show *wherein he joined a highly secretive boys club of outer space enthusiasts whose shenanigans baffle Donna and Dr. Alex until they're let in on the secret.*

Petersen was literally "saved" by David Oliphant, of book publishing firm Simon & Schuster, who encouraged the former actor to write about his experiences as a race car driver. Although Petersen once, in a self-destructive fury, had driven his $15,000 Cobra sports car over a Hollywood cliff, he had nonetheless become a crack driver and penned a book called *High Performance Driving.* He followed this with a series of paperback adventure novels about a young man named Eric Saveman. Aimed at the youth market, the first two books sold 250,000 copies.

Petersen has fond memories about the cast of the show. For many years there were consistent reunions. "We shared so much during those eight years together, we're closer than a family," Petersen said in 1974. Looking back, he noted: "The characters we played were artificial. They didn't get down to the warts and tumors of real life. The show perpetuated the myth of ideal relationships. In today's world, it's better to admit that there are complex problems that can erupt in a family that only time and maturity can take care of."

In recent years, Petersen has been operating a limousine service in Los Angeles. He has a son, Brian, from his second marriage.

CARL BETZ

"For eight years I was pretending I was somebody I wasn't," Carl Betz told our father in a 1968 interview. "On *The Donna Reed Show*, I was a patient, calm, pleasant father. And I'm not that." Our father remembered Betz as a "real sophisticate. His bookshelves were lined with Shakespeare, Kazantzakis, Nabokov. He was a gourmet and liked expensive clothing, elegantly styled coats with red silk linings, and he was a fine dresser. He loved to travel abroad and drove a Lancia Flaminia sports car."

Carl Betz was his real name, and he was born in Pittsburgh, on March 9, 1921. He was six feet tall, 165 pounds, and had dark brown hair and blue

◄ *Known as the ever-smiling, ever-hokey TV dad Dr. Alex Stone, Carl Betz was a serious actor whose great love was playing roles on the legitimate stage. Besides making him financially secure, TV meant little to Betz till he starred on his own dramatic series,* Judd, For the Defense *(1967–69), a highly acclaimed program for which he was rewarded with an Emmy for Best Actor in a Dramatic Role.*

►
America's apple pie perfect Mom relaxes between takes at the Screen Gems studio where her show was filmed. Employees of Todon Productions (the company co-owned by Reed and husband/producer Tony Owen which produced the series) stated that their perfectionistic star/employer had a "whim of iron" when it came to running the show.

eyes. He had always wanted to be an actor, and after serving in World War II with the Army Corps of Engineers in North Africa and Italy, he spent many years in regional theaters and then on Broadway. Betz played in a few movies and even had a stint on a TV soap opera, *Love of Life,* in 1955.

"I did sixty plays in sixty-five weeks once in stock," Betz said in 1967. But when his son, Richard, was born in 1957, the prospect of steady work in TV was appealing. "I did it for the money," Betz admitted.

After eight years as Alex Stone, Betz was happy to move on. "I was little more than the monosyllabic Dr. Stone, which is what one reviewer called me. Most of the time, I was seen hanging around the background with egg on my face. I'm not ashamed of fifty percent of those shows," he said in 1967. "The other half you can burn."

Betz had his greatest TV triumph starring in *Judd for the Defense* (1967–69) on CBS, playing a flamboyant Texas attorney, replete with cowboy hat and boots. The role won him a well-deserved Emmy for Outstanding Actor in a Dramatic Series in 1969. In the years following, Betz worked mostly in theater and TV movies. A longtime smoker, he died of lung cancer at age fifty-seven on January 19, 1978.

TV ROLES & ROCK 'N' ROLL

Donna Reed's husband, producer Tony Owen, arranged for auditions for both Paul Petersen and Shelley Fabares at Colpix Records in Hollywood. Back in 1962, Owen figured rightly that these immensely popular teens could do no wrong, so why not cash in on the rock 'n' roll craze, the same way Ricky Nelson had.

"But Mr. Owen," Fabares protested, "I'm not a singer. This is just going to be awful." A song called "Johnny Angel" was chosen for Fabares, who reluctantly sang it, and it sold one million copies.

Petersen didn't fare as well with "My Dad" (the single was a tribute to his TV dad, Carl Betz), but it and Petersen's seven other singles and five albums sold over one million copies before his recording career ended. Fabares and Petersen's albums and singles are now sought-after collector's items.

CAST LIST

FAMILY: The Stones

MEMBERS:

Donna Stone . . . . **Donna Reed**
Dr. Alex Stone . . . . **Carl Betz**
Mary Stone (1958–63) . . **Shelley Fabares**
Jeff Stone . . . . **Paul Petersen**

SIGNIFICANT OTHERS:

Trisha Stone (1963–66) . . . **Patty Petersen**
Dr. Dave Kelsey (1963–65) . . . **Bob Crane**
Midge Kelsey (1963–66) . . . **Ann McCrea**
Smitty (1965–66) . . . . **Darryl Richard**
Celia Wilgus . . . . **Kathleen Freeman**
Wilbur Wilgus . . . . **Howard McNear**
Karen Holmby . . . . **Janet Langard**

THEME SONG: **"Happy Days"** by William Loose and John Seely
TIMEFRAME: **1958–66**
NETWORK: **ABC**
ADDRESS: **Hilldale, USA**

275 episodes

BONANZA

"Up there's the high Nielsen peak," Lorne Greene tells his costars, "and that's where we're fixing to stake our claim. There's more riches up there than in all the silver mines in Virginia City!" He wasn't kidding, either. After he and Michael Landon and Dan Blocker sold their residual syndication rights to the show, they all became millionaires. They also made guest appearances in rodeos together.

White hats ruled the TV prairie in those days of yesteryear, 1957–61, the heyday of the Western. Those white hats rode after lowdown, ornery black hats, lassoed outlaw varmints, and then tipped their ten-gallon chapeaus to the pretty school-marm in the gingham dress.

In 1959—the year oaters peaked with thirty, that's right, thirty of 'em in primetime—NBC, in a blaze of inspiration pretty as a desert sunset, put *four* white hats in the saddle. Their names were Ben, Adam, Hoss, and Little Joe, and they were part of a strange new breed of Western, the sagebrush soap opera. They were Lorne Greene, Pernell Roberts, Dan Blocker, and Michael Landon.

A family show with fisticuffs and fusillades might have been one way of describing *Bonanza,* which purported to tell the "real" story of the Old West during the silver rush in Nevada in the 1850s. Creator Dave Dortort said at the time he wanted to fight "Momism" on television, in which "Father always turns out to be a fool." *Bonanza* would be "a show where a man could be a MAN without women mucking things up."

For all of their rugged, manly virtues, the Cartwright sons were still three grown men following their father around saying, "What do we do next, Pa?" Pa was Ben Cartwright, a man of magnetic personality and basso profundo voice. His every utterance seemed to compel awe and to seem, well, profundo. The script says each of his three sons was born to a different wife, who subsequently perished from the rigors of frontier life. (Women continued to die with regularity on the one-thou-sand-square-mile Ponderosa ranch, if and when they became engaged to any of the men. Some-times it would be an accident, as when a horse and buggy went off a cliff, or a rattlesnake bite, or fire or flood. Thus was creeping "Momism" kept at bay. And female viewers, who liked their favorites single, kept happy.)

Adam was the eldest son, a dark, brooding presence, usually dressed all in black. Next was Hoss, a gentle giant, adored by the younger viewers as the good-natured buffoon. Lastly was Little Joe, the teen heartthrob nattily dressed in fawn gray rancher's pants, matching boots, and a moss green jacket. Quick to flash his mischievous smile or his ever ready fists, he was the one the others were

Are Lorne Greene and Pernell Roberts laughing about big Dan Blocker's proclivity for the cold cuts as they rustle up some lunch on location? At six-feet-four and 275 lbs., Blocker had a healthy appetite. Michael Landon told an audience at the South Texas State Fair: "My brother Hoss (Blocker) loves to dance. You should see that boy do the Twist. He looks like a runaway truck and trailer." They were best pals.

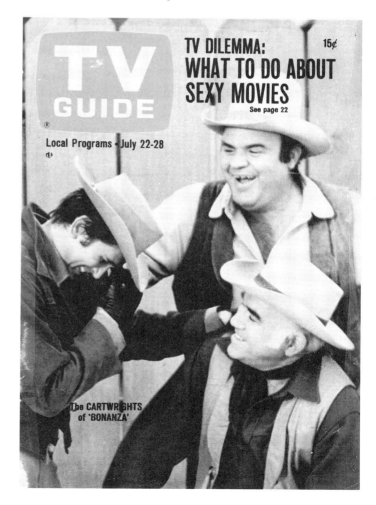

When they weren't fighting bad guys, the boys sometimes fought each other. Here Little Joe is seen trying to take a poke at Adam, with Hoss intervening. As creator Dave Dortort described the show: "A father and three sons whose allegiance is not to silver but to the land. The three sons are forever at each other's throats but when the chips are down they fight shoulder to shoulder."

always bailing out of trouble. And he was always flirting with the ladies.

Despite the lack of a feminine touch in the family, the men lived comfy lives in their neat, immaculate ranch house. None of their clothes ever showed the gritty results of cattle ranching either. Fact is, *Bonanza* was not really a Western at all, but, as one critic put it, "a family-situation-comedy-action-adventure series, with a Western setting." By blending all these genres, the network cleverly staved off the boredom that eventually builds with a familiarity of storylines. Having guest stars like Dean Stockwell, Yvonne De Carlo *(The Munsters)*, Jack Carson, and Ruth Roman, who, for one episode each, become involved in the lives of the Cartwrights, kept things fresh too. Beside the usual gunfights and bronco-busting, one might encounter an historical figure like Mark Twain (played by Howard Duff) or Henry Comstock (Jack Carson), for whom the Comstock Lode was named. For comic relief, there was the time a knight in armor rammed his lance through a stagecoach door, or when the boys adopted a circus elephant. Most memorable was Hoss's run-in with a bunch of wily leprechauns.

At the heart of *Bonanza* was the commanding figure of Ben Cartwright. By the mid-1960s, he was undoubtedly the most popular star on television. With his majestic white locks and thundering voice, he lent a biblical presence to the show and became a kind of national father-figure. Many episodes were mini-morality plays in which issues such as mercy killing or racial prejudice were explored. But mostly it was the honest and decent Ben Cartwright & Sons going against assorted sad-dlebums and renegades.

One typical plot concerned a man named Matthew, a former Union soldier and defrocked minister, running afoul of one of Ben's neighbors, an ex-Confederate officer. The Southern gentleman, whose plantation had been burned down, is furious when his daughter Lori falls in love with the much-decorated Matthew. He believes the damned Yankee's Medal of Honor was for the savage butchery of so many of the South's finest sons. In order to drive home his feeling that the romance is ill-conceived, he and his sadistic son tie Matthew to a wagon wheel and prepare to send

Since their Ponderosa Ranch is approximately the size of Rhode Island, the Cartwrights spend lots of time in the saddle. If you want to see a replica of the ranch, there's one described in TV Guide *(1986) in Incline Village, Nevada (near Reno), which features a petting zoo, a church, a Hossburger stand, and "real gallows for photo ops." A good place for parents to take the kiddies.*

Michael Landon, seen here dressed smartly in fawn gray pants and moss green jacket, was the show's teen heartthrob. When he joined Bonanza *he weighed only 132 lbs., so his clothes were padded to make his chest and shoulders bigger, while he weight-trained. The guy with his hands on his hips is David Canary (Candy), who was brought aboard to "replace" departed Pernell Roberts (Adam).*

him out of town with a new coat of tar and feathers. As the son moves forward with a clump of molten tar on a stick, Lori arrives with a wrathful-looking Ben. A shot rings out, cutting the flaming stick in half. His white sideburns bristling, Ben advances. "This thing stops right now," he growls. He has a telegram just received from the United States War Department proving that Matthew is not the killer everyone says he is. Then in sonorous cadence, Ben reads the Medal of Honor citation, for saving both Union and Confederate soldiers on the field of battle during heavy bombardment. It is signed, "Abraham Lincoln."

Another story involves Ben's old friend Horace, who stops at the Ponderosa, with his wife Deborah and beautiful daughter Melinda, on the way to California. Deborah, an ambitious woman, sees a way to rescue her family's failing fortunes. She bullies Horace and Melinda into supporting her scheme to land Little Joe as son-in-law. Feeling that they don't have the financial or social position to match the Cartwrights, Deborah invents a phony past for Melinda, including the best finishing schools and well-bred ex-boyfriends.

> MELINDA: Why does it have to be Little Joe?
> DEBORAH: Because Hoss doesn't feel that way 'bout you, and Adam is too cunning.

All this deceit is too much for the genteel Melinda. It makes her feel woozy, and so she excuses herself from dinner "to get some air." Still, she is her mother's daughter, and she feels more attracted to Adam than to Little Joe. She tries to seduce him by getting her dress caught on a barbed wire fence, but Adam guesses her game.

Any similarity between this and classic soap opera fare is purely intentional: the poor girl seeking to join the well-to-do family, the old-fashioned value of truthfulness in love, the triumph of virtue. Melinda confesses all to Little Joe, as violin music swells. Ben is magnanimous and arranges a job for Horace in San Francisco, and, better for having met the Cartwrights, the family moves on.

All of this hokey moralizing, week in and week out, was a little much for the cast to take, so there

was plenty of practical joking and horseplay on the set. Dan Blocker (Hoss) was described as the most boisterous and fun-loving by his good friend, Michael Landon (Little Joe). At six-feet-four, 275 pounds, he was indeed the genial giant. (When Landon first landed his *Bonanza* role, he was a wispy 132 pounds, so his fawn gray rancher's outfit was padded to make his chest and shoulders larger, until, through weight-training, he gained ten pounds.) Lorne Greene (Ben), the third of these Three Mesquiteers, was a lordly six-foot-one and a paunchy two hundred pounds.

Through several joint business ventures, Greene, Blocker, and Landon became very rich. And by staying with the show almost till the end (Dan Blocker died suddenly of a lung clot on May 13, 1972) and by each selling his residual syndication rights for a reported seven-figure sum, the three became very, *very* rich. Not included in all this comraderie was Pernell Roberts. As somber and moody offstage as on, he kept mostly to himself and, in the early 1960s tried to get out of his *Bonanza* contract. Told by NBC he would never work there or anywhere else again, he stayed on until 1965. To "preserve my sanity," he told reporters, he would just "walk through" his role. Apparently this was okay with NBC, which told him his work was "great." For Roberts, however, there was no room for "dramatic honesty." The series had to turn out thirty-four episodes per season, or one every six days. Sarcastically, he dubbed the Ponderosa a "fairytale kingdom."

When Pernell Roberts left the show with hopes of doing something more "significant," it was speculated that it was a wrong career move. And indeed it was. He took off his toupee and did numerous guest shots over the years, but it would be fourteen years before landing in his next series—his only other one—in the starring role of *Trapper John, M.D.* (1979–86).

▶

Dan Blocker was described by friends as boisterous and fun-loving, and also bright and articulate, two qualities that, of course, were hidden in his role as the "dumb but lovable" Hoss. Blocker and Michael Landon developed such a close friendship while on Bonanza *that Landon chose Blocker to be his best man when he wed his second wife, model Lynn Noe.*

According to Michael Landon (seen here drawing his gun as Little Joe), Bonanza suffered through one of TV's periodic clampdowns on "violence." For example, NBC objected to Landon's story of chain gang escapees tracked by vicious German shepherds. "I then suggested we use collies and destroy Lassie's image on CBS, our rival network!" he said in a 1969 interview. "Finally, we were down to rabid Pekinese..." Eventually, the story was scrubbed, and Bonanza remained "a family-situation-comedy-action-adventure series, set in the West."

By 1964, the fairytale kingdom was drawing huge audiences. For the following three years, 1964–67, it was television's number one program, replacing *The Beverly Hillbillies*. (Before that, *Wagon Train* had been top doggie, and *Gunsmoke* had won the triple crown prior to that, 1958–61.) By the time of *Bonanza's* ascendancy, most other "cowboy" shows were on the wane. The only one showing some life was *The Virginian*, which copied *Bonanza's* slick production and genre-mixing formula. The saga of the Ponderosa would remain a top ten Nielsen show for all but the last two years of its run.

When *Bonanza* debuted in 1959, the Cold War was still running hot. We wore the white hats, the Russian wore black. There was fear a real shooting war could break out at any time. How satisfying, then, to watch bad men bite the dust every week, on TV. In a complex world, we longed for simple solutions. "If you have a problem with a man in a Western," explained Dan Blocker, "you just say, 'Draw!'"

The first year was tough for the show, however. Ratings were lousy, but NBC stuck behind it, and with good reason. The top NBC executives had ordered a big color series to help sell color TVs, the new product of their parent corporation, RCA. By 1960, both the show and the product were doing very well. And Lorne Greene & Company began to reap the rewards of their stardom.

THE PONDEROSA VS. SOUTHFORK

Bonanza was the most successful show of the 1960s and, after the phenomenal *Gunsmoke,* the biggest Western hit in television.

It was a megahit, and its enormous popularity (it's still seen in reruns) rivals or exceeds *Dallas* at its height. Depending on which source you believe, *Bonanza* was aired in between forty to sixty countries (including the then-Communist nation of Poland) and had some three to five hundred million weekly viewers!

Now hear *Bonanza's* creator, Dave Dortort, explain the show's concept, in 1959: "A father and three sons whose allegiance is not to silver [of the famous Comstock Lode] but to the land. The three sons are forever at each other's throats, but when the chips are down they fight shoulder to shoulder. [NBC vice president in 1959] Alan Livingstone has called it 'a love affair between four men'—and that's what it is."

Sound familiar? Except for the last statement, he

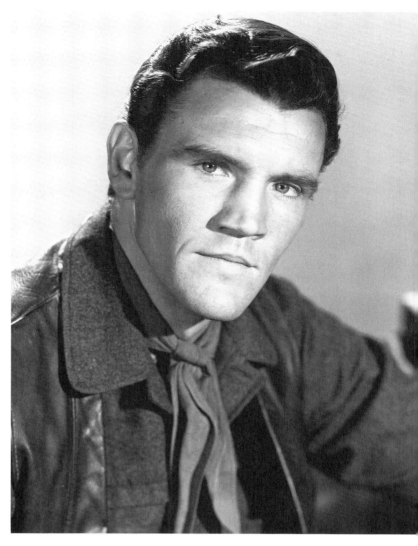

might be talking about *Dallas.* Just take out the word "silver" and substitute "oil."

There *was* one thing unique to *Dallas,* however. Being called "chewing gum for the brain" by Hans Wallow, a member of the West German Parliament, during debate on whether the show should be banned from German airwaves! That's one distinction *Bonanza* never had.

LORNE GREENE

Born in Canada, Lorne Greene had a distinguished career as a stage actor. (He played Othello, among other Shakespearean roles, and starred opposite Katharine Cornell on Broadway in *The Prescott Proposal*). Moving to Hollywood in 1957, he did some film work (most notably as the prosecuting attorney in *Peyton Place*), then came his golden moment, a guest starring role on *Wagon Train,* then America's number two program, behind *Gunsmoke.*

Bonanza creator David Dortort was then looking for someone to be Ben Cartwright. The role, as first conceived, was to be that of a tyrannical father. (It was later amended to be "stern but fair.") Dortort wanted to see if Greene could "dominate" *Wagon Train*'s star, Ward Bond, in their scenes together. A tall order for a tenderfoot, but Greene pulled it off, and was duly offered his chance for television glory.

When fame came, Greene was ready for it. He promoted *Bonanza* tirelessly. In 1965, he took a fledgling nightclub act to the Nugget Hotel in Sparks, Nevada, where he sang this parody of "I'm an Old Cowhand": "I'm an old cowpoke, I never drink or smoke/I don't mess around with all them women folk/I'm rough and tough, but I'm never coarse/And I represent such a moral course/That my sponsor would faint if I kissed my horse." He also told anecdotes about the show and encouraged the audience to take off their shoes, put their feet up on the table, and look at him through their spread toes, just like they did at home. "Sons" Landon and Blocker rode with him in state fairs and rodeos, dressed as the Cartwrights, six-guns blazing blank cartridges, to the delight of fans. In fact, Lorne Greene became so absorbed in his TV persona that some feared he'd blurred the bound-

Pernell Roberts's departure from Bonanza *is still celebrated in Hollywood as one of the worst career moves ever made by a television star. Only McLean Stevenson's departure from* M*A*S*H *and Patrick Duffy's quitting* Dallas *in 1985 are considered comparable. (Duffy returned to* Dallas *a year later, however.) Roberts's absence made room for David Canary (pictured here) to join* Bonanza *as the cowpoke Candy. Today's soap opera fans will know Canary as the Emmy-Award-winning star of* All My Children, *playing Adam Chandler.*

ary between himself and Pa Cartwright. One guest star on *Bonanza* told a reporter, "He [Lorne] has a tendency to carry his television role into real life. When he offers an opinion, he thinks he is a sage. When I talked to him between scenes, I got a feeling he actually thought he was my father."

An exact replica of the Ponderosa ranch house, complete with staircase that led nowhere, was built in Mesa, Arizona, to help promote a new development, and Lorne Greene was there to greet visitors. He was awarded an honorary degree from Missouri Valley College for "bringing wholesome entertainment to a world during times of stress, and because the nature of your…public image is one of dignity deserving recognition." And an

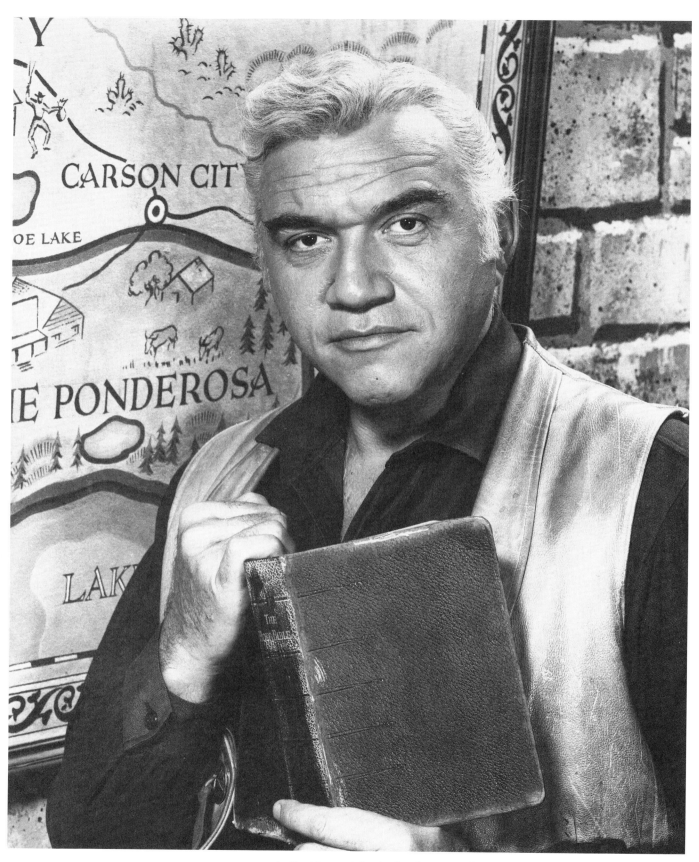

As Ben Cartwright, the family patriarch, actor Lorne Greene strikes a stern pose in front of a map of the Ponderosa Ranch, clutching an open Bible, in this publicity shot from the show's first season. With his deep voice and majestic white locks, Ben has the stage presence of an Old Testament prophet.

advice column was offered to him by a newspaper, now that he had become America's favorite Dad.

Once known as the "Voice of Canada" for his work as a radio commentator, Greene turned his mellifluous tones to music, recording the hit ballad "Ringo" in 1965, which reportedly sold two million copies worldwide. It was a cadenced monologue in which the speaker, a lawman, recounts his early friendship with Johnny Ringo, and how their paths diverged. Finally, on opposite sides of the law, he guns down Ringo in a Western duel.

Despite his close identification with the character of Ben Cartwright, when *Bonanza* ended its run, Greene was able to move on. He did commercials (most notably for Alpo Dog Food), a documentary series on wildlife called *Lorne Greene's New Wilderness,* and assorted action series, like *Griff, Battlestar Galactica,* and *Code Red.*

Lorne Greene died on September 11, 1987, in Santa Monica Hospital. He had gone there the month before to have abdominal surgery for an ulcer and then contracted pneumonia. Three days before dying, he was visited by Michael Landon, who reported: "He couldn't speak. I took his hand in mine and held it. He looked at me and then slowly started to arm-wrestle like we used to. He smiled and nodded. I think he wanted me to know everything was okay."

MICHAEL LANDON

To Michael Landon, Lorne Greene truly was like a surrogate father, and he and Dan Blocker, a nonstop prankster, felt close enough to Greene to play a practical joke aimed at their "Pa's" most vulnerable spot. It was one of the best-kept secrets on *Bonanza* that Greene's handsome head of hair was a fake, and he was very sensitive about it. He would never appear without his toupee, not even among close friends. Well, the two cut-ups shoved their unsuspecting target into a swimming pool and then watched as he sank down and down.

For the longest time he stayed under, until his tormentors began to worry. With his breath finally expended, he broke the surface, clutching his soaked and slipping dignity. It is not recorded what reaction he gave. We presume he either laughed his deep belly laugh, or else marched away with all the manly dignity of Ben Cartwright.

As usually happens when a program reaches the zenith of popularity, its stars' power and influence grow as well. By the mid-sixties, everybody in the cast was complaining about the diminishing quality of the scripts. Michael Landon was especially interested in the behind-the-scenes end of production, so he took the lead in suggesting changes and rewrites, finally convincing the producers to let him do whole scripts from scratch. He found he had a knack for it and was soon doing half a season's worth of stories, and was even directing.

"The Wish," written and directed by Michael Landon, was about a freed slave (Ossie Davis) and his young son (played by nine-year-old John Spell). As Cartwright neighbors, they are befriended by Hoss, who unwittingly becomes the fumbling and insensitive, if well-intentioned, white "liberal." "I did research in black history," Landon said at the time (1969), "but I really wanted to show a black man in terms of contemporary society." The title referred to the young boy's wish that his father was white, he explained, and was happy to report that John Spell thought the script was "funny." "He couldn't imagine wishing his own father was white."

Landon also did melodrama, as with his script, "To Die in Darkness," which marked his directorial debut in 1968. It guest-starred James Whitmore as a man wrongfully imprisoned on testimony given by Ben. He seeks revenge by trapping Ben and Candy (David Canary) in a mine shaft. By isolating Ben and Candy, Landon hoped to let the audience learn more about Candy, the ranch hand meant to fill Adam's boots after Pernell Roberts exited. A thirty-foot mine shaft was constructed especially for this episode, and the two actors had to work in a space that was only seven feet by seven feet.

Perhaps the toughest episode of all to shoot was "Forever." Landon wrote it as a special showcase for his friend, Dan Blocker. It was supposed to have been the tragic story of Hoss's love affair and marriage. Sadly, a true-life tragedy intervened with Blocker's untimely death.

Landon reworked the script into the ill-fated romance between Joe and his bride, played by Bonnie Bedelia. Some lines were added to indicate Hoss's death, but words of grief were kept to a minimum. Landon felt more could be said "with silence."

Before we close, we should mention the Cartwrights' Chinese cook, Hop Sing. The character was played by the venerable Victor Sen Yung, for *Bonanza*'s entire run.

EPISODIC WEIRDNESS
BIG HOSS, LITTLE FALSIES

Hoss rushes home. "Paw! Little Joe! I've seen leprechauns! They was down by an abandoned mine with a sackful of gold just like those folk tales. They was real!" Paw and Little Joe look at each other. Hoss must have fallen off his horse again and hit his head.

An insulted Hoss goes back to look again; this time he sees a leprechaun perched in a tree. Like all the others, it is small with a sneaky smile and wears a medieval costume of peaked felt cap and slippers with long, pointed toes. While Hoss watches openmouthed, another leprechaun sneaks up behind him and, with a blow to the head, renders him unconscious. Little Joe finds Hoss later. Clearly *something* is going on. The Cartwrights head back for the abandoned mine.

There the mystery is solved. The leprechauns are really circus midgets. Their sack of gold is money owed to them by an unscrupulous circus manager. When he returns to retrieve it, the Cartwrights rescue their new little friends, send the manager packing, and offer Virginia City as a place for the newly unemployed midgets to live.

When some citizens object, Hoss shames them with an eloquent speech on brotherhood. It takes a lot more than a fall from a horse to get big-hearted, hard-headed Hoss to change his Big Softy ways.

Looking back, we can see the show had other problems besides bad scripting. The flaws were many and obvious:

• The Cartwrights were raising cattle in an era when buffalo were still plentiful, and there was little market for beef.

• Their hairstyles were suspiciously modern (Ben wore a ducktail!).

• Since part of the action takes place during the Civil War, one has to ask, were the boys draft dodgers?

• And what about the fact their cowboy pants had zippers?

These things are quibbles, of course. *Bonanza*'s heyday was a simpler time. The most popular shows were those with rural or frontier settings. People didn't expect realism, they wanted escape, with a little dime-store psychology or homey sermonizing thrown in at the end.

Bonanza reflected those times and delivered what was needed: a reassuring tale of four men for whom knowing right and wrong was second nature, and to whom loyalty to ideals and to family was the highest virtue. Not a bad credo, actually. After all, audiences responded all over the world by taking Ben, Adam, Hoss, and Little Joe into their hearts.

In 1987, the original creators of *Bonanza* attempted a syndicated "reunion" show of sorts, but Lorne Greene's death on the eve of production complicated matters. John Ireland was written in as Ben Cartwright's long-lost seafaring brother who comes in to take over the Ponderosa and (greenhorn that he is) begins selling off drilling rights to a crafty land baron. Most interesting was the casting. Michael Landon, Jr., played the son of Little Joe (his dad's old role), who was said to have been lost charging up San Juan Hill with Teddy Roosevelt. Gillian Greene, Lorne's daughter, was the love interest between the new Little Joe (aka Benj) and Hoss's bastard son, played by Brian A. Smith. Barbara Anderson played the old Little Joe's widow. *Bonanza: The Next Generation* turned out to be a proposed new series pilot which simply didn't fly.

CAST LIST

FAMILY: The Cartwrights

MEMBERS:

Ben Cartwright . . . . **Lorne Greene**
Little Joe Cartwright . . . . **Michael Landon**
Eric "Hoss" Cartwright
 (1959–72) . . . . **Dan Blocker**
Adam Cartwright
 (1959–65) . . . . **Pernell Roberts**

SIGNIFICANT OTHERS:

Hop Sing . . . . **Victor Sen Yung**
Candy (1967–70,
 1972–73) . . . . **David Canary**
Sheriff Roy Coffee . . . . **Ray Teal**
Jamie Hunter Cartwright
 (1970–73) . . . . **Mitch Vogel**
Deputy Clem Poster . . . . **Bing Russell**

Lavishly produced, with a sumptuous color process that still looks terrific today, Bonanza was created expressly to help RCA (the parent corporation of NBC) sell its newest electronic product: color TV. The show's debut, in 1959, was "disastrous," according to the New York Times *TV critic. It lost out badly to its powerhouse competition,* Perry Mason, *but went on to be one of the most successful programs in television history.*

THEME SONG: **Jay Livingston and
 Ray Evans***
TIMEFRAME: **1959–73**
NETWORK: **NBC**
ADDRESS: **The Ponderosa Ranch
 Virginia City, Nevada**

440 episodes

*Sung on the opening show by Lorne
 Greene, Pernell Roberts, Dan Blocker,
 and Michael Landon

95

THE ANDY GRIFFITH SHOW

There's a seamless, loving quality to *The Andy Griffith Show*. Life in the mythical town of Mayberry, North Carolina, unfolds slow-w-l-y—nothing is ever rushed. People take their time when they talk. They are gracious. They talk to, not at, one another. They ponder the goings-on of the day, pause to watch the frogs leap in a pond, sniff the sweet scent of a hot apple pie cooling on the windowsill. They smile a lot, look closely at the new stranger in town, then sidle up and greet him warmly. Never in a hurry, the good and decent citizens of this rural, friendly American town are church-going (but not fire-and-brimstone Bible quoters), loyal-to-their-neighbor kind of folks. They may act foolish and certainly are a bit naïve at times, but, with only a few *decided* exceptions, they are nobody's fools.

Sheriff Andy Taylor (Andy Griffith) is the strong, supportive, father figure to his fellow Mayberryans. He is the linchpin around which all the characters, all the actions, sooner or later revolve. Without homespun Sheriff Andy, life might go on in Mayberry, but he would be sorely missed, and it would only be an imitation of life. The key success of this program lays squarely on Griffith's shoulders, in his remarkable characterization of Sheriff Andy. He is the calm at the center of the storm, the voice of reason when all others have lost theirs, waiting patiently while calamity strikes all around him, forever giving gangly Deputy Barney Fife (Don Knotts) a free rein to explode all over the tube. When the smoke clears there would be Griffith, the oak standing tall after the hurricane, with that little grin across his face, kind of saying, "Well, y'all have cut up a might now, but ah'm here to tell ya everythin's gonna be jus' fine, y'hear?" And so it would be, week after week, year after year.

One could read volumes in the pauses of the characters' speeches in the show. Characters, especially Sheriff Andy, would take so long to talk sometimes, pausing between words, that one could swear to hearing the synapses sparking in their brains. How the characters spoke, and how quickly they finished their speeches, was a bone of contention between Griffith and the show's creators right from the very beginning. Since the main concept in television, especially sitcoms, has always been "speed," the idea of taking your time in

In the first episode to feature the sweet, homespun, and slightly dippy Aunt Bea (Frances Bavier), Sheriff Andy patiently tries to teach her the fundamentals of baseball by showing her which way to hold the bat.

We all know about Sheriff Andy's shy ways around the womenfolk, yet here it sure looks like he's the one pointing out the mistletoe to Miss Ellie Walker (Elinor Donahue) during this December 1960 broadcast.

exposition, slowly building the timing and nuances in a scene, went against the prevailing order.

Griffith, ever the perfectionist (and owner of fifty percent of the show), took great pains to hone each script to its perfected essentials. Usually executive producer Sheldon Leonard, producer Aaron Ruben, director Bob Sweeney, and Griffith and Knotts would go over every script together, editing, reworking, collaborating till it was right. Only when Griffith was perfectly satisfied would he rise from the story conference table. In the beginning, New York/Hollywood types like Leonard and Ruben were uncomfortable with the slow pacing. But Griffith would insist that people "back home" enjoyed their languor. The humor was not vertical, always heading towards some "peak" at breakneck speed, but more horizontal, and laid back.

Griffith's all-time favorite scene, from the 249 episodes that were shot over eight seasons, illustrates his passion for timing and "realism." Griffith recalled the scene to Richard Kelly, in the latter's excellent book, *The Andy Griffith Show* (John F. Blair, 1981).

It's a drowsy afternoon in Mayberry, and Andy and Barney are lazing on the front porch. Barney stretches, turns to Andy and says: "Know what I'm gonna do?" And quietly acknowledges the question with an "Mmmm…" little grunt. Barney continues: "I'm gonna go home, take a shower, go over to Thelma Lou's, and watch a little TV." A good several seconds of silence follows, then Barney slaps his stomach: 'Yep, that's what I'm gonna do—go home, take a shower, go over to Thelma Lou's, and watch a little TV." Several more seconds of silence. Then Barney continues: "That's it—home, shower, over to Thelma Lou's…" Without missing a beat, Andy comes in with "…watch a little TV?"

This was the leisurely, amiable signature of the show. Viewers everywhere believed that this manner of speech and way of life represented small-town life in rural America. Just plain folk sitting around, and nothing much seems to happen—and it's all so quiet, sweet, and safe. An undertone pervading those important elements of sweetness and safety was that Mayberry folks genuinely loved

Four stouthearted he-men of Mayberry…or should that be two he-men and two half-wits. (Left to right) Sheriff Andy (Andy Griffith), Opie Taylor (Ronny Howard), and Deputy Barney Fife (Don Knotts) taking aim at the sane with his slingshot, while bewildered village idiot Gomer Pyle (Jim Nabors) tries to figure out just what a slingshot is.

and respected each other. That warmth was always present and especially embodied in the character of Sheriff Andy Taylor. The warmth is what drew the loyal audiences week after week.

The proof of the popularity of the show is easily determined by scanning the ratings for the eight seasons the program ran. In each, *The Andy Griffith Show* consistently ranked among the top ten shows. Ironically, in its final season, 1967–68, it ranked number one. Its numbers were always in the high twenties, meaning that whenever the program aired it captured never less than a quarter of all sets turned on during its time slot. *The Andy Griffith Show* owned Monday nights in its slot, 1960–63 at 9:30, 1964 at 8:30, 1965–68 at 9:00, invariably beating the competition.

The program's popularity and resilience resulted from the unique chemistry of its ensemble company of actors. All fondly thought of themselves as "a family," crew included. To this day, Griffith and Knotts remain the closest of friends. "We're more than friends," said Griffith in 1964. "I think I'm closer to Don than anyone else. We've worked side by side ten hours a day for years." Their friendship began in 1955, when Knotts acted with Griffith on Broadway in *No Time for Sergeants*, which ran two years. They reprised their roles for the film version in 1957. There's a common thread to their friendship, as both men come from rural backgrounds—Griffith from North Carolina, Knotts from West Virginia. Many others in the cast also came from similar "country" backgrounds. Jim (Gomer) Nabors and "cousin" George (Goober) Lindsay are both Alabama natives, while Ron (Opie) Howard was born in Duncan, Oklahoma.

The ensemble company acted out a rich tapestry of caricatures. Sheriff Taylor is a widower living with his young son, Opie, and his spinster Aunt Bee. He never carries a gun (crime's only minimal since everyone knows everyone), and enforces the law through example, quietly demonstrating a strong moral code while remaining understanding and pliant, never superior or pontifical. Andy occasionally dates women such as local schoolteacher Helen Crump, but his main concerns are keeping the town safe from his well-meaning but dunderhead deputy (and cousin), Barney Fife,

They're all a-grinnin' because Mayberry sho' is a funny li'l town with, among others, Sheriff Andy Taylor (Andy Griffith), his son Opie (Ronny Howard), and Deputy Barney Fife (Don Knotts). Opie's got his cowboy neckerchief and cap pistol and, heaven help him, Barney Fife to watch over him. It's a toss-up as to which "boy" gets into more mischief on the show.

Life sure can be tough in Mayberry when the one wise man in the whole town has to deal with three of its biggest, but funniest, fools. Sherriff Andy tries to discourage an impending fight by discussing the cause with Goober (George Lindsey), Floyd the barber (Howard McNear), and would-be fighter/ resident hillbilly geek, Ernest T. Bass (Howard Morris). The episode aired in color on September 27, 1965.

The premiere episode of the fourth season, "Opie the Birdman" (broadcast September 30, 1963) was a morality tale and one of the finest half-hours in the series' eight year run. A beautifully crafted teleplay of life, death and coming of age.

who's just a little too paranoid to be a "peace" officer. Don Knotts said of his character: "Barney was like a kid. He showed all of his feelings. He was a little boy in a man's body. There was no control in Barney, that's what made him so funny." At five-feet-eight, 120 pounds, Knotts—with his trademark persona—was perfect as the jittery-bundle-of-nerves deputy with the Napoleonic complex, and he earned five Emmy Awards for Outstanding Performance by an Actor in a Supporting Role as Barney Fife.

BARNEY AND THE JAYWALKER

A typical example of Barney behavior is when he attempts to arrest senior citizen Emma Watson for jaywalking (one of Barney's favorite offenses, which he views as a heinous crime). Barney drags the poor old gal into the police station in handcuffs:

BARNEY: Now, Emma, I seen you do it. Don't tell me you didn't do it. Don't think you're gonna get away with that kind of stuff on my beat. Because when you commit a crime in this town, you pay for it. And I'm the one that sees to it you pay for it 'cause that's my duty!

EMMA: But Barney, I always cross Maple in the middle of the block.

BARNEY: Emma, that's jaywalking. It's against the law. Step over here. You've got to be booked and fingerprinted. This is modern police methods.

ANDY: (Strolling in) Mmmm...Barney, what...what do you think you're doing?

BARNEY: I'm booking and printing, Sheriff. (Glares disapprovingly at Emma) Jaywalking!

ANDY: Now, Barney, you know we don't ever stop Emma. We figure if she can save a step here or there, she'll be with us that much longer. Now, you go home, Emma.

EMMA: (Hobbles off with her cane) Thank you, Sheriff. (Shakes her cane at Barney and sniffs) Naughty deputy!

BARNEY: Now why'd you do that, Andy? You know she was guilty. I seen her do it! Now she's gonna go out and tell all her friends how she got away with it. Next thing you know people is gonna be jaywalking all over the place, disregarding 'Keep Off the Grass' signs and everything. Mayberry's just going to turn into a regular sin town!!

The show always opened and closed with "The Fishing Hole," the now famous whistling theme by Earle Hagen. The visual that accompanies the jaunty tune shows Andy and Opie sauntering down a country lane, heading for the fishing hole. When they arrive, Opie tosses a stone into the water as any rambunctious little boy would do. This little scene demonstrates and reinforces the bond between father and son, who are so obviously comfortable together and honoring and loving of each other. The same deep affection is felt for Aunt Bee, who fusses and putters about baking pies and (s)mothering Opie. You can almost hear "Bringing in the Sheaves" and other hymns playing when Aunt Bee is around.

"I know my hometown folks," said Griffith in 1960. "Do not think they are ignorant. Naïve, yes. But not ignorant. They are set in their ways and opinionated. They also have native wit and great humor." And most of them are a pretty eccentric lot. There's barber Floyd Lawson, who's forever making weird pronouncements.

> FLOYD: Andy, did you know the dingo dog is indigenous to Australia?
> ANDY: No, I didn't know that, Floyd.
> FLOYD: (Pause) Well, it is.

Otis Campbell is the resident rummy, a town drunk who locks himself up in his own personal jail cell, then lets himself out when Andy tells him he's served his time. Otis is Barney's perfect foil, always there for Barney to run his scientific "rehabilitation" experiments on, or to receive some new mutant form of Barney "psychobabble." Of course, the best cure for Otis's drunkenness, aside from a night in his cell, is a warm, homecooked meal from benevolent Aunt Bee. While Otis is a drunk, there's not much excuse for the behavior of the gas-station-attendant Pyle cousins, Gomer and Goober…they're just plain dumb hicks.

While "gawl-lee" Gomer was just flat out a Bozo, Goober had a bit more animation to him. He read

Don Knotts never needed funny costumes to make the audience roar with laughter, yet the five-time Emmy Award winner could no doubt see the humor in "going drag" in this April 29, 1963, broadcast. Here, Deputy Barney Fife pretends to be a backwoods bride in order to thwart the unwelcome attentions of Ernest T. Bass (Howard Morris) to a mountain girl.

comic books, wore a crown-type beanie with holes in it (to let a little air get to his brain, maybe), and could do a mean imitation of Cary Grant—"Judy, Judy, Judy!" They were both too sweet and innocent

What's a boy to do who goes fishin' and reels in a baby in a basket? That's Opie's dilemma when he heads for the uncertainty of explaining his presence with an infant in tow.

to take offense to (although it certainly seemed they played right into the "dumb Southern country boy" image that had been around in movies for decades). Fascinating that Jim Nabors later got his own hugely popular spinoff series, *Gomer Pyle, U.S.M.C.*

While Gomer is semi-dimensional, Ernest T. Bass, the cretinous mountain-man-on-the-loose-in-Mayberry, is positively other-dimensional. Ernest wanders into Mayberry on occasion and makes his presence known by acting out his riot-minded behavior, such as tossing rocks through windows, seeking out women to "take" back to the hills with him, or demanding that he be given a proper "edge-ah-cay-shun." Played with inspired lunacy by comedy veteran Howard Morris (one of the original cast members of Sid Caesar's *Your Show of Shows*), Ernest T. appeared in only five shows over the years, but his impact on audiences was colossal.

"OPIE THE BIRDMAN"

In one of the more moving episodes (# 96, aired 9/30/63), Opie accidentally kills a mother bird with his new slingshot after being warned by his father to be careful how he used this potentially dangerous weapon. Andy goes upstairs to Opie's room and bids the boy to listen to the cries of the newly orphaned baby birds wailing outside the window. Setting himself in front of Opie, Andy says: "I'm not going to give you a whipping." (Pause) He opens the window and asks: "Do you hear that? That's them young birds chirping for their mama that's never coming back...and you just listen to that for a while."

In this one scene, Andy firmly but lovingly crafts an important lesson in morality and responsibility in a direct way his young son can understand. Opie's heretofore boyish respect for life is crystallized in an adult manner when he takes on the responsibility of raising the young birds. Later he must also find the courage to break his attachment to his charges, once they are mature enough to be released back into the wild. Opie then remarks to his father how empty the bird cage in his room now looks. Andy glances towards his son and remarks: "But don't the trees sound nice and full?"

By the fifth season, dramatic cast changes were taking place. In five years, Don Knotts earned four Emmys and millions of devoted fans who religiously followed the manic doings of Deputy Barney Fife. Knotts then left the show through a bit of a misunderstanding. Griffith had signed a five-year contract in the beginning and made it understood to Knotts he wouldn't be around after the fifth season. By 1964, Knotts's popularity was great enough that he could write his own ticket in Hollywood, and he took an offer to do a film for Universal (*The Ghost and Mr. Chicken,* developed especially for Knotts). As the fifth season began, Griffith came to Knotts and told his friend he was staying on the show, and asked Knotts his plans, because he (Griffith) had a new offer for him. By this time, Knotts had signed his movie deal, was well on his way to developing other film scripts for himself, and felt it was time to move on. Knotts did return for several appearances over the last three seasons, and won his fifth and final Emmy for the episode, "Barney Comes to Mayberry" (episode #208, 1/23/67). It was in that same season, 1966–67, that Frances Bavier won her Best Supporting Actress Emmy for portraying Aunt Bee.

In the spring of 1966, Jack Dodson appeared as Howard Sprague, the sheepish, mother-dominated county clerk. The Sprague character was brought in to shore up the vacuum left by Knotts's exit. Dodson stayed with the show for five seasons, on into the period when it was retitled *Mayberry R.F.D.,* after Griffith's departure. Dodson always thought of his Howard Sprague character as a "thirty-five-year-old bachelor who wasn't through puberty yet."

Comedian Jack Burns, of the team Burns & Schreiber was brought in specifically to "replace" the Barney Fife character. Although Burns was quite adept at stand-up "schtick," he just wasn't right as a Barney clone. Burns appeared in only six episodes as Deputy Warren Ferguson, nephew of Floyd the barber, and was let go by Griffith just before Christmas 1965.

Fellow cast members say Howard McNear, who played Floyd, was indeed much like his character offscreen, "a nervous man." With the show from the beginning, McNear suffered a stroke and was out for the entire 1963–64 season. Through Griffith's kind intervention, McNear found his role

It's no mistake that "Opie Loves Helen" as indicated in chalk on the blackboard. Helen Crump (Aneta Corsaut) was Opie's fifth grade teacher, and the object of love crushes by both father and son. In the eighth season, Sheriff Andy wed Miss Crump and Opie got himself a new mother.

waiting for him and was brought back onto the show. The stroke had paralyzed his entire left side, so he was usually filmed sitting down. A special contraption was erected to hold him up so that he could seem to be standing when the script called for it. McNear survived on the show through 1967, when a second stroke killed him.

Various women were brought in over the years to play at being girlfriends to Sheriff Andy Taylor, but none of them ever seemed to work. Executive producer Sheldon Leonard said that women had to be introduced as girlfriends for Andy or "we'd [sic] have been suspected of homosexual inclinations." Griffith said the writing was the problem, that "we never knew how to write for women." He also added that his character and personality made it difficult for writers to come up with a female

After an eight year absence, the stars of The Andy Griffith Show *decided to reprise their roles in an NBC made-for-television movie,* Return to Mayberry, *broadcast April 13, 1986. The plot has Andy Taylor coming home to Mayberry to run again for sheriff, only to discover his former deputy Barney Fife has also entered the race. Clockwise from left: Don Knotts (Barney Fife), Jim Nabors (Gomer), George Lindsey (Goober), Ron Howard (Opie Taylor), and Andy Griffith (Andy Taylor)*

counterpart whose chemistry would work harmoniously with his "peculiar nature." Throughout Griffith's screen and TV career, he has never been known as a ladies' man, and Don Knotts described him as being "very shy" with women.

Nevertheless, Griffith tried to romance women on the show, starting with Elinor Donahue (formerly Princess/Betty on *Father Knows Best)*, who lasted only the first season as Ellie the druggist. Gorgeous Sue Ane Langdon appeared as Peggy the country nurse, but also didn't work out. Finally, Aneta Corsaut, as Helen Crump (Opie's schoolteacher) made the grade, lasting from 1964 through 1968. Many times over the year there was talk of marriage between Andy and Helen (they finally did wed at the end of the 1967–68 season and "left town"), but all viewers instinctively knew that the only real "marriage" on the show was between Andy and Barney. Griffith and Knotts made a great comedy team, and Griffith wisely knew he must be first and foremost "straight man" to Knotts.

Toward the end of the eighth season, everyone with the show knew Griffith was planning his exit. Ken Berry (Captain Parmenter of *F Troop,* 1965–67) had been hired to play Sam Jones, a gentleman farmer and leading citizen of Mayberry. Berry appeared in the final episode, "Mayberry R.F.D.," which served as the pilot for the follow-up series of the same name. Essentially, Berry replaced Griffith per the sponsor's (General Foods) wishes and began a three-year run on *Mayberry R.F.D.*

Soon after the final episode of *The Andy Griffith Show* aired on April Fools Day, 1968, the star was off to begin his five-year, ten-movie contract with Universal. (Actually, he made only one on the contract.) After eight successful years, the show went out ranked number one in the ratings for the 1967–68 season. It had averaged better than thirty million viewers every week, and so-called non-sexy Griffith was receiving one thousand fan letters per month. The comedy series brainchild of Danny

To the bewilderment of Sheriff Taylor, Otis Campbell (Hal Smith), the town boozehound, rides into Mayberry on a cow and insists he's riding a horse. Maybe another night in Otis's second home—his personal jail cell at the sheriff's office—will bring him to his senses, but knowing Otis, we doubt it.

Thomas, Andy Griffith, and Sheldon Leonard* had become something of an American television institution—the most enduring, warmhearted, and delightful rural situation comedy ever created, an unforgettable piece of Americana, as indelible as apple pie.

In 1986, Griffith and fifteen other members of the original cast—among them Ron Howard, who had grown up to become a major film producer/director—reunited for the TV movie *Return to Mayberry*.

Griffith, of course, went on to star in a hugely successful second series, playing the crafty, hayseed Atlanta lawyer, Ben Matlock. He didn't forget old Don Knotts and invited him to play Matlock's Barney Fife-like neighbor on a recurring basis.

*The show had spun off from an episode of *The Danny Thomas Show*.

The one and only Don Knotts portraying the inimitable Deputy Barney Fife. Here Barney takes a two-straw break from chasing all of Mayberry's desperate criminals, most of them notorious jaywalkers. Ever wonder what Mayberry would've been like had the druggist slipped a couple of horse tranquilizers in ol' Barney's cola?

CAST LIST

FAMILY: The Taylors

MEMBERS:

Sheriff Andy Taylor . . . . **Andy Griffith**
Deputy Barney Fife
(1960–65) . . . . **Don Knotts**
Opie Taylor . . . . **Ronny Howard**
Aunt Bee Taylor . . . . **Frances Bavier**

SIGNIFICANT OTHERS:

Floyd Lawson . . . . **Howard McNear**
Clara Edwards . . . . **Hope Summers**
Ellie Walker (1960–61) . . . **Elinor Donahue**
Otis Campbell (1960–67) . . . . . **Hal Smith**
Thelma Lou (1960–65) . . . . **Betty Lynn**
Gomer Pyle (1963–64) . . . . . . **Jim Nabors**
Goober Pyle (1965–68) . . **George Lindsey**
Howard Sprague (1966–68) **Jack Dodson**
Warren Ferguson (1965–66) . . **Jack Burns**
Mayor Stoner (1962–63) . . . . **Parley Baer**
Helen Crump (1964–68) . . **Aneta Corsaut**
Emmett Clark (1967–68) . . . **Paul Hartman**
Jud Crowley (1961–66) . . . . . **Burt Mustin**

THEME SONG: **Earle Hagen**
TIMEFRAME: **1960–68**
NETWORK: **CBS**
ADDRESS: **Mayberry, R.F.D.**
   North Carolina

249 episodes

GREAT PERFORMANCES

Emmy Winners

Don Knotts

Best Supporting Actor (Comedy)

1960–61, 1961–62, 1962–63,
1965–66, 1966–67

Frances Bavier

Best Supporting Actress (Comedy)

1966–67

MY THREE SONS

The handsome family Douglas, "all-male and a nation wide in appeal," said this 1965 CBS photo caption. During this, the show's sixth season, several changes took place—Uncle Charlie, played by veteran character actor William Demarest, replaced William Frawley, and the show was now broadcast in color. Left to right: Stanley Livingston (Chip), Fred MacMurray (Steve), Don Grady (Robbie), William Demarest (Uncle Charlie), and bespectacled Barry Livingston (Ernie) and Spud the dog (Tramp the dog).

My Three Sons is the original granddaddy of the "widowed father with three young sons" type of all-male family sitcom. The main action takes place in a bland-looking white suburban house (sans picket fence) on a quiet street situated in a peaceful development on the outskirts of a medium-sized city called Bryant Park in midwestern U.S.A. Nothing terribly momentous happens at the house, at the boys' school, or at Dad's job—but that is the key to *My Three Sons:* one hundred percent safe, even-keeled, habitually bland, and in the early 1960s, that look and that feeling were ever so appealing to a broad television-watching audience.

Widower Steve Douglas, a former test pilot, now a consulting aeronautical engineer ("consulting" means he has an office in his house so he can spend plenty of time with his boys), earns a comfortable enough living so he can support his three sons and his irascible father-in-law, Bub O'Casey, a retired army drill sergeant. To assure total family lovability, the household is completed by Tramp, a large shaggy dog of dubious ancestry, who galumphs about the house, crashing into furniture and people, providing slapstick in an otherwise mild, low-key family comedy.

When the series had its premiere telecast on ABC, September 29, 1960, the boys were aged eighteen (Mike), fourteen (Robbie), and seven (Chip). The star of the program was Fred MacMurray, a sturdy leading man, mostly in motion picture comedies since the mid-thirties, who was, in 1945, Hollywood's biggest box office star, the highest paid actor of the year, and one of the five highest salaried men in America, earning about one-half million dollars. True to his Scots ancestry, MacMurray was known to be very respectful of a dollar, investing wisely in Los Angeles real estate and other ventures so that by the 1950s he had no need to work at all. Though he was still making pictures, it took a very strong and cleverly devised lure to snag him into a television series.

MacMurray was born on August 12, 1908 (some sources give 1907 as his birth year), in Kankakee, Illinois, because his mother, Maleta Martin, traveled everywhere with his father, Frederick MacMurray, Sr., a concert violinist, and that's where their tour happened to be at the time. Shortly afterward, they settled in Madison and then in Beaver Dam,

One of the rare times we didn't find Bub (William Frawley) in the Douglas kitchen in his apron. Bub was the "Mother" to the boys in that he was chief cook and bottle-washer, and crusty, golden-hearted sep-tuagenerian advice-giver to any and all listeners. Frawley left the show in 1965 due to ill health, and died the following year at age seventy-nine.

Eldest son, Mike, played by Tim Considine, stuck around long enough during the 1965 season to marry his girlfriend, Sally (Meredith MacRae), before taking off for New York City to work as a psychologist. Proud pop Steve Douglas (Fred MacMurray) joins the wedding portrait. Mike's exit left only two sons, but paved the way for Ernie to be officially "adopted" as the new third son.

Wisconsin, where Fred at sixteen graduated from high school, the top student in his class, with ten letters in athletics and the American Legion Medal for the best athletic and scholastic record at Beaver Dam High.

Bent on a musical career ever since he played his first violin concert, at age five (standing on a chair, accompanying his father), MacMurray spent his first earnings—eked out in a pea-canning factory—for a baritone horn, which he later traded in for a saxophone. Fred paid his way through two terms at Carroll College in Waukesha, Wisconsin, by playing in a jazz orchestra at night. But football (he was a fullback) and music left so little time for studies that he finally left college and headed for Chicago where he found occasional jobs with different jazz bands. To survive those periods when band work was not forthcoming, Fred tried selling electrical appliances house-to-house and clerking in a department store, meanwhile studying art at night in the Chicago Art Institute.

While visiting relatives in Los Angeles, Fred decided to stay on and worked as a movie extra until orchestra engagements began to come his way. When word got around that Fred was also a talented vocalist, he was signed to record with both the George Olsen and Gus Arnheim orchestras. He was soon chosen by a band called the California Collegians to display his talents as a triple threat—singer/saxophonist/comedian. He signed with the band to appear in New York in the revue, *Three's a Crowd*. This was followed by nightclub dates, vaudeville appearances, and a role in Jerome Kern's *Roberta* on Broadway.

Impressed with MacMurray's good looks (Cary-Grant-cleft-chin, six feet three-and-a-half inches tall, 190-pound muscular athlete's frame, black hair, blue eyes) and acting promise, a Paramount Pictures talent scout arranged a studio screen test.* Fred was signed to a contract and made his screen debut in *The Friends of Mr. Sweeney* in 1934. His ascent to screen stardom didn't take long. By his third film, a romantic comedy entitled *The Gilded Lily* (1935), in which he costarred with Claudette Colbert and Ray Milland, he established his now well-known screen persona of the down-to-earth, all-American average Joe, sincere and somewhat

---

*The top hat he borrowed for his 1934 Paramount screen test belonged to *Roberta* star, Bob Hope. It took Fred thirty years to retrieve it from an old trunk. He sent it over to Hope in a box. Inside was a note: "Here's your hat. What's your hurry?"

lumbering, bright, masculine, and easygoing. He did the role to perfection, and to this day remains far too modest to acknowledge what a fine actor he is.

"I'm a personality," MacMurray insisted to the *Los Angeles Times* in 1966, "rather than an actor in the sense Marlon Brando is an actor. It's all the same, since I'm playing myself, reacting the way I think I would react if I actually were in the situations you see on the screen."

He and Colbert had a wonderful screen chemistry, and they appeared together in seven movies over the next thirteen years, perfecting their romantic comedy relationship, with her as the suave sophisticate and him as the stubborn man of the streets who brings her down to earth.

By the mid-forties, Fred was the number one male box office star and one of the highest paid men in America. Only rarely did he stray from his forte as one of the screen's premier light comedians, most notably in *Double Indemnity* (1944), playing a murderous insurance investigator; *The Caine Mutiny* (1954), as a cowardly, manipulative naval officer; and *The Apartment* (1960), as a philandering married business executive. He won rave reviews for all three roles and proved he had great range as an actor.

MacMurray married dancer Lillian Lamont in 1936. The couple adopted two children, Robert and Susan. Some months after his wife died in 1953, his friend John Wayne invited him to a costume party where he met actress June Haver, eighteen years his junior. She had just emerged from seven months in a convent following the death of her fiancé. They fell in love and were married in a civil ceremony on June 28, 1954. Haver is a practicing Catholic, MacMurray a Presbyterian. They adopted twin girls, Katherine and Laurie Ann, born May 7, 1956.

Fred and June still live in a spacious colonial house, decorated with early American furnishings, in Brentwood. Once an avid fisherman, hunter, and golfer, Fred loves to putter about the house playing Mr. Fixit. He also paints watercolors and fashions leather holsters.

MacMurray reportedly is one of the wealthiest actors in Hollywood, who invested wisely in real estate holdings—cattle ranches, orange and lemon

A *close-up portrait of irascible Uncle Charlie, ex-sailor and semi-tough authoritarian mug played with just the right character mix of bluff-and blarney by one-time vaudevillian William Demarest, who gave delight to stage, screen and television audiences over a seventy-three-year career. Demarest played Uncle Charlie the role on* My Three Sons *from 1965 to 1973.*

groves, oil wells, a hotel in Mexico—over the years, and has always lived a quiet life devoted to his family and a small circle of friends. He credits his strong, loving marriage as the key in helping him beat throat cancer in 1979.

MacMurray is both flattered and moved when fans recognize him. "I can't tell you how many people come up to me and say, 'You were my Dad.'" Of 380 original color and black and white episodes, 220 have been running on the Nickelodeon Channel since 1985, and a whole new generation of young viewers have discovered Fred MacMurray and *My Three Sons*. He told *TV Guide* in 1986: "I really don't like looking at my old work. I'm not my greatest fan. I can always see how I should have played the scene better." Differently maybe, but certainly not better.

To this day, MacMurray describes himself this way: "I haven't changed, I'm a simple man." This simplicity, self-effacement, and Everyman solidity were exactly the qualities producer Don Fedderson was looking for in the leading man he was hoping to sign for a new television series. Fedderson had already successfully produced the very popular series, *The Millionaire*. And he not only had a great concept for a family situation comedy, but he had already contracted William Frawley, late of *I Love Lucy*. Fedderson's first notion was three girls and a grandfather. Not satisfied, he changed the sex of the kids, kept Frawley, and decided on a strong and thoughtful if occasionally befuddled father figure,

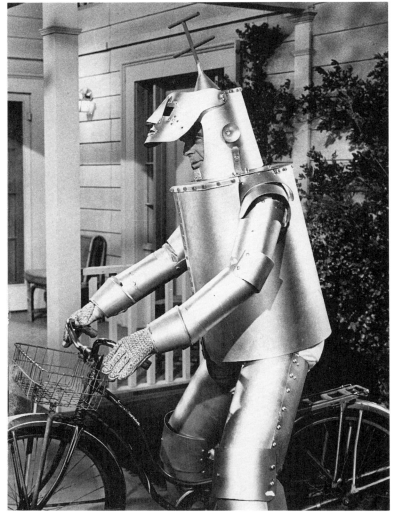

Sometimes, Fred MacMurray acted more like the fourth son rather than like their father, providing for some nice slapstick relief from the usual low key comedic tone. Garbed as a robot for son Chip's school play, MacMurray is forced to use a bicycle to get him to the stage on time, in this episode that was broadcast November 11, 1965.

much resembling Fred MacMurray, as star.

It was 1959, and MacMurray was happily busy in films, getting ready to shoot *The Absent-Minded Professor* for Walt Disney, and later, *The Apartment* for Billy Wilder, and the last thing he wanted was to slave week after week in a TV series. Fedderson was not one to give up, so he decided to make MacMurray an offer he couldn't refuse.

"He called me," said MacMurray, "and offered this deal whereby I'd only have to work three months out of the year. So I said to June, 'Gosh, I've got to have lunch with this guy. If I can't work three months out of the year, then maybe I *am* lazy.' I've been turning [series offers] down for years, saying I'm too lazy."

The word had been that he was merely rich. "Somebody asked me how rich I was. I said, 'I'm just so rich I don't have to do a TV series.' I talked to people like Bob Young," MacMurray said in 1960, "and I know all about the money [Young had just sold rights to air episodes on his series, *Father Knows Best,* for $7 million] but..."

Fedderson's offer was a groundbreaker, custom-tailored for this movie star reluctant to plunge into series TV. The MacMurray System (as it was to be known) simply had the production crew shoot all of Fred's scenes when he was available, which meant sixty-five days per year, and all the other scenes when he was not. MacMurray didn't give Fedderson sixty-five days in a row either. He would report in late May to the Desilu Studio on Gower Street in Los Angeles, and work thirty-five days (five days per week, weekends off), then take off for ten weeks. Back in the studio again, he'd complete shooting his remaining thirty days and be finished altogether by around Thanksgiving.

The first season was tough because all the wrinkles had to be worked out. Fedderson and MacMurray, equal partners in the show (Gregg-Don Productions), learned by doing. Though *MTS* achieved fine ratings the first season, the show initially lost $254,000. The immense success of the show later paid that back many times over in its twelve-year run. Initially, the logistics needed to be made workable. A scene might call for Steve, Bub, Mike, Robbie, and Chip to be eating steak and mashed potatoes at dinner, and if the shooting time ran out, Fred might be disappearing for months, and when he returned, everything and everybody would all have to look exactly as they had before.

"For instance," MacMurray told the New York *Daily News* in 1961, "if we were going to shoot right here, we'd do every scene in the script which called for this setting, whether they were in continuity or not. All it takes, really, is a good script girl to remember exactly how things are placed, where you were standing, and what the last spoken line was."

For continuity, haircuts could be a major problem. In the spring, hair could be long, but summer brought crew cut weather, so Fedderson solved the problem by having the boys' hair trimmed every seven days. There were little hair problems for

A very handsome and very young Fred MacMurray early in his movie career (circa 1935). His wavy black hair, blue eyes, 6'3½" linebacker's frame, coupled with his all-American small-town sincerity and straightforwardness, made him a genuine heartthrob to female moviegoers, and a nonthreatening "regular Joe" to males. This is a typical Paramount Pictures publicity still.

TV GUIDE

15¢ • LOCAL PROGRAMS • JULY 16-22

FRED MacMURRAY,
WILLIAM DEMAREST
OF 'MY THREE SONS'

This TV Guide cover from the late sixties captures the beaming, bewigged countenances of the elders of the My Three Sons clan, Fred MacMurray and William Demarest, a couple of old Hollywood pros who kept audiences chuckling while they laughed all the way to the bank.

Frawley, who was bald, or MacMurray, who never made a big secret over his toupee (covering the top front of his scalp), or William Demarest who later played Uncle Charley and also wore a toupee.

The MacMurray System (more accurately the Fedderson System for Fail-Safe Filming) developed built-in controls as filming experience created the need. Every scene that was to be picked up at a later date (perhaps months down the road when MacMurray returned from his break) was photographed with a still camera, to record hairdress, wardrobe, set decor, colors, and the exact positioning of props and people. Even neckties were numbered. Incidentally, MacMurray was probably television's first bow tie daddy. That form of neckwear was as much a part of his characterization as his ever-present pipe was a friendly prop. Actors who were not immediate cast members and who might be hired for two-days' shooting in May and three days in September—for one script—were duly warned not to get fatter or thinner or change their hair color in the interim. The silent prayer on the set was that all cast members remain healthy. In the autumn of 1963, comedian Wally Brown ap-

peared in a scene and was to report back six weeks later. Brown died in the interim, and the bit had to be reshot with another actor.

The System had built-in taboos as well. The first, according to then (1964) production supervisor John G. Stephens was never to show MacMurray with teenage actors, other than his TV sons, on the same piece of celluloid. Stephens's rationale: "If we shoot MacMurray together with five kids in a master scene, and then have to pick up the action later, who knows whether we'll be able to find all five kids again? If one quits acting, and MacMurray is fishing in Colorado, that master scene kills us. So when you see on your screen Fred saying, 'Hi, kids,' and the boys answering, what really happens is that Fred looks down to where the kids would be if they were there, and says his line. Later, the dialogue coach stands on a soapbox until she is six feet three-and-a-half inches off the ground, and the kids look up and say, 'Hello, Mr. Douglas.'"

MacMurray wasn't always the only person or thing with availability problems. One script called for MacMurray to watch his son Robbie tinker with an ancient jalopy. Unfortunately, the tin lizzie wasn't available, as it had been rented to another studio, and the poor script girl had to make her acting debut mimicking the sounds of a dying car, while MacMurray strolled around the auto muttering, "I think it's the carburetor."

It was not unusual to shoot scenes from five or six different scripts in the same day. (Fedderson's lifesaver was having an abundance of scripts written well in advance of any shooting days.) There was a day, however, in the second season, that holds the all-time record, when pieces of eleven separate shows were filmed. As long as scripts were in hand and not on the drawing board somewhere, production schedules could always be tailored to the availability of people and props.

It is known as the MacMurray System because he is the key that made it work so well. An organized, by nature perfectionist Virgo, MacMurray defines the term "professional actor." "He is a pro," said John Stephens in 1964. "He always remembers where he stood, what he was doing, what his motivation was [although MacMurray had publicly decried 'The Method' school of acting]. He is not an actor in temperament. He is a man, an unneurotic man, with an uncluttered mind." All in all, the

Fred MacMurray surveys the youthful members of his all-male household in the first color episode of My Three Sons, *broadcast September 16, 1965. Stanley Livingston (Chip) is on the left with real-life brother Barry Livingston (Ernie) next to him. Don Grady (Robbie) is on the right.*

perfect Steve Douglas. Fedderson said MacMurray was "exactly right for the part—handsome, mannish, believable."

In reality, Fred MacMurray is just plain shy, but he's too modest to even say that. Queen of the Hollywood gossip columnists, Hedda Hopper, once said of Fred, "He's as down to earth as applesauce or the boy next door." Barbara Stanwyck, with whom he costarred in *Double Indemnity* (among others), described him as the perfect Rotarian. Mary Martin referred to Fred as "sort of big and awkward and cheerful and happy. The big lug *has* something." Interestingly, MacMurray's shyness doesn't come across on screen. Throughout the thirties and forties, many of his roles were that of the brash, confident, self-assured but usually blue collar kind of guy, dashing around in comedies and musicals, and every so often surfacing in fine dramas. For all his believable simplicity, MacMurray is a deceptively skillful actor.

One could say that deceptive quality underlies the character of Steve Douglas. In the show, the hysterics and overt theatrics were usually left to Bub (William Frawley) or Uncle Charley (William Demarest), who were so good at playing cantankerous but heart-of-gold old geezers. The sons were so normally saccharine and even-tempered by today's standards, yet they always had some kind of problem—awkwardness around females (not surprisingly, with two manly old coots in aprons as "motherly" role models): school science projects that won't work for some darned reason; confusing boyhood rituals dealing with friendship and loyalty—and "Gee whiz, gosh, junk like that kind of stuff, Dad." And when the impasse came, or it was finale time, Steve would quietly saunter into the room and utter the right words covering just the right morals, and the situation would be cleaned up right and tight.

In 1965, Fred summed up his Steve Douglas character to *TV Guide:* "Uh—the father in our show isn't a dope. He can handle things better than I can at home. Then, too, we don't have any big messages. No dramatic problems. I play myself, most actors do. Maybe I happen to be the kind of fellow I'm playing. I don't tell jokes. I react to jokes. If there is an explanation, it is the all-male, mother-

115

Successful father to three growing sons and adoptive father to a circus lion with a poor sense of direction who ended up on the Douglas doorstep instead of in the big top. Looks like Leo and Fred had no trouble becoming friends, in this October 21, 1965 episode.

less family that Don Fedderson and George Tibbles [who wrote the pilot] devised. Five men without a woman lend themselves to a lot of funny things."

In one of the best episodes from the early black and white days, trust and understanding between father and son is the theme.

TERM PAPER PLAGIARISM

When Robbie (Don Grady) complains to his father that he cannot finish his history term paper because he is overwhelmed with work in all his other subjects, Steve suggests he has the whole weekend in which to buckle down and complete it. Robbie then reveals he's been invited for a weekend in the country with a girl he's been trying to date for three months. Steve says there'll be other days to spend with girls and suggests he call her and cancel the outing. A short time later, she shows up at the Douglas house and coos to Robbie how

she's looking forward to their time together over the weekend. Older brother Mike (Tim Considine) rescues him from his dilemma, informing him of the existence of one of Steve's old term papers in a trunk conveniently stored in the attic. Robbie uncovers the paper, sees that it's just what he needs, and decides to copy it, thinking no one will ever be the wiser.

At school, Robbie's history teacher returns his paper with a failing grade and demands Robbie deliver a letter to his father informing him of his son's misdeed. At home, Robbie guiltily confesses the truth to his disappointed and disillusioned father.

> ROBBIE: I not only let myself down, but I let the whole family down. I found one of your old papers, copied it, and submitted it as my own.
> STEVE: That's pretty serious, Rob.
> ROBBIE: I know it's not much to say that I'm sorry.
> STEVE: I know. So am I, Robbie.

At school, the teacher confronts Steve with the fact that the original paper had been plagiarized, showing him a text written in 1874 with the same wording. Dumbfounded and ashamed, Steve goes home and confesses to Bub that he doesn't know how to tell Robbie about the paper. Bub tells him that if he doesn't admit the truth to his son, he'll get the Hypocrite of the Year Award. Yet neither father nor grandfather can figure a way to tell Robbie the truth.

Steve walks into Robbie's room just moments after Robbie had been agonizing to Mike over ways to make up for his indiscretion to his honorable father, who has always had faith and trust in him. Steve sits down and quietly admits to Robbie that he, too, had plagiarized the paper in question. Although visibly shaken, Robbie promises to keep the incident a secret between him and his embarrassed father. Crestfallen, Steve slowly closes the door to Robbie's room as he exits.

Late that night in bed, Steve has a nightmare over the incident that so shakes him he awakens. Somehow, on a hunch, he heads up to the attic and begins ruffling through his old school papers. Bub hears the noise and comes up to find Steve smiling. He tells Bub he's unearthed his original assignment, which called for him to copy the original history text, word for word; hence he hadn't cheated on his paper after all.

> BUB: Bully for you. This leaves us exactly where we were earlier. You're in the clear, but Robbie's still in the doghouse.

> STEVE: Oh, I wouldn't tell Robbie about this for anything, Bub. You know something? He and I were closer tonight in his room than we've ever been. He thought that I had feet of clay, and he was still on my side.

Yet there was drama in this comedy, and it always came in the way in which the moral lesson was learned at the end of most episodes. Though the character of Steve Douglas (through MacMurray's seamless acting) always seems a bit old-fashioned, even Victorian at times, he's down-to-earth and plain enough to seem the EveryDad. The half-hour always seemed to be eaten up by the boys' never-ending self-entrapments, or by Bub's or Uncle Charley's humanoid agitations, yet Steve/Fred always seemed to pop into the room at the precise moment to cement all the loose ends together.

Said executive producer Don Fedderson, in 1965, "Ask me why we are so big [the show was readying to enter its sixth season], and I say it is because we have the best men—guys like George Tibbles and Peter Tewksbury [producer/director the first season, who for so many years worked his magic on *Father Knows Best*]. But mostly we've got Fred. This guy can do more with the raise of an eyebrow than a dozen other actors."

"The thing about Fred," said Tibbles, "is that he makes the conventional man seem interesting. But you know television. You have to have a device to get on the air at all. Once on, the personalities keep you there. If you've got a MacMurray, you can do no wrong."

In 1965, Tewksbury described the show as "pathetic. I mean the situation is basically tragic—the family without women. Women tend to want to mother it. They can see a million things to do in the house. Clean it, for one thing. And that's the way we played it." That same year, twenty-one-year-old Don Grady earnestly called *MTS* "a meat-and-potatoes show. Nothing gimmicky. Maybe I'm being too philosophical, but they say ours is a male-dominated society. I never found a woman yet who wasn't interested in a man's troubles."

Whatever they were doing on *My Three Sons,* by 1965, the chemistry had been perfected because CBS had successfully stolen the hit show from ABC, and reportedly had spent between $6 million and $8 million for the five years of the show already filmed. Plus they had contracted for two years more and an option for five years after that, which came to twelve years altogether—exactly the dozen the show ran before ending in 1972. By this time, changes were in the making. William Frawley, who second-banana-ed so perfectly through most of the 1965 season before falling ill, was written out of the show and replaced by fellow vaudevillian, William Demarest, who took golden-hearted crabbiness to new heights. In this writer's opinion, the Frawley years of the show were better, certainly less gimmicky. No reflection on Demarest, who was fine, but he was part of the new concept—episodes in color and the addition of women to the regular cast. In the 1966 season, eldest son Mike, now twenty-five, was married off to his TV girlfriend, Sally Ann Morrison (Meredith MacRae), and headed for points east where he got a job as a psychology instructor. His character had been known to occasionally sprinkle his conversations with lightly condescending "explanations" of the behavior of his siblings, his father, and Bub. Mike's departure graduated Robbie to number one son position. Chip (Stanley Livingston), now fourteen and the new middle son, befriended an orphan named Ernie (Barry Livingston, Stanley's real-life younger brother, who moves in with the Douglases and is eventually adopted by Steve, and now there are three sons once again.

What's a father to do when one of his three sons falls for a cheeky chorus girl? Well, naturally, concerned dad Steve Douglas (Fred MacMurray) goes backstage to check out the questionably motivated chorine, on My Three Sons. *However, Steve found lovely Lauri Mitchell to be sweet-natured and possess a character above reproach. This episode was broadcast in color, October 14, 1965.*

CHIP AND THE CHICKEN CLUNK

In an episode with overlapping themes, one of Mike's girlfriends thinks the paint drippings left by Bub on a piece of paper represent great "art" worthy of a gallery show. She doesn't realize the art was "created" when Bub was painting a chair and placed the paper beneath it to catch the drippings. Bub, of course, won't admit to her that his "painting" was a mistake, and spends the rest of the episode dashing off "masterpieces."

Meanwhile, Chip is avoiding a kid named Freddy, who wants to be friends with him. Found hiding in the house, Chip tells Bub, "I don't want that clunky Freddy Selby to see me."

BUB: "Why don't you like him?"
CHIP: "Because he's a clunk, and I think he's chicken too."
BUB: "Now there's a new one—a clunky chicken!"

Bub urges Chip to be friendly to his peer, and Chip reluctantly complies. That evening, Freddy's father calls Steve to ask permission to have Chip accompany Freddy and his parents on a camping trip. Chip interrupts his Dad, who promises to call Mr. Selby back after dinner. Steve then asks Chip why he doesn't want to go on the trip.

CHIP: We've got a whole week out of school. Why do I have to spend it with the clunky Freddy Selby?
STEVE: Does Freddy have any friends?
CHIP: Heck, no. Who wants to play with a chicken clunk?
STEVE: Well, don't you think it would be kind of nice if someone did play with him?
CHIP: Lots of people play with him...all the girls.
STEVE: Ah, Chip, this has never happened to you because you have your brothers, Mike and Rob. A lot of little boys don't have any brothers or sisters, and so they get very lonely. Or maybe they're self-conscious and can't always say the right thing. Or maybe they don't wear the same clothes as the rest of the gang. Uh...Freddy sounds a little bit like that to me. Is that right?

Realizing his father won't pressure him to go on the trip or force him to be friends with Freddy, Chip gets the message on tolerance, understanding, and fair play. He goes on the trip, but unfortunately, at the lake, Freddy turns out to be just the little wimp Chip had always supposed. Freddy's not helped at all by his overprotective mother, who worries over his every move. Freddy won't go boating or horseback riding "or anything!" Chip, however, is the model of tolerance, remembering his conversation with his dad.

STEVE: You're sure you want to [go]?
CHIP: Yeah. I got to thinking how awful it'd be to be a chicken clunk. I kinda felt sorry for him.
STEVE: You're growing up, Chipper.
CHIP: Yeah. How come?
STEVE: Well, one of the hardest things to do in this world is to put yourself in someone else's place. (Smiles and pats Chip on the cheek.)

Finally, Chip loses his eleven-year-old cool and punches Freddy, and the boys have a brawl. Having given one another a black eye, the two have solidified their friendship. The brawl has delivered them through a male rite of passage, and it certainly has moved Freddy up a rung on the ladder of self-esteem. Back at home, Steve, Mike, Robbie, and Tramp all greet Chip at the door. Though gone only one week, the father and brothers affectionately greet the youngest Douglas, offering handshakes, hugs, and lots of embraces and smiles. This is followed by a shot of Bub in the garage, greeting Chip with a smile and a big hug, while they all laugh at the art "masterpieces" Bub has placed all over the floor.

In the 1967–68 season, Steve finds himself transferred to Los Angeles, presumably to be nearer the heart of the aerospace industry. Robbie is now twenty-one and finishing up his college education, when he meets and marries Kathleen "Katie" Miller (Tina Cole), and in no time the young couple has triplets! Two sets of identical twins who all looked very alike were used as the triplet boys: Steve Douglas, Jr. (after dad), Charley Douglas (after Uncle Charley), and Robbie Douglas II (after Robbie). The show required the babies to be fair complexioned, with blue eyes and light hair, and had to have been born between June 17 and 24. The babies were allowed on the set only for two hours per day, and only could remain under the hot lights of the set filming for twenty minutes. The set was rife with welfare workers, nurses, and concerned stage mothers. Three days were devoted to shooting the babies in order to have

enough appropriate footage to last for four episodes. Six months later, two sets of older twins were hired for the new segments in which the babies had "grown."

By 1970, the tenth *MTS* season, the series was growing weary, and in need of some enlivening change. Ernie, now in high school, has problems coping with a teacher, Barbara Harper, played by the ever-dependable Beverly Garland, who is, of course, a youngish widow with a darling little daughter, Dodie (Dawn Lyn). When Steve consults the teacher over Ernie's troubles, his own love troubles are solved by the fetching Miss Garland, and they marry. Chip, now in college and all of eighteen, decides to wed his girlfriend, Polly Williams (Ronne Troup). Steve, perhaps slightly addled by his new matrimonial state and perhaps with his feet no longer squarely on terra firma, okays his son's marriage. In some strange way, the writers may have thought this was in keeping with the changing values of the country, as many kids were openly rebelling against their parents' "conservative" ways, and "flower power" was at its height.

ROBBIE REBELS

One episode that exemplified the move of the show to be more "hip" and "relevant" involved actor Sal Mineo, who had built a career around playing troubled and rebellious youths. In the episode, Mineo is an old college buddy of Robbie's who one day roars up to the Douglas household on a motorcycle. He quickly fills Robbie's head with images of freedom from responsibility and the joys of life lived moment to moment on the open road. This is music to Robbie's ears, as he's all tied down with Katie and his "triple" responsibilities. He rails at Katie over his need once more to feel free from the shackles of middle-class suburban life, all this as Steve quietly watches from the sidelines, confident his Robbie will do the right thing. Finally, departure day comes, and Mineo is pushing hard with his "Yeah, man, let's get up and blow this little nowhere town" hipster lingo. As the man-boys take off on their trip to Oz, Katie, with armfuls of triplets and teary-eyed, listens as they roar away. But, wouldn't you know it, seconds later Robbie is back humbly acknowledging that one can't break the mold.

By 1972, the final season, the writers had pulled out all the plugs, and comedy had taken a turn toward parody. A Scots relative, "Laird" (Lord) Fergus McBain Douglas, had arrived in America looking for a wife. This gave an opportunity for MacMurray to enact a dual role, and he had a ball, showing once again his gift for broad screwball-type comedy. The laird eventually meets a cocktail waitress, late of a bowling alley, and promptly marries her (Terri Dowling, the waitress, was played by luscious Anne Francis.) MacMurray, although of Scots ancestry, didn't use his own voice when playing Fergus, it was dubbed by actor Alan Caillou. On August 24, 1972, the show was finally dropped by CBS. (It played its first five seasons on ABC; its last seven on CBS.) A 1977 TV reunion followed, and that was the last time MacMurray came out of retirement.* Fred MacMurray died November 9, 1991, age eighty-three.

In the years since *MTS* ended, Don Grady, who secretly moonlighted during the show's run as a rock musician, continues to ply his lifelong interest in music. Independently wealthy from wise investments and revenues from *MTS* reruns, Grady today is a record producer and composer of film scores. He also scored the theme for *Donahue*. He lives in Los Angeles with his wife and young son.

Stanley Livingston nowadays is a successful documentary film director, while brother Barry continues his acting career and, in 1990, became a first-time father.

*Between the end of *My Three Sons* in 1972 and the 1977 TV reunion, MacMurray starred in a prospective pilot called *The Chadwick Family* (1974), recycling *MTS* by having him a patriarch of a clan consisting of a wife, three daughters, one son, and two sons-in-law (one Oriental).

CAST LIST

FAMILY: The Douglases

MEMBERS:

Steve Douglas . . . . **Fred MacMurray**
Mike Douglas (1960–65) . . **Tim Considine**
Robbie Douglas . . . . **Don Grady**
Chip Douglas . . . . **Stanley Livingston**
Michael Francis "Bub"
   O'Casey (1960–65) . . . . **William Frawley**
Uncle Charley
   O'Casey (1965–72) . . **William Demarest**

SIGNIFICANT OTHERS:

Sally Ann Morrison
   Douglas (1963–65) . . **Meredith MacRae**
Ernie Thompson
   Douglas (1963–72) . . . . **Barry Livingston**
Katie Miller Douglas (1967–72)   **Tina Cole**
Dodie Harper
   Douglas (1969–72) . . . . **Dawn Lyn**
Barbara Harper
   Douglas (1969–72) . . . . **Beverly Garland**
Steve Douglas, Jr.
   (1970–72) . . . . **Joseph Todd**
Charley Douglas (1970–72) . . **Michael Todd**
Robbie Douglas II (1970–72) . **Daniel Todd**
Terri Dowling (1971–72) . . . . **Anne Francis**
Polly Williams
   Douglas (1970–72) . . . . **Ronne Troup**

THEME SONG: **Frank DeVol**
TIMEFRAME: **1960–72**
NETWORK: **ABC (1960–65),**
            CBS (1965–72)
ADDRESS: **Bryant Park, USA**

369 episodes

Those were the days: Archie Bunker (Carroll O'Connor) surrounded by his family—Edith Bunker (Jean Stapleton), Mike Stivic (Rob Reiner), and Gloria Stivic (Sally Struthers, on floor). One best-kept secret of the 1975 season: an "insecure" Sally Struthers trying to break her CBS contract. After a bawling out by father-figure Carroll O'Connor, and a good cry backstage, she agreed to stay on.

The picture says it all: Archie ponders "which end is up" as he struggles to do the "woman's work" of diapering Baby Joey. In real life, Carroll O'Connor is the exact opposite of Archie: a champion of liberal causes and an involved father. Still, O'Connor says, "Archie is a great role. I'll probably never play a better one in my life."

When Archie Bunker arrives home from work, there is no benevolent smile on his face, as there might be on Jim Anderson's (*Father Knows Best*). He is more likely to snarl and fume at his son-in-law, Mike—"Get away from me, Meathead"—as he slumps into his favorite chair and sends his wife trotting subserviently into the kitchen for a beer.

Archie is a bigoted loudmouth. He has long since given up the hope that he will be a man of substance, that he can find esteem and regard in his own home, like Jim Anderson.

Instead, he feels besieged on all sides. When he turns on the TV, he sees long-hairs, "pinkos," and weirdos (his son-in-law Mike Stivic is all three) thumbing their noses at *his* government and *his* cherished beliefs.

And what of Archie's beloved but empty-headed daughter, miniskirted Gloria, his "Little Girl"? She too has been infected by this insidious virus of disrespect and impropriety. While poor Archie winces at a "good girl" gone sexually aggressive, Gloria greets her husband by leaping into his arms and wrapping her legs around his waist.

Then there are the uppity "minor-orities." Once a working man could have taken some comfort from people who were even worse off than he. Now he is told to his face, by Mike and Gloria, that those non-whites are his "equals," and he shouldn't use the names for such people that he's always used.

What has the world come to?

The world has come of age, at least in television terms. All molds have been broken. It is not too much to say that all of sitcom history can be divided thus: B.A.B. and A.A.B. (Before Archie Bunker and After Archie Bunker). For the first time, a bigot holds center stage in a TV family, and the words "coon," "spic," "dago," "hebe," and "mick" are heard outside of a documentary on racism. For the first time, substantive topics ranging from prejudice, sex discrimination, and homosexuality to rape, cancer, and menopause are explored on a *comedy show.*

With our first glimpse of the Bunkers in January of 1971, we felt ourselves "snap to" as if we had dozed off for a long time, lulled to sleep by the narcotic familiarity of blandness in TV. Here were vibrant creations! Four distinct personalities argu-

Archie and his "Little Girl" fought like cats and dogs over practically everything, including her marriage to that "dumb pinko-Commie Polack." But underneath it all there were deep bonds of affection. In 1982, Sally Struthers went it alone as a now-single mom in the All in the Family *spinoff,* Gloria. *The show, however, only lasted one season.*

Wouldn't you know it, those bleeding heart Stivics gave their son Joey a truck made by the Marx toy company! The raising of Joey was always a bone of contention in the Bunker household. Mike and Gloria Stivic decided to write the Bunkers out of their will as guardians to Joey after Archie gave the boy a toy gun.

ing, cursing, sulking, declaiming, seemingly all at the same time. A riot of voices, all sounding a different note, but somehow belonging together.

All in the Family, inspired by the British series, *Till Death Do Us Part,* was "developed" by Norman Lear in 1966 and peddled to ABC. The network financed a couple of pilot episodes (then called *Those Were the Days)* starring Carroll O'Connor as Archie and Jean Stapleton as Edith. Lear had chosen O'Connor as his temperamental blue collar "shlub" while watching him in an airplane screening of *What Did You Do in the War, Daddy?* and he knew Stapleton from her work as a stage actress. Nothing came of the project, however, until 1970, when CBS showed some interest.

The show premiered as a midseason replacement, and Norman Lear admits that he was not optimistic about its chances. He wondered, "Is America ready to watch this?" CBS braced itself for an immediate flood of negative phone calls. Nevertheless, this first airing contained all the "shock" elements we came to know: sex, religion, racial slurs. Newlyweds Mike and Gloria are discovered having sex on a Sunday morning as Archie and Edith return from church. Mike reveals himself as an atheist, and Archie exposes his narrowminded bigotry. By letting it all hang out in the first show, Lear risked cancellation. His gamble paid off as there was no firestorm of protest, and the show began to slowly build an audience. By its second year, *All in the Family* was at the top of the ratings.

NORMAN LEAR'S FAVORITE FAMILY

From 1971, when *All in the Family* began, until 1978, creator Norman Lear would personally greet the audience on taping days at CBS Television City in Hollywood. Lear had a special place in his heart for this show, because he had put so much of himself, and his past, into it.

Lear remembers his own father, a Russian-Jewish salesman and failed entrepreneur, as "outgoing and affectionate but enormously insensitive." Like Archie Bunker, his father told his wife to "stifle" herself, raged against blacks, and held forth from a special (red leather) chair in the middle of the living room. "I grew up in a family that lived at the top of its lungs and the ends of its nerves," says Lear.

NORMAN LEAR

His mother was sweet and gentle, like Edith Bunker. Does Lear's memory of his boyhood with her echo in this *Family* exchange? We think so.

ARCHIE: You think it's fun living with a saint? You ain't human.
EDITH: YES I AM.
ARCHIE: Prove it. Do something rotten.

To critics who claimed there was too much yelling in the Bunker household, Lear countered: "I don't experience it as yelling but as passion. A celebration of life." And again: "I *am* shameless about my feelings. I know I wear my emotions on my sleeve—but frankly I can't find anything wrong with that."

We can't either. That is Archie's style, too and rightly or wrongly, that's what endears him to us.

The first reason we could tolerate Archie was that we feel superior to him. How many times have we laughed at his malapropisms? One might create a whole dictionary of them. When Archie hears the term "Homo sapiens" he knows the definition immediately: "killer fag." The Reverend Felcher pontificates from his "ivory shower." Of Mike he asks, "Why are you all duded up like Errol Slim?" When he feels Mike, Gloria, and Edith have ganged up on him, he demands, "What have we got here, the Three Muscatels?" He lists the following among America's famous men: "Elder Cleavage" and "Henry Woolworth Longfellow." And when Mike avers he trusts his painter friend Szabo (David Soul), who is doing a nude portrait of Gloria, Archie sneers, "Famous last words. That's what Abel said when he got it in the back of the head with a cane."

Our ability to laugh at this semi-illiterate, ill-informed lunkhead also helped to offset the anger we felt at Archie's verbal abuse of Edith. We saw how she ran herself ragged to please him, how her hand would cover her mouth when she thought she'd overstepped her wifely bounds. But this kind of vengeful laughter is not enough to carry a program to the heights of popularity *All in the Family* enjoyed.

For the main character must have redeeming qualities. Eventually we must do more than tolerate Archie—we must embrace him. And it is, not

The show broke from its accustomed Archie-centered storyline and format in this special one-hour episode of 1978 when Edith is confronted by a "molester" (David Dukes). Edith died of a stroke in 1980, leaving Jean Stapleton free to pursue a career on stage and TV. In 1990, she costarred with Whoopi Goldberg in the ill-fated sitcom, Bagdad Cafe.

Sally Struthers looked glorious as Gloria, in this gorgeous publicity still from All in the Family. *Since leaving the sitcom in 1978, she has appeared on Broadway in the female version of* The Odd Couple *(with Rita Moreno), raised daughter Samantha (approaching teenage) as a divorced parent, and traveled the world to raise money for the Christian Children's fund.*

A happy moment for the Bunkers and the Stivics. Who'd imagine that select reruns of their 1971-83 series would be the hit of CBS-TV's summer 1991 season, meant initially to hype Norman Lear's new show, Sunday Dinner—*which flopped?*

Goateed neighbor Henry Jefferson (Mel Stewart) is only one of the many "minor-orities" who get Archie's goat. After AITF *ended, Norman Lear was asked if he thought it had had any effect on promoting racial tolerance. He answered: "If two thousand years of the Judeo-Christian ethic had so little effect, I would be a fool to think a half-hour show would have any…. We put a spotlight on it and the world moves on."*

surprisingly, Edith, that gentle soul, who helps us do it.

In one episode, Mike is accused of badmouthing Archie as much as Archie badmouths him. Yelling at Archie is simply self-defense, counters Mike. No, there's more, explains Edith. For five years Archie has supported Mike, feeding him and giving him a roof over his head, so he can be free to study and eventually graduate from college. (Would Archie continue to do that if he *really* thought Mike a *"dumb* Polack"?) "When you owe someone so much," continues Edith, "you begin to think you'll never be able to pay them back. And that makes you resent them even more."

Then Edith explains to Mike why Archie yells at him. "You're going to college. Archie had to quit high school to help his father support the family. He sees in you all the things he'll never be."

Mike is so moved by Edith's keen perceptions that when Archie comes home that evening, Mike impulsively hugs him. "I've got something to tell you," he says in a choking voice to his startled in-law. "I *understand.*"

All this doesn't make Archie into a tragic Willy Loman, of course. He's still as feisty and pugnacious as ever. And Edith is content to stand in the background, wringing her hands and assuring him, "I'm your wife. I've always done what you've said, even when you were wrong." (Archie, in turn, insists he is *never* wrong.)

As time goes on, Edith finds her own voice and learns to stand up to Archie. One memorable moment comes when she finds he has placed a bet on a horse. Many years before, Archie had become addicted to betting, and Edith made him promise never to gamble again. She had once left him because of the "sickness." Now she finds he has lied to her. She takes a phone message for him: "Glow Worm in the fifth." Later, when returning from work, Archie asks, "Any messages for me?"

"Yes," says Edith, repeating the tip, and slapping Archie in the face.

"I never thought I'd see the day Mom would hit Daddy," Gloria notes.

That was the first time he ever saw Archie, says Mike, "with his mouth open and nothing coming out!"

"Did I ever hit you?" Archie asks Edith.

She never gave him cause, Edith replies. "I could forgive you for hitting me, but I could never forgive you for making me hit you."

Reminding Archie how she once quit their marriage is enough to bring him back in line.

Does Archie have a roving eye? Only once did he stray—with a waitress. At all other times in the presence of young women, he is a lump. "Sex" and other "four-letter words" (like "breast") are banned in the Bunker household. He winces at the word "pregnant," used by Gloria to joyously describe her new condition.

He is sexually repressed, Gloria insists. But if he was afraid of sex, parries Archie, "you wouldn't be here." His generation had respect for their women. "Do you think I would have spent the night with your mother before I married her?"

Edith supplies the answer: "I wouldn't let him."

It is Carroll O'Connor's tour de force as Archie—his ability to find the humanity beneath the sneers and the swagger—that kept us riveted for such a long time (twelve years). But the cast was uniformly excellent. They did true "ensemble" acting under Norman Lear's encouraging eye. Lear welcomed their input at story conferences. Some of the funniest lines that landed in the script were ad-libbed by the cast in these discussions.

As time went on, and the show won such great acclaim, the cast and the writers were spurred to make it even bolder and more intense. Characters' hidden secrets and sensitivities emerged. Emotions became more genuine.

According to Norman Lear, the breakthrough episode in terms of making Archie sympathetic was the one in which Gloria suffers a miscarriage. For it is here in the wordless look that passes between father and daughter that we see Archie at his most vulnerable.

After buying her a giant teddy bear, Archie returns home to hear from Edith and Mike the terrible news. The doctor has come and gone, and Archie finds his "Little Girl" sitting up in bed with a magazine. He stares numbly.

"You want to say something?" Gloria prompts.

"No, nothing," he mumbles. But Gloria knows better. She lovingly furnishes his thoughts for him. "You love me...I love you too, Daddy."

It is a moving moment.

Jean Stapleton was easily the most popular character on the show, and her "death" as Edith in 1980 sent a wave of sadness over viewers everywhere. Edith's demise so upset AITF creator Norman Lear, that he donated half a million dollars to the National Organization of Women as part of a memorial fund in Edith's name. Post-AITF roles for Stapleton have included playing Eleanor Roosevelt in a TV movie and chef Julia Child on stage at Washington's Kennedy Center and Off-Broadway; and starring on Broadway and on tour in Arsenic and Old Lace *and* Drood.

Although they "divorced" after leaving All in the Family, *Mike (Rob Reiner) and Gloria (Sally Struthers) will remain Archie's "Meathead" and "Little Girl" forever. Struthers, a native of Portland, Oregon, was described by her sister, Sue, in 1974, as "stone-willed...always individualistic." Today, Rob Reiner is bearded and bald, and one of Hollywood's most successful directors of film comedies.*

The Bunker-Stivic household was joined by Stephanie, Archie's niece, played by Danielle Brisebois, in 1978, the same year Mike and Gloria Stivic packed up and left for California with little Joey. In this Thanksgiving scene are (seated): Archie (Carroll O'Connor), Joey (Justin Draeger), Stephanie, and Edith (Jean Stapleton). Standing are Gloria (Sally Struthers) and husband Michael (Rob Reiner).

On the set, Sally Struthers (Gloria) called Carroll O'Connor "Daddy" out of affection and respect. "He saw me through an engagement, dates, boyfriends," she told *People* in 1978. "He always disapproved of them because he thought none of them was good enough for me. Just like my own father would have."

O'Connor was born in New York City but studied drama at the National University of Dublin. He joined the Dublin Gate Theatre, where he did Shakespearean roles, and also toured Europe in various classic plays. Returning to the U.S., he appeared on Broadway and was a supporting player in more than two dozen films, including Elizabeth Taylor's *Cleopatra*. During a lull in his acting career, he worked as a substitute teacher (1955–57) in New York City schools.

Like Norman Lear, he was pessimistic about *All in the Family*'s reception by the American public. He kept paying rent on an expensive apartment in Rome, where he had been living, "just in case." He was certain the TV audience "would explode in indignation" at Archie. Part of the reason they didn't was surely his own sterling performance.

Archie's accent was "pure Canarsie," according to O'Connor, referring to a section of the New York City borough of Brooklyn. The voice was real, that of a "supreme court judge" he had overheard in a restaurant. The man wasn't going to return to this establishment because it was "a regula rendevooze fa buhms."

The exterior of the Bunker house was filmed in the borough of Queens, and it appeared on the opening of every show, us the camera dissolved to the Bunker living room with Edith and Archie, at the piano, singing the opening theme "Those Were the Days."*

All in the Family made Carroll O'Connor a millionaire, and he wasn't afraid to use his new-found superstar status to influence the direction of the series. Outspoken and strongly opinioned, he knew what was "right" for Archie and what wasn't, and he would demand script changes he thought necessary. At the height of Bunkermania, he

*This song was issued as a record, by Archie and Edith and rose to #43 on the *Billboard* charts.

EPISODIC GEM
ARCHIE SEES 'DE LAWD'

Archie is bugged at his Italian neighbor, Irene Lorenzo (played by Betty Garrett). She is a *female* who knows how to fix things better than he does and puts a new safety lock and automatic closer on his basement door. He is waiting for the oil men to come and service his heater. After Irene leaves, and the house is deserted, he goes into the basement to check the heater and accidentally locks himself in. The house is cold, and his family won't be home for hours. Archie finds some liquor—his "blanket in a bottle"—and gets smashed trying to keep warm. "I could croak down here, and nobody would know."

Reeling drunkenly, he decides to make out a will. To Mike, he leaves his American flag ("with forty-eight stars"). To Gloria, "who I forgive for marrying above-mentioned, my personal living room chair" to be the centerpiece of her new home. "To Mrs. Irene Lorenzo, who killed me," he gives a wet raspberry. Edith, he feels, will be provided for, because "God takes care of dingbats."

Impatient to meet his maker, Archie calls on God to "take me out of this joint." To his amazement he hears a knock. "Is that you down there. Mr. Bunker?" "Yeah, Lord." "Hold on, I'm coming for you." Footsteps on the stairs. A black man, the *oil man,* with a beard and a mellifuous voice, steps out of the shadows. Mouth agape, Archie falls to his knees, crying, "Forgive me, Lord. The Jeffersons was right!"

created a nightclub act using his "Archie dialect," which he took to Reno, Lake Tahoe, and Las Vegas. Merchandizing included "Archie for President" bumper stickers (Archie Bunker actually did get one vote at one of the presidential nominating conventions in 1976!), posters, T-shirts, beer mugs, magazines, and buttons.

And there was the final, crowning glory when the Smithsonian Institution, that receptacle of assorted Americana in Washington, D.C., accepted *both* Archie and Edith's living room chairs for glass-encased exhibits. The originals, bought from Goodwill Industries for next to nothing, cost

America's favorite Everymen of the 1970s, Archie Bunker hates the cards life has dealt him. If he can find a way to cheat, he will. In contrast, wife Edith, "The Dingbat," usually hold a winning hand and doesn't even know it.

Son-in-law Mike Stivic represents everything in the world Archie hates: hippies, the antiwar movement, racial tolerance, freedom of sexual preference, and atheism. Put Archie and Mike in the same room and they're bound to argue.

$3,000 to be replaced by exact duplicates. Also, we mustn't forget the Joey Stivic doll, inspired by Mike and Gloria's firstborn (played on the show by twins to circumvent child-labor-law restrictions on how long one child can work per day). It was the first anatomically correct male doll in America.

All in the Family was not without its critics, which included Bill Cosby and Dr. Alvin Poussaint, noted psychologist who is now a consultant on *The Cosby Show.* In their view, the show made racism a laughing matter, and thus encouraged an acceptance, by blacks and whites alike, of bigotry.

Norman Lear strongly disagreed. "I've never known a bigot who didn't have something endearing. My point is, bigotry exists in *good* people."

Jean Stapleton agreed. A native of Manhattan, she grew up in an Anglo-Saxon family. "My grandparents had strong prejudices and my parents had some too. But I was fortunate enough to attend desegregated public schools. I learned through contact with classmates of different backgrounds....But I don't think my parents, or Archie, are hateful. I believe they say the things they do simply because they're uneducated."

The Jeffersons (Sherman Hemsley and Isabel Sanford) arrived as Archie's next-door neighbors in 1971. Eventually he learns to tolerate them, even break bread with them in his own house. George Jefferson is Archie's mirror image, as the black bigot. "I wouldn't step in your house," says George, "even if you got down on your knees and sang 'Mammy.'" His son Lionel gets his licks in too, but with subtle humor. "You know more about black people than anyone I ever met," he tells Archie. "You sure you haven't got some black blood?" Archie denies it, but Mike insists, "Yes you do. Look at those kinky eyebrows."

When the Jeffersons' college-age son Lionel bugs Mike to go jogging with him one afternoon, Archie wants to know why he is so insistent. "If you were a cop walking down the street, and you saw a black man running in this neighborhood," answers Lionel, "what would you think?"

For Archie the inferiority of the non-white races is a fact of nature. He can even quote Scripture to prove why black and white must be separated.

While Sammy Davis, Jr. (in one of the series' best-remembered episodes) waits at the Bunker house to retrieve a briefcase he left in Archie's taxi (it's being brought from the main cab office), the polite chitchat eventually turns to race. "If God had meant us to be together, He would have put us together. But He put you over in Africa and the rest of us in the white countries." "You must have told Him where we were," replies Sammy Davis, "because someone came and got us."

Privately, Lionel tells Sammy that Archie isn't so bad. "He'd never burn a cross on your lawn." Sammy isn't impressed. "But if he saw one burning, he'd probably toast a marshmallow."

Archie uses his fractured knowledge of the Gospel to make sure the women in his life know their proper place. When Gloria is in her second (successful) pregnancy, she relates how using natural childbirth methods can reduce the pain. Archie will have none of that kind of talk. "In the Book of Generous, God says, 'In pain shall youse bring forth children.'" Mike raises his eyebrows. "God said 'youse'?" "Because Eve ate the apple," continues Archie, "the snake was there and he rattled on her."

Knee-jerk liberalism also comes in for its lumps on *All in the Family*. When Mike and Gloria decide to make two of their friends guardians of Joey should they die, they do it because Archie and Edith don't share their "values." This move is triggered when Archie buys a toy gun for Joey. "You're going to hand our grandson to strangers?" Archie bellows. Edith is deeply hurt.

Eventually the Stivics learn that ideological purity is not always the best test for parenthood. They realize no one will ever love Joey more than his grandparents.

Mike is just as rigid and self-righteous in his opinions as Archie. He also has some lingering macho elements in him, as Gloria gradually learns. Like her mother, she is a stronger and more actualized person, in many ways, than her husband.

When we first saw Gloria in 1971, she was the buxom but girlish newlywed in Shirley Temple hairdo and miniskirt, hanging on Mike's every word. Several years later she is the sexually asser-

tive woman, bumping and grinding her way through the song "Making Whoopee," while her husband sits glumly in a chair.

"What's wrong?" Gloria demands. In the bedroom, he was always the one to make the first move, says Mike. "You never jumped till I said, 'Ready, set, go.' I don't know who's the man around here…"

Thus was equality fought for in the Stivic marriage.

By the 1977–78 season, Archie has bought a saloon, and the Stivics are packed and ready to move to California. (CBS had decided to put Sally Struthers, now a single parent, in her own spin-off series, *Gloria*. Rob Reiner—Mike—defected to ABC and subsequently has become a very successful film director.)

The following season found a new character living in the Bunker home, Archie's brother's daughter, Stephanie (played by nine-year-old Danielle Brisebois). By now, Archie has mellowed and become almost benign. Although he's spent many seasons using the epithets "kike," "hebe," and "that tribe," he overcomes his scruples to attend a funeral in a synagogue, and even dons a yarmulke. And despite being upset that Stephanie, raised a Christian, now decides to adopt her deceased Mom's religion and become Jewish, Archie eventually supports her and takes her to his bosom. Without the Meathead to keep him on his toes, this Archie Bunker has gone soft.

In 1979 the series was rechristened *Archie Bunker's Place*, with Martin Balsam as Archie's new Jewish partner, Murray Klein, and *another* young girl, teenage Billie (Denise Miller) brought into the Bunker household and adopted. The following season, Edith was killed off at Jean Stapleton's request. Three years later, having dropped to 22nd place in the ratings (tied with *That's Incredible*), *Archie Bunker's Place* was shuttered.

The enduring popularity of Archie and Edith and family was illustrated in the spring and summer of 1991 when, after years of syndication, *All in the Family* returned to CBS in selected reruns and landed in the Top Ten in the ratings.

Archie doesn't have to say a word—his look says it all: "Stifle, Edith!" And where did that word "stifle" come from? The show's creator, Norman Lear, says his own dad used it often. "I grew up in a family that lived at the top of its lungs and the ends of its nerves," recalls Lear. So it's no surprise the noisy Bunkers live exactly the same way!

CAST LIST

FAMILY: The Bunkers

MEMBERS:

Archie Bunker . . . . **Carroll O'Connor**
Edith Bunker (1971–80) . . . **Jean Stapleton**
Gloria Bunker Stivic
   (1971–78) . . . . **Sally Struthers**
Mike Stivic (1971–78) . . . . **Rob Reiner**
Joey Stivic
   (1975–78) . . . . . **Justin or Jason Draeger**

SIGNIFICANT OTHERS:

Lionel Jefferson (1971–75) . . . **Mike Evans**
Louise Jefferson
   (1971–75) . . . . **Isabel Sanford**
George Jefferson
   (1973–75) . . . . **Sherman Hemsley**
Irene Lorenzo (1973–75) . . . **Betty Garrett**
Frank Lorenzo
   (1973–74) . . . . **Vincent Gardenia**

Stephanie Mills
   (1978–83) . . . . **Danielle Brisebois**
Billie Bunker (1979–83) . . . . **Denise Miller**
Murray Klein (1979–81) . . . **Martin Balsam**

THEME SONG: **"Those Were the Days"**
               by Lee Adams and
               Charles Strouse
TIMEFRAME: **1971–83**
NETWORK: **CBS**
ADDRESS: **704 Hauser St.**
               Queens, New York

207 episodes
("Archie Bunker's Place" [1979–83],
89 episodes)

GREAT PERFORMANCES

Emmy Winners

Jean Stapleton

Outstanding Actress (Comedy)

1970–71, 1971–72, 1977–78

Carroll O'Connor

Outstanding Actor (Comedy)

1971–72, 1976–77, 1977–78, 1978–79

Sally Struthers

Outstanding Supporting Actress (Comedy)

1971–72, 1978–79

Rob Reiner

Outstanding Supporting Actor (Comedy)

1973–74, 1977–78

The Evans family (and their next-door neighbor): Clockwise from left are Michael (Ralph Carter), James "J. J." Evans, Jr. (Jimmie Walker), Thelma (BernNadette Stanis), Willona Woods (Ja'net DuBois), James (John Amos), and matriarch Florida (Esther Rolle).

J. J.'s pumped-up self-portrait, as "Kid Dyn-o-mite," gets a belly laugh from the building's beefy super, Bookman (Johnny Brown). Coproducer Norman Paul noted that Good Times *audiences warmed almost immediately to Walker as J. J. "We never expected that reaction. The audience just took to him as a natural comedian."*

The small ghetto apartment is J. J. Evans's stage. Upon it he struts, leers, rolls his eyes, puffs out his scrawny chicken chest, and spews out a stream of self-glorifying nonsense that never fails to bring gales of laughter from the audience. And when he's particularly excited—perhaps he thinks one of his shady schemes has come to fruition—his eyes glisten, and he crows, "Dyn-o-mite!" That word, and J. J.'s exuberant delivery of it, created a catchphrase of the mid-seventies and made Jimmie Walker a bona fide TV star.

With the Evans family struggling to make ends meet in the squalid Cabrini-Green housing project (aka "Cockroach Towers") in Chicago, J. J. supplies much of the warmth and laughter, the "good times" that make their struggle bearable. The show's message is: you may be poor, but as long as you've got family you can be happy. And this African-American family is intact. "It's complete," said Esther Rolle, who played the matriarch, Florida Evans, "with two parents and all the love and pride I know to be a fact." She herself grew up ninth in a family of eighteen, the daughter of a truck farmer and his wife, in Pompano Beach, Florida.

Completing the family circle are father James, J. J.'s younger sister Thelma, and the baby of the household, Michael (J. J.'s junior by six years). With James often out of work (through no fault of his own), J. J. helps out by "finding" things that have been "lost" around the neighborhood. A high school dropout and a talented, self-taught painter, he hopes someday to succeed as a commercial artist. In the meantime, he uses his overstimulated imagination to dream up new schemes to make money. He fronts a rock band for his brother ("Michael and the Dyn-o-mites"), manages a stand-up comedian, and even tries to rent out a room in the apartment. ("We don't have your ordinary bodacious machine," he tells an interested party who asked about air conditioning. "We have our own ventilation shaft. We believe Nature's way is best.")

J. J. has plenty of confidence—a kind of charming, street-smart sassiness—that is irresistible. He uses it on everyone, including his parents, who despair that he will ever grow up. He seems to be the perpetual adolescent, with his flights of fancy and his funny, rhyming jive talk. After spying on Thelma and her new boyfriend while wearing a trench coat and slouch hat, he exclaims, "I had the knack of Kojak, and was better than Baretta." And after some smooth talking on the phone, J. J. claims "the diplomacy of Henry the K., the slick moves of Dr. J."

As J. J. himself might rhyme it: he is quick with the lip, ever ready with a quip.

Which may explain why this gawky stringbean with the mobile playdough features is a hit with the "foxy chicks." He is the self-proclaimed "Connoisseur of Amour" and the "Emperor of Ecstasy," and his tales of romantic conquest include such colorful names as Boom Boom Belinda, Velma the Vacuum Cleaner, and Samantha the Human Panther.

All this doesn't impress his parents, however. His mom, a churchgoing, God-fearing woman, tells him, "There are two ways to get out of the ghetto. We're going the right way." "Yeah," answers J. J., "that's why it's taking us so long." He then briefly finds employment taking bets over the phone for two bookies.

It is J. J.'s constant skirting at the edge of lawlessness that grieves his parents. In a two-part episode, J. J. becomes acquainted with a gang leader and winds up in the middle of a turf war between Satan's Knights and the War Lords. J. J.'s parents try to stop the rumble, but there is a scuffle, and J. J. is shot. Part one ends with him lying on the street, bleeding.

Esther Rolle and John Amos (James) both had a hand in developing this script in order to bring more realism to the series. They wanted to show not only the danger of gangs, but what it is that

Nathan Bookman (Johnny Brown), also known around the housing project ("Cockroach Towers") as "Buffalo Butt," came aboard Good Times to help fill the void in the 1977–78 season, caused by the absence of Esther Rolle (pictured here). Miss Rolle returned a year later (at Norman Lear's request) with more power to get the kind of storylines she felt essential. Basically, Mr. Lear said "Uncle."

drives children into them. It turns out that the reason J. J. was shot was the gang leader's jealousy over something J. J. had and he didn't—a father.

This story came in the first year of the show's run. By the second season, J. J.'s popularity as a comic figure was at its peak. There were "Dyn-o-mite" hats, socks, p.j.s, pocketbooks, belt buckles, even underwear, for sale. Jimmie Walker was sharing in this merchandising bonanza, and Good Times went with its comic strength. Episodes with social themes vanished, leaving two people very unhappy: Esther Rolle and John Amos.

Amos, an athlete who'd made the training camps of fourteen professional football teams before turning to acting and writing, was a veteran of the Mary Tyler Moore Show, appearing as Gordy, the weatherman (1970–73). Previous to that, in 1969, he was a writer on The Leslie Uggams Show, contributing a weekly sketch, "Sugar Hill," about a middle-class black family.

Jimmie Walker defended his flamboyant, if unrealistic, portrayal of J. J., by asking, "Does The Fonz represent white teenagers?" He did allow, however, "There's not as much merriment in the ghetto, as we pretend." In this scene from 1975, J. J. launches his show business career as the manager of a singer, played by Judith Cohen.

Good Times was "developed" by Norman Lear, but it is a sure bet that Amos's creative input was encouraged, as was Esther Rolle's. Miss Rolle had been contacted to play Florida Evans, the flippant housemaid of Maude Findlay, on Lear's hit sitcom, *Maude,* which, in turn, had spun off from *All in the Family.* (At first Rolle told Lear, "I've struggled so many years in acting, I'm not playing any maid!" But when Lear explained that her character would be every bit as strong and opinionated as Maude, Rolle accepted.) Two years later, Florida bid farewell to a sorrowful Maude, explaining that "Henry" (his name was later changed to James) had gotten a good job in Chicago and the family was moving. (Inexplicably, when they arrived, the job had disappeared!) Thus was born *Good Times* (its working title had been *Great Day*).

The first episode was written by two African-Americans, Mike Evans (Lionel on *All in the Family*) and Eric Monte, who was retained as story editor. According to Esther Rolle, this was going to be American TV's first "real" black family. Diahann Carroll's 1969–71 *Julia,* the first post-*Amos 'n' Andy* black sitcom, was "about as white middle class as anything," scoffed Rolle. "You didn't learn anything about black people from that." What was needed was a strong father figure to head the family "instead of a stereotyped black woman without a husband and with a houseful of kids.... I'm tired of the black male going unsung."

John Amos knew some of the frustrations minority men faced in a society "that tells him he must compete, then minimizes his opportunities." Growing up in East Orange, N. J., he'd worked as a sanitation man and in other semiskilled jobs until finding his calling in show business. He wanted to bring these experiences into his characterization of James Evans. Unfortunately, as the show shifted its focus more and more to J. J., John Amos felt he wasn't getting a fair chance. The show's credits might read "Starring Esther Rolle and John Amos," with Jimmie Walker's name coming last under the featured player listing, but the writing was already on the wall. After many months of fruitless backstage battles, Amos announced he was leaving in 1976, citing his dismay "at the new direction" the show was taking. Eric Monte, *Good Times* cocreator, was reportedly fired because he also objected to the new order. Fortunately for John Amos, he was able to segue into the role of the adult Kunte Kinte in the epic TV miniseries, *Roots*.

The show's producers now had a problem to solve. What should they do with the James Evans character? They decided he should go to Alaska to work on the pipeline. Esther Rolle protested. That was the old cliché all over again of the black man deserting his family, she said. The only alternative—and a more "realistic" one, according to Rolle—was to kill him off in an accident, far away from home. So the story was concocted that James had found work in a garage in Alabama, and was ready to send for his family when he was killed in a car crash.

The wake held after the funeral of James Evans remains one of the most fascinating *Good Times* episodes. Not one tear is shed until the final scene. Instead, Florida plays a cheerful host to her guests, serving them ham with pineapple. The mood is festive, and the script takes comic swipes at some of the guests. One running gag is that everyone brings the same contribution of food: a canned ham. Florida's best friend, Willona Woods (Ja'net DuBois), looks in the refrigerator and comments, "It's like roundup time at the old hog ranch!" When Ned, the local wino, can only offer some turkey, he explains, "I tried to get ham, but they were all out."

Meanwhile, the undertaker is trying to drum up business, announcing: "We don't advertise. We just pick up things in the neighborhood." To the building superintendent, "Booger" Bookman (played by comedian Johnny Brown), he says, "I have some choice plots. They're repossessions. The man who

Esther Rolle and John Amos were all smiles in 1974 when Good Times *premiered. They had high hopes that for the first time on television a poor black family would be portrayed in a fairly realistic fashion. That was before J. J. became so popular that the show became* his *showcase.*

bought them is having financial troubles, and he wants to get out from under."

This seems to be the wrong note to be sounding for the passing of James. The Evans children are irritated. When James's friends from the plant begin joking about the good times they had together, young Michael (Ralph Carter) can stand it no longer. "Our daddy's dead and you're standing around here laughing. Doesn't anybody care?"

Florida, still maintaining an eerie calm, explains, "People always acted this way. In Africa, they don't mourn the dead, they celebrate life."

But this thought is not enough to sustain Florida after her guests have left. Finally, embracing her three children, she breaks down and cries.

Deftly, the writers have managed to rid themselves of a major character, get their quota of laughs, and teach us something as well.

With James gone, other people took on prominence, like Willona, the sexy single lady next door. A vibrant chatterbox always on the lookout for a boyfriend, she had no use for the hefty super, Bookman, calling him "Buffalo Butt." When Bookman has been thrown out by his wife, he hopes Willona will take him, but she snaps, "Make your home where the buffalo roam!" And when a woman, Wanda, a professional mourner, tries to

Series scripts promoted young Michael (Ralph Carter) as the smart brother, leaving J. J. to be the Clown Prince of the Evans family. Esther Rolle objected to the fact "J. J. isn't interested in school, has his little brother helping him read, is wearing outrageous costumes, and stands around yelling "Dyn-o-mite!"

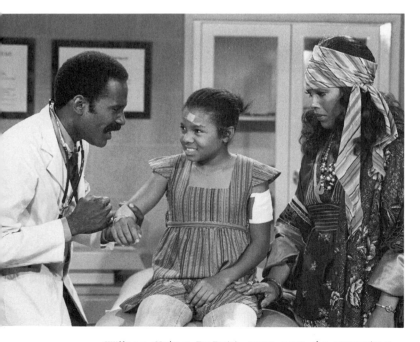

Willona (Ja'net DuBois), upset over the mysterious scrapes and bruises that keep appearing on ten-year-old Penny Gordon (Janet Jackson), takes her to see a doctor (Bob Delegall) in this fifth season premiere episode of Good Times. *Miss Jackson, of course, went on to appear on TV's* Fame, *and to become the nation's best-selling female recording artist.*

crash the funeral of the street hustler, Fishbone (Robert Guillaume), Willona warns, "Cool it, Mama, I'm working this wake."

Then there was Carl Dixon (Moses Gunn), brought in to be Florida's new love interest.

Backstage tensions continued to run high, however, because of J. J.'s continued dominance in the stories. Rumors flew that J. J.'s popularity had gone to Jimmie Walker's head, that he was coming late to rehearsals. And critics were beginning to call J. J. "obnoxious," "grotesque," and "immature."

Esther Rolle concurred wholeheartedly. "Little by little they've made J. J. more stupid," she said. "What kind of image is that for black children to follow?" Tension mounted on the set, aggravating Miss Rolle's blood pressure, and once she had to be rushed to a hospital for four days of recuperation. Finally, while *Good Times* began filming for the 1977–78 season, Rolle stayed in the Bahamas, where she had gone for a vacation. After missing the first two episodes and not getting any of the concessions she felt so necessary, she and the producers agreed on a parting of the ways. CBS, in "a Kremlin-like announcement," according to one acerbic newspaper critic, declared that Rolle was withdrawing because of "ill health."

But a peppy Esther Rolle continued to pepper the show with criticisms. She was especially unhappy at how they'd handled Florida's departure. Florida had married Carl Dixon and they'd taken their honeymoon in Arizona, where they decided to remain because the dry climate was better for Carl's health. "What kind of mother would go traipsing across the country, leaving her three children to fend for themselves?" asked Rolle. It was bad enough James Evans had been erased; now they had the mother marrying a man she barely knew and moving away. And, on top of that, they showed J. J., according to Rolle, just "lying around."

To be fair to Lear's Tandem Productions, J. J. did not just lay around. He was still liable to proclaim, "One day, one of my dumb schemes will make me J. Paul Ghetto!" But the scriptwriters were already toning him down.

With Willona assuming the role of surrogate mother in the Evans family, J. J. took the first steps toward being the man around the house. A new character was introduced: Penny, a battered child, played by Janet Jackson (yes, *the* Janet Jackson). Willona befriends her, then takes legal custody after her mother abandons her. Despite this sad background, Penny is basically an upbeat girl who takes an instant liking to J. J. His crazy antics cheer her up. "Here's a fly going through a fog of Black Flag," he shouts, buzzing and weaving. When he finally goes belly up, Penny laughs.

J. J. shows his tender side by telling Penny his version of a fairy tale as she readies for bed. It's called "Afrolocks," with Michael as the "smallest bear," Thelma as the "most ugly, bodacious bear," and J. J., of course, as the "most savoir-faire bear."

J. J. also rises to the occasion when Michael runs afoul of the law. Seems Michael went along for a "joy ride" when his friend Howard "borrowed" his father's car without permission. After a stern lecture from the police, Michael is released. J. J. promptly dubs him "Baby Face Evans" and tells him he is "officially grounded" for one week. This is a real turning point for J. J. For to monitor Michael's grounding, he must give up what he loves dearly: dating his "bodacious ladies."

To her role as Florida's best friend, Willona Woods, Ja'net DuBois brought high energy and playful sassiness. For the season that Florida was absent, Willona became surrogate mother to the Evans kids, and adopted Penny Gordon, an abused child whose mother had abandoned her.

EPISODIC WEIRDNESS
J. J.'S DREAM

When a better position opens up for him at work (as an art director), J. J. fully expects to be promoted. Then his boss, who is white, gives him the bad news. He can't have a minority person in this "high-profile" job because "I have to deal with clients who are prejudiced...I don't like this league, but I have to play ball."

Feeling that a "foul" has been committed, J. J. returns home, eats a chili dog and falls asleep. The next morning, when he awakes, he is *white*. (Well, actually, he's still J. J., but his Alternate Self is white.)* J. J. remains outside this strange doppelganger, as an observer, but the voice that comes out of its mouth is his.

Willona uses a dishrag on J. J. because she thinks he's wearing "clown makeup." Brother Michael scolds J. J., reminding him what their father once

*This situation was similarly explored by Godfrey Cambridge in Melvin Van Peebles's 1970 movie, *The Watermelon Man.*

J. J. and "WHITE J. J." (played by Dennis Howard)

Situation normal at the Evans apartment: a screaming match between elder brother J. J. (Jimmy Walker, right) and siblings Thelma (BernNadette Stanis) and Michael (Ralph Carter). J. J., of the trademark floppy hat and big mouth, usually has the last word—or at least the loudest.

said: "You have to play with the uniform you were issued."

But J. J. is tantalized by the possibilities. He watches, fascinated, as his white alter ego eats croissants at work instead of donuts. His boss comments, "I see you've redecorated your face." "Some are born white," says J. J., "some become white and some have white thrust upon them." Now the new job seems within his grasp.

At that moment J. J. awakens. It was all a weird dream. He rushes to work and is elated when his boss tells him he won't knuckle under to prejudice. He's decided to fill the new position with a minority worker: a woman!

J. J. remembers his father's words and feels better.

At least he didn't have "to go through that dream in a dress!"

With J. J.'s character remolded, the stage was set for Esther Rolle's return in the show's final season. Ratings had dropped significantly during her one-year hiatus. She had been asked repeatedly by Norman Lear to do guest shots, and had refused. Now, on a trip to New York to attend the Peabody Awards, Lear convinced her to return for one last season, reportedly with script approval of all episodes and a larger salary.

During Esther Rolle's year-long absence, Jimmie Walker had not been silent. J. J., he said, wasn't "supposed to be a genius"; he was simply a character on a sitcom. "Is the Fonz representative of white teenagers?" he demanded. J. J. was popular because he was "safe." "He's not a threat to anyone, black or white. His brother is the thinker, the militant. J. J. is likable."

Walker had never professed the idealism of Rolle or John Amos. If he had any militancy he hid it well. "I don't work for the 'Movement,'" he told an interviewer in 1974. "I work for the Jimmie Walker fund."

He wanted to do stand-up comedy and be a star the proportions of a Richard Pryor. Acting was secondary; he found it "tedious and boring." During his run as J. J., Walker would go to the Comedy Store in the evening to hone his stand-up routines. Like J. J., he was a realist, a survivor. To make it to the top he would have to attract a "mixed" audience. "I want everyone to dig me," he remarked.

But while Jimmie Walker was not in the "Movement," he knew the score. In 1975, when there were three black sitcoms in the Top Ten at the same time (*Good Times, The Jeffersons,* and *Sanford and Son*), he said, "The ideal point is for all Americans to view these shows as non-color....But realistically, that will never happen. Not in this society...."

Born in the South Bronx, Walker dropped out of high school but studied speech and drama at the City College of New York, under the SEEK anti-poverty program. He did his first "stand-up" in front of one of his college classes, using a three-minute Dick Gregory monologue. "I studied speech for five years to lose all signs of ethnic traces in my voice," he recalled. "When I finally got in the business, they paid me to talk the way I talked in the first place."

And the utterance that got him the furthest was "Dyn-o-mite!" (His trademark "wasn't my creation....One of the writers laid it on me...." It came in the second show after J. J. has a brush with the police, and exclaims, "They knew they were in trouble once they realized they were dealing with Kid Dyn-o-mite!") It was to become a national catch-phrase.

JIMMIE WALKER'S TALE OF A LUCKY HAT

Jimmie Walker has always worn his celebrity lightly, with the same jaunty, breezy style as his most famous comic creation, James "J. J." Evans, Jr. But like many performers he has a superstitions side, especially when it relates to work.

One of his first jobs was as a stand-up comedian in Manhattan's African Room (now closed). Bette Midler, who also was appearing there, liked his act and recommended him to the Improv, which Walker describes as a training ground for "eighty percent of the talent on TV." From the Improv, Walker got his first chance to go before a national audience when he auditioned for the small role of a junkie in the 1973 Robert Duvall police thriller, *Badge 373.*

To do this role properly, Walker felt that he needed a hat. Somehow it would help him "get into" his character, he believed. He found what he wanted at a small subway stand in Manhattan. It was a floppy thing that he bought for $1.99, but it was worth its weight in gold. "I stomped on it a few times so it would look dirty," remembers Walker, and he was set. With the hat he won his part, and he's kept the hat ever since, like other people keep a "lucky" rabbit's foot. He wore it on *Good Times,* where it became an integral part of J. J.'s "look." In 1987, Walker returned to TV in the syndicated series, *Bustin' Loose,* wearing the same hat as another wisecracking "J. J." type, Sonny Barnes.

JIMMIE WALKER

Florida's return from Arizona is made with a simple declaration. "I'm home!" she calls as she steps into the Evans apartment in the fall of 1978. Her new husband's illness has worsened, requiring his permanent hospitalization in Arizona. Now she is free to take up mothering again.

Although J. J. is still prone to flights of fancy, he is more mature and responsible now. His diligence at teaching himself painting has paid dividends—he has found work as art director in an ad agency. Things are changing for Thelma (BernNadette Stanis) as well. She's marrying her boyfriend, professional football player Keith Anderson.

At season's end, all loose strings are tied up in the final episode, titled "End of the Rainbow." Thelma and Keith are expecting their first baby, and Florida will be moving out of the ghetto to live with them in their new home. Willona has found a new, better paying job, and will be near her friend Florida. And J. J. is moving into his own bachelor apartment.

Good Times was the first sitcom to make a sincere effort to portray the lives of African-Americans of the inner city. It had its "good times," its comedy, and its "bad times," when part of the cast fought with the network powers-that-be. But it did tackle some important issues. One episode showed black professionals (in this case, two doctors) guilty of turning their backs on the community, and how Florida shames them. In another, it was a dishonest black alderman soliciting for a phony cause ("The Fred Davis Clinic for Unneutered Cats"). Then there was the time the show warned high schoolers not to stake their future on the promise of a career in sports.

But most of all *Good Times* was about a commitment to family life, of people helping each other. Despite the difference in tone and setting, it is clearly a precursor of *The Cosby Show.* In fact, no matter how many times he shouts "Dyn-o-mite!" when the chips are down, J. J. is always there for his family. Because that's the way his mother taught him.

In this moving scene, a subdued Willona (normally the show's spitfire) watches as Penny (Janet Jackson) says her bedtime prayers. The story of Penny's rescue by Willona (Ja'net DuBois) showed the tender side of this often-raucous comedy.

CAST LIST

FAMILY: The Evanses

MEMBERS:

Florida Evans (1974–77,
   1978–79) . . . . **Esther Rolle**
James Evans (1974–76) . . . . . **John Amos**
James "J. J." Evans, Jr. . . **Jimmie Walker**
Thelma Evans
  Anderson . . . . **BernNadette Stanis**
Michael Evans . . . . **Ralph Carter**
Carl Dixon (1977) . . . . **Moses Gunn**
Keith Anderson (1978–79) . . **Ben Powers**

SIGNIFICANT OTHERS:

Willona Woods . . . . **Ja'net DuBois**
Penny Gordon Woods
  (1977–79) . . . . **Janet Jackson**
Nathan "Booger" Bookman
  (1977–79) . . . . **Johnny Brown**

THEME SONG: **David Grusin, Marilyn
             and Alan Bergman;
             sung by Ja'net DuBois**
TIMEFRAME: **1974–79**
NETWORK: **CBS**
ADDRESS: **Cabrini-Green Housing
            Project
            Chicago, Illinois**

120 episodes

The Winning Formula: The happy, loving, close-knit pioneer prairie family in front of their Little House hearth. The stars of the NBC-TV series Little House on the Prairie *circa 1980 are: (standing left to right) Linwood Boomer, Melissa Gilbert, Michael Landon, Melissa Sue Anderson; (seated left to right) Sidney Greenbush, Karen Grassle, Matthew Laborteaux.*

On the harmonious set of Little House on the Prairie *during its second season (1975), executive producer Michael Landon stands between actresses Melissa Gilbert, then eleven years old, and Melissa Sue Anderson, then thirteen, who play his TV daughters, Laura and Mary.*

Mitch Vogel (formerly Jamie Hunter on Bonanza*) guest-stars as a new boy in Walnut Grove to whom Laura Ingalls (Melissa Gilbert) is somewhat attracted, in "The Love of Johnny Johnson" episode.*

Michael Landon owns a unique place in the gossamer firmament known as Hollywood. As star/ executive producer/director and writer of *Little House on the Prairie,* he single-handedly was able to create and shape the visions in his own dreams and deliver them into the reality of a strong, successful weekly television family drama. No small achievement for any actor, no matter how big and powerful, in an industry as fickle, fault-finding, and failure-ridden as network television broadcasting.

After fourteen successful seasons of playing Little Joe Cartwright on NBC's weekly Western family drama series, *Bonanza,* Landon took his idea for a brand new one and added his own closely-supervised dimensions of story and character that were not present in the original material. Landon fathered *LHOTP,* nurtured the cast and crew, directed and wrote most of the stories, and entirely supervised every detail of the series. As he has always made perfectly clear—if the show should fail, the responsibility lay with him and no one else. The fact that the series was a resounding success, and continues resonating in syndication, affirms Landon's belief in his own visions and his remarkable ability to translate them successfully for a mass audience both in the U. S. and abroad.

Little House on the Prairie is essentially a soap opera with horses, a pure prairie drama. Like many weekly dramatic series it has (and must have) strong emotional hooks to pull you in and capture your attention for fifty-two minutes. Landon's vision of the strong, honest pioneer family whose spirit of love and devotion overcomes all physical harshness and obstacles of the heart, and always taught a moral, proved irresistible. *LHOTP* featured an excellent cast, plus a roster of fine guest stars to carry out the actions of usually simple plots. The stories were based on Laura Ingalls Wilder's eight *Little House on the Prairie* books published in the 1930s and 1940s, reminiscences of her early youth, when her father took her family into the vast American plains to make a new life for them.

"In the books," said Landon, "Charles Ingalls could lose a crop and sing a song. Nothing ever bothered him. He was a dreamer. He always wanted to do well, but he never had a knack for it.

He sometimes moved five times a year. He borrowed money, and he always lost his shirt. It must have been tough on his family." In the show, executive producer Landon creates his Charles Ingalls character to be almost the complete opposite of the farmer in the books. As the family patriarch, he is a hardworking, God-fearing man of the soil (mysteriously rarely wearing soiled clothes) who usually looks fresh after a seventeen-hour workday of plowing, pushing, and heaving. Ingalls has a strong-willed, handsome young wife, Caroline, played with quiet lustre by Karen Grassle, and three beautiful, bright-eyed, bright-toothed, well-disciplined daughters whose souls are as wrinkle-free as their always clean calico dresses. The older daughters, both pre-teen at the beginning of the series, are played with a delightful combination of spunk and sensitivity by cute-as-a-kitten Melissa Gilbert as Laura (the narrator of the stories) and ethereal Melissa Sue Anderson as Mary. The youngest daughter, Carrie, is played alternately by sisters Lindsay and Sidney Greenbush.

First and foremost, this is the story of a struggling pioneer farm family seeking the promised land and a better life in Walnut Grove, a small town in 1870s Minnesota. Although pains are taken to recreate the look and feel of those hearty days of yore, the grittiness is missing. What the show lacks in Old West "realism" (remember this is not a shoot-'em-up Western but a "family drama"), it makes up for in characterization. Granted, you'll never find any real frontier "geeks" in Walnut Grove like you would in the Dodge City of *Gunsmoke,* where Marshal Matt Dillon would swiftly dispatch them with a .44 slug or a choice whack from his pistol butt. In *LHOTP,* Ingalls and the townsfolk rarely move to gunplay. The quiet approach—a 1970s sensibility somehow transplanted to the 1870s—serves better and certainly stretches out the plot. There were flaws, of course—Landon has that Hollywood blow-dried look, Grassle has the understanding of Job, and both Melissas always seem to handle situations and problem-solving as if they had graduate degrees in clinical psychology. These, however, are rather easily overcome because the family chemistry is irresistible, and the acting is usually first-rate. It is

Laura (Melissa Gilbert) and Albert (Matthew Laborteaux) sneak a peek at busybody Harriet Oleson's (Katherine MacGregor) notes for her newspaper gossip column and learn some shocking details, in the episode, "Harriet's Happenings," broadcast October 30, 1978.

nearly impossible to watch this show without getting quickly caught up in the drama.

All the right ingredients come together under the skillful guidance of executive producer Landon, whose boyish good looks and long wavy chestnut hair (dyed) belie a driven perfectionist whose personal vision is embossed on every one of the 204 color episodes. Landon created a strong, loving family unafraid to display their affections and ever ready to stand up for their convictions. *LHOTP* was a lot about sermonizing, never the fire-and-brimstone kind of preachiness, but always the moral lesson learned through tolerance of those different from us, compassion for those less fortunate, patience with those less able. This show in many ways was about a strong Christian family struggling to practice Christian principles, interesting in that Landon was born and raised a Jew. But Landon came to *LHOTP* no stranger to Western family drama after costarring for fourteen seasons on *Bonanza* (which, save *Gunsmoke,* was American television's longest-running Western). *LHOTP* is a kinder, gentler, less leathery version of *Bonanza,* and in this incarnation it was all daughters and no sons.

Mary and Laura Ingalls go swimming in the creek with a friend, but the fun turns to tragedy, in "My Ellen" episode broadcast April 3, 1978.

"MY ELLEN"

In this episode, Laura and Mary invite their friend, Ellen Taylor, to come swimming with them. On the way, Laura wants to take a shortcut across the property of Busby, a dimwitted eccentric who looks like he suffers from acromegaly (enlarged facial features and hands), and Mary admonishes her, "Ma said not to, and if you do, I'll tell." Laura replies, "You would too!" From deep in his property, Busby watches the girls march by. At the swimming hole the three girls try to hide when the youngest Ingalls daughter, Carrie, innocently informs her sisters that there are two boys watching them. The three girls shriek and dive below the water's surface. After the boys run off, only Mary and Laura resurface. They call out, but Ellen doesn't answer.

The townsfolk search the waters, and they find Ellen's body. Later, at the funeral service, Ellen's mother, hysterical with grief, blames Laura for her daughter's death. "If it hadn't been for you, my Ellen would have been home with me. You did this. It was you!" Charles and Mr. Taylor both look on helplessly. When the Reverend Alden visits Mrs.

Taylor to console her, she accuses God of not saving her child, and throws Alden's gift, a Bible with marked passages, back in his face, screaming, "Take your damned book with you!"

At the Ingalls farm, Charles tries to comfort his weeping daughter.

> CHARLES: Well, half-pint, people in mourning say a lot of things they don't mean…it wasn't your fault.
> LAURA: But it was my idea to go swimming.
> CHARLES: Now, you listen to me (he tenderly cradles her face in his hands)…. Folks can't foretell the future. There's nothing anybody can do about it, and there's no one to blame for it. It's just the way life is, that's all. (He holds her close and strokes her head.) Miss Taylor will be all right, you'll see. She'll lean on the Lord. That's all.

On her way to school, Laura visits Mrs. Taylor, flowers in hand, in an effort to comfort the distraught woman, not knowing she has slipped from profound grief into dementia. When Mrs. Taylor looks at Laura, she begins to hallucinate she's seeing her dead daughter, Ellen, instead. She quickly imprisons Laura/Ellen in the root cellar and holds her captive. Meanwhile, Mary informs her father that Laura is missing. Charles rouses the men who form a search party. Childlike Busby has found Laura's flowers and books, which were tossed away by Mrs. Taylor, and when Jonathan Garvey (Merlin Olsen) finds them at Busby's farm, Busby guiltily runs off. The search party turns its attention to Busby and Mr. Taylor finds and shoots him, revenging himself thinking Busby to be responsible for Ellen's drowning.

When Mrs. Taylor wanders into town seeking birthday candles for her daughter's cake at the store, she rouses the suspicions of town busybody Mrs. Oleson, who races to the doctor's office where the men are questioning the wounded Busby. With Charles, Mr. Taylor makes haste for his farm, concluding Laura is still alive and being held by the demented Mrs. Taylor. Laura, meanwhile, has escaped but again is caught by Mrs. Taylor at the grave site of Ellen. As they struggle, Laura cries

Some of the excellent players who made up the fine cast of Little House on the Prairie, *from left are: Victor French (Isaiah Edwards), Richard Bull (Nels Olesen), Dabbs Greer (Rev. Robert Alden), Kevin Hagen (Dr. Baker), and Michael Landon (Charles Ingalls). This shot is from the final episode, "Little House—The Last Farewell," which broadcast February 6, 1984, as a two-hour TV movie.*

that she is not Ellen, and this somehow miraculously (it's only a fifty-two-minute show) snaps Mrs. Taylor out of her psychotic state and back to reason. Laura tells her that faith in God will help her, just as Charles and Mr. Taylor ride up. The husband and wife reconcile as Charles and Laura weepily embrace. The final scene shows Laura delivering flowers and a book to the gentle and dumb giant, Mr. Busby. "We want to be your friend, if you want us to." Busby's smile says "Yes," and fade to black.

The sincerity inherent in this episode, which, like in so many others, is the key element that keeps our disbelief suspended. We are swept along by the pace of the action and convincing acting by the cast. In one brief scene, the Reverend Alden, returning from the Taylor farm and his confrontation with Mrs. Taylor, visits Charles and remarks ever so easily that Mrs. Taylor's behavior is not "rational." This is pure bunk, as there was no word "rational" to describe such behavior back in the 1870s; it simply didn't exist. Yet, even obvious flaws

like this, though they diminish it, do not destroy the story's impact. These are all elements of Landon's great control over the series and even greater desire to create a warm, wise, and happy farm family.

Landon may well have wished to create this idealized, pure prairie family, brimming with compassion and understanding, as a balm to his own unhappy and tormented family background. Born Eugene Orowitz on October 31, 1937, in Forest Hills, N.Y., Landon was raised in the virtually all-Protestant town of Collingswood, N.J., and early on he surveyed the role of outsider personally. One of his early memories was being singled out by Christian kids at school and called a "Jew bastard." But, if life was bad outside, it was far worse at home. Decades before the term "dysfunctional family" came into mainstream grammar, Landon was living a daily emotional nightmare with his

In the episode "The Wedding," broadcast November 6, 1978, Charles Ingalls gives his blind daughter, Mary (Melissa Sue Anderson), in marriage to Adam Kendall (Linwood Boomer), teacher of the blind.

In one of the best and most challenging episodes, "May We Make Them Proud," broadcast August 18, 1980, Adam Kendall tries in vain to console his wife, Mary, when she learns their infant son has perished in a fire. A powerful and moving episode written by Michael Landon.

parents. His father, Eli Orowitz, was Jewish and a district manager for a chain of theaters. Landon's mother, Irish-Catholic Peggy O'Neill, had been a showgirl in stage musical comedies. "She was off her rocker," Landon admitted candidly. "She was very abusive. She would sit on the sofa holding a Bible and asking God to kill me." "My mother and father did not like each other," Landon told late-night talk show host Bob Costas on NBC's *Later* in 1990. "My mother was anti-Semitic and my father wasn't too thrilled with Catholics. Many a time when I was a teenager, a taxi would pull up in front of a soda shop at eight o'clock at night. In the dead of winter, my mother would leap out in a night-gown with a hanger and start beating the hell out of me in front of all these people, calling the girls whores. An hour and a half later, she'd be talking baby talk, and she'd be all right again."

Landon also admitted on the show that his mother had stabbed him when he first moved away from her to his own quarters, and he had to call the police because he was afraid he would injure his mother while defending himself against her attacks. Costas asked him what his saving grace was at that terrible time. "I am a survivor," Landon said. "Nothing was expected of me, so I could go anywhere. I was never going to be anything in that family as far as my mother was concerned. Sad lady."

Landon used the traumas of his childhood to further himself and his career, becoming a positivist and a doer. The energies that destroyed his early family life he turned around in adulthood. He grew up a loner and made fantasy an ally to stave off his anguish. "I had to dream just to get myself out…I dreamt everything," said Landon in 1985. "I'll tell you something about his capacity for fantasy," said a crewman on the *LHOTP* set. "I remember this one day of shooting when there was a lot of concern over schedules and money, and Michael, like he was oblivious to it all, was spending hours studying real simple shots, thinking them over. Then he shot this scene of himself and Victor French [Isaiah Edwards in the series], and you could see it moved everybody. They were kind of teary. Everybody. The grips. Victor. And Michael. Especially Michael. I think the man lives for those moments when the fantasies seem real."

Landon says he deliberately portrays Ingalls as an emotional man. "I think it's important for young guys growing up to see a man cry and know that it's not a sign of weakness. On the show I've jumped on the kids and been wrong. I've apologized for it. It's not a sign of weakness to apologize to a child."

In real life, Landon is a strict but loving father to nine children from his three marriages. He does not allow his own school-age children to watch television on a school night "unless there's something special on. As long as anybody lives in my house, they go by my rules." During the *Little House* years, Landon took a lot of rapping from press and public because there seemed to be so little bickering depicted between family members on the show. He strongly disagreed with criticisms that the Ingalls were too harmonious, and shot back, "It happens at my house and if it doesn't happen at your house, you ought to straighten up your act."

To criticisms that the show didn't religiously follow the books, Landon replied it was impossible to be true to the text "because one whole chapter is 'Laura sees a cricket.'" Landon does admit, however, "It's a soft show. Either you buy it or you don't. There's only nine people living in town, so how much action can you get?"

Depictions of churchgoing, religious faith, and prayer always played a strong part in the show, reflecting Landon's own real-life experiences. "Religion evolved in my personal life over the years," says Landon, "and when one of my daughters had an accident, and it was hit-or-miss for a long time, I found great comfort in faith." Prayer then became important on the show. "It's just something I've discovered about my nature," Landon said in 1980. "But it fits in well with the story because those were very religious times." Depending on the marriage, Landon's children have been raised Jewish, Catholic, and Protestant. Incorporating his real-life history into the program, Landon wrote a two-part episode, during the 1979–80 season, depicting a short Jewish boy marrying a tall Christian girl, modeled after his parents' marriage.

Although interactions between Ingalls family members were mostly happy and wholesome, their lives had their share of misfortune as well. Resulting from scarlet fever she had suffered a year

Star/executive producer Michael Landon (Charles Ingalls) shares a tense moment with Little House on the Prairie *neighbor Victor French (Isaiah Edwards). Cancer took the lives of both stars—close loyal friends in real life—who died within two years of each other, French in 1989, Landon in 1991.*

before, daughter Mary eventually went blind (exactly as had Laura Ingall's sister in real life), and this tragedy was depicted in several of the show's most dramatic and touching episodes. Melissa Sue Anderson did some of her finest acting to date during that 1977–78 season, earning her an Emmy nomination as Best Actress in a Drama.

Another heartbreaking storyline involved an infant who perishes in a fire. "I just started writing the script about the fire and it got sadder and sadder," Landon told Joel Swerdlow, author of *Remote Control: Television and the Manipulation of American Life,* in 1980. "I had no idea the baby would die until it happened. That was a two-hour episode, and I thought we would lose the audience for the second hour. But the audience built up. I think it's because everyone has a tragedy, and they were happy to see that characters could suffer and get through it."

When storylines weren't dealing with the immediate dramas of an individual Ingalls family member, or that of any regular costar like Victor French or Merlin Olsen, a guest star was brought in usually as a one-episode "outsider" to stir things up in otherwise bucolic Walnut Grove. Now this "outsider" could be a havoc-wreaking hailstorm or a prairie fire, but usually it was an eccentric stranger who'd end up teaching the townsfolk a lesson about tolerance, or a minority person whose presence would raise the issue of racial prejudice.

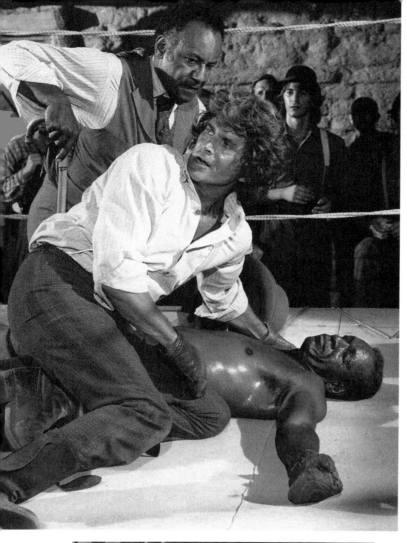

KEESIA THE WITCH

When an eccentric eighty-year-old woman named Keesia arrives in town in an old wagon, parks in front of the church, sets up an imaginary household, and rocks in a chair with a pet crow perched atop her head, the children naturally label her "a witch." When Reverend Alden wants to invite Keesia to Sunday service, gossipy Mrs. Oleson leaps up and screeches, "She's about as welcome among the congregation as a plague of locusts." She then leads a discussion among the congregation, urging them to join her in tossing the poor woman out of town.

Enchanted by Keesia, the Ingalls girls seek her out, accompanied by the ever-bitchy Nellie Oleson and her brother Willie, who make nasty remarks to Keesia when she offers all the children imaginary coffee.

NELLIE: I can't see any coffee!

And when Keesia talks to her crow, she calls it Parrot Polly.

NELLIE: (mockingly) It's not a parrot, it's a crow!
KEESIA: Sshh! He thinks he's a parrot.

Captivated, the Ingalls girls rush home and tell their mother how Keesia has read their tea leaves and told their fortunes. Caroline Ingalls scolds the girls for not finishing their chores before going off to play. She's especially upset with Laura, who didn't finish removing the "foxtails" from her pet dog Jack's ears. Laura goes to Jack, finds him very sick, and calls her Pa to attend him. Charles marches bare-chested into the barn in pants and suspenders, tanned and with nary a hair on his manly chest. A few moments later, he tells Laura that Jack has died. The family holds a funeral service for the dog in the open field where he had loved to romp. While the family weeps, Laura is inconsolable.

"I didn't mean the things I said to you, Jack," Laura sobs. "You're the best dog in the whole world. The best dog a girl could ever have. I'm going to say a prayer for you every night. May God keep you safe and warm in your new bed." (Piano tinkles sadly in background.)

Caroline Ingalls (played by Karen Grassle, right) tries to comfort her eldest daughter. Mary (Melissa Sue Anderson), who goes blind in the two-part episode "I'll Be Waving as You Drive Away," March 6, 1978.

Back in town, Keesia the crone hasn't been accepted, but she hasn't been run out yet either. At the store, a stray dog follows Charles as he picks up supplies, then jumps into his wagon as he makes for home. Naturally, Charles tries to give the dog to Laura, but she'll have no part of the animal as she's still mourning for her beloved Jack. Charles labels the wily canine Bandit. Bandit, however, is immediately smitten with Laura and follows her everywhere, even though she yells at him and treats him badly.

Although Keesia has miraculously cured Jonathan Garvey of a painful crick in his back, Mrs. Oleson's lobbying has forced the Reverend Alden to ask Keesia to leave town. She replies to his request by telling him, "People are the same everywhere. Kind of set in their ways. Afraid of anyone who's different from them. It's got nothing to do with good or bad, generous or stingy. It's human nature." The reverend tells her never to change, as it's "the people who are different who move the mountains."

When Laura comes to town, Keesia sees her scolding Bandit, and sadly watches while the girl throws a stone and strikes the fleeing dog. Keesia then berates Laura for not being kind to the dog. The girl explains her feelings of loss over Jack, and Keesia tells her that home is like "a feeling of belonging" and not necessarily a physical place, hence her "imaginary" house. Keesia then says that she is just like the unwanted dog in that the townsfolk don't want her in church. She tells Laura not to be afraid of re-experiencing hurt.

Melissa Sue Anderson as Mary in the series (left) and in real life (right) circa 1978, age sixteen. She portrays a married woman on the show, but avers, "I think it would be a mistake to get married at sixteen today. But one-hundred years ago you were an 'old maid' if you weren't married by then."

Melissa Gilbert and Michael Landon share a laugh as he tells her about his recent (1980) vacation in Japan, where the residents made him nervous by refusing to recognize him. Both Little House on the Prairie *and* Bonanza *have been popular shows in Japan, where they were both dubbed into Japanese.*

ferent? Mrs. Oleson calls for a vote to keep the witch away, but no one supports her. Garvey and the kids race off after Keesia to bring her back to town.

Much of the ongoing success of *LHOTP* had to do with the crew surrounding Landon, many of whom had known Landon since his *Bonanza* days. Loyalty is something Landon is big on, and he seems to inspire it in most of those who've worked for him. His devotion to his cast and crew was as ferocious as his passion for controlling the show. The experience with the crew on *LHOTP* was very black and white—those that were loyal and in agreement with Landon remained happily by his side, while those that didn't were gone quickly. Among the body count were some very respected names in television. Early on during the first season, Landon clashed with co-executive producer, Ed Friendly, who wanted to adhere faithfully to the storylines in the books, while Landon wished to take incidents from them and build expanded fictional stories around them. Friendly was followed by producer Winston Miller, who had been brought in by NBC. Celebrated director Alf Kjellin was contracted to helm one episode, but after three days he walked out, stating simply, "Directing is a job for one man, not two."

Landon acknowledged his obsession with controlling nearly all aspects of the show and rationalized his position, telling *TV Guide* in 1974, "If Michael Landon bombs, I don't want anyone else to have to take the blame but Michael Landon." Nothing succeeds like success, and after eight highly-rated seasons, Landon could thumb his nose at everyone. His boosters, so many of the cast and crew, were fiercely devoted to him. Multi-Emmy Award-winning cinematographer Ted Voigtlander grabbed the prize two seasons in a row, 1977–78 and 1978–79, for his work on *LHOTP.*

Voigtlander adores Landon, and said in 1979, "He's the busiest man I've ever known, probably because he's the most generous with his time. In addition to being star and executive producer of the show, he also directs every other segment and writes a great number of them. And still he finds time to spend hours and hours helping people

"You're afraid to love Bandit because he might die and you'd hurt all over again. Well, let me tell you this, child, hurting goes away. Love, never. Loving is the greatest gift the good Lord gave us. Don't waste it. Not for a moment."

Laura races off to find Bandit, but when she does the dog runs away from her. She lays down in the field and weeps, and suddenly Bandit reappears and places his paw on her shoulder. Laura then heads back to town, Bandit in tow, in time for Sunday church service.

Recalling Reverend Alden's sermon, Laura stands up and tells the congregation to heed the scripture that says, "Knock, and you will be answered." "We knocked on her [Keesia's] make-believe door, and she let us in. But when she knocked nobody heard her." The reverend then adds that if a certain stranger who made the blind to see and the lame to walk were to come to town, would the congregation cast him out just because he was dif-

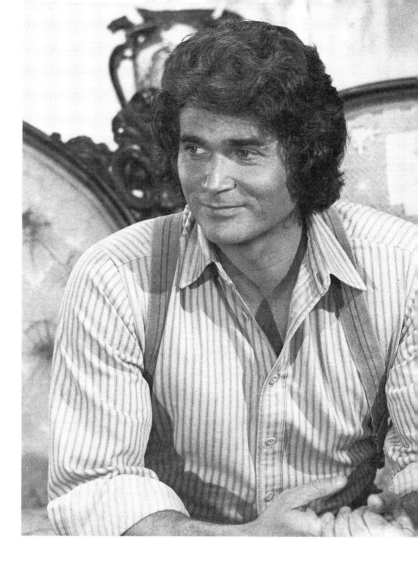

who want to get ahead in this business. A crew member who works as a stand-in mentioned to Michael that she was interested in becoming a makeup artist. He took every opportunity to show her the do's and don'ts of makeup, got her into makeup school, and showed her reels of film to point out how makeup helped or hurt this actor or actress."

Voigtlander said Landon had spent valuable hours of his evenings and weekends helping people on the show when they expressed a real desire to learn a new trade.

Voigtlander has a good idea of why Landon is as generous as he is. "He drove us all nuts with questions when he was a youngster," said the man who had been handling cameras for Landon since back in the *Bonanza* days when Landon first became interested in production. "He'd hang around between shots watching everything I did with the camera. He wanted to know all about it. I spent days and days answering questions about lenses, film speed, camera angles, and so on. Finally I gave him the most complicated book I could find, hoping that it would keep him out of my hair for a while. But he finished it in one weekend, and then began asking questions beyond what was in the book. He was grateful for the time we gave him, and I'm convinced that's the reason he takes so much time now, helping anyone who wants to better themselves."

There were more than one hundred members of the cast, crew, and office personnel working on *LHOTP,* and every one of them received a five-piece silver tea service, valued at over $1,000, for Christmas in 1980. The year before, Landon gifted each crew member with an antique copper coal bucket filled with wines and cheeses, and buried at the bottom was a gold Swiss watch. And the year before that, they got gold coins. In years before, stereos and television sets. "I love Christmas," said Landon in 1981, "because it gives me a chance to thank everyone for the wonderful job they do for me each year."

The show's sound man, Frank Meadows, said, "We'd work for Mike just for the pleasure of his company and talent. In a town where most stars or producers give their crew a bottle of booze or a

Charles Ingalls beams with pride and joy as he finally gets to be a grandfather when daughter Mary gives birth to a healthy young son (eight-week-old Nicholas Corney, pictured here), in the episode "Author, Author!" broadcast November 26, 1979.

wallet for Christmas, what can you say about a man who smiles like a kid as he hands out more than $100,000 in gifts each Christmas?"

Accolades aside, Landon is quick to point out that he's a man with flaws "like every other human being. I get moods, bad depressed ones, and I go around screaming at people—at home and at the studio—mad at everybody, my wife, the kids, the help. Banging down phones, swearing, cursing, and yelling."

"THE WISDOM OF SOLOMON"

Todd Bridges (who later gained fame as Willis on *Diff'rent Strokes*) portrayed Solomon Henry, a young black boy with an insatiable craving to go to school and learn, who runs away from his mother and older brother, both former slaves, to try and fulfill his dream of educating himself. Solomon's mother had discouraged him from pursuing his desire, telling him, "You're free to be what the white folks want you to be." She tells him he'll cause nothing but trouble if he "doesn't stay in his place." That's when the inquisitive and naïve eleven-year-old flees to chart his own course.

In Walnut Grove, Solomon is caught stealing an apple by the storekeeper but is rescued by Charles Ingalls, who advises him to ask for what he wants instead of stealing it. Solomon then follows Charles home and hides in the Ingalls' barn. Next day, Laura sees Solomon's face in the schoolhouse window, and on the way home tells her sister she saw a "black boy." "A Negro," her sister corrects.

That evening, Laura stumbles upon Solomon in the barn and finds him sucking an egg. "Are you a real Negro person?" she asks. She then runs her finger across his face to see if his blackness comes off. When it doesn't she squeals, "You are a real one!" Afraid she'll tell her Pa and he'll get whipped, Solomon begs Laura not to tell she's found him. Charles then walks in and Laura repeats his fears to her father.

CHARLES: Whipped. What in the world for?
SOLOMON: I sucked one of your eggs.
CHARLES: Well, in that case, you'll be wanting a glass of milk.

Solomon is warmly welcomed into the bosom of the Ingalls family, but lies about not knowing his family's whereabouts. Solomon offers himself as a slave to Charles, who quickly informs him about the Emancipation Proclamation. The youngster then says he wants to sell himself to Charles so he can get money to go to school. Solomon is allowed to stay on and do chores to pay for his keep, and the following day Charles enrolls him in school.

LAURA: Wait till they see him in school, Ma. A genuine Negro person.

A protean creative force in telelvision family dramas, executive producer and star of Little House on the Prairie, *Michael Landon, right, twenty years after his debut as Little Joe Cartwright on* Bonanza *(1959), both shows NBC ratings blockbusters.*

Charles Ingalls has to reach for the strong soap after accidentally becoming the victim of his daughter's scheme to trap a thief, in the episode "The Creeper of Walnut Creek" (October 24, 1977).

"He was just saying that to make things easier on me. You see, Solomon is my son by a former marriage. I know you understand, but a lot of people in this town wouldn't. Good day." Preposterous, but it worked, like so many other modernized, "enlightened" bits of scriptwriting on the show.

Miss Sims, the schoolmarm, instantly accepts Solomon, while the children, especially stuck-up Nellie Oleson and her brother, look on him with disdain. When Miss Sims asks the children what they most dislike, all reply "Homework." Solomon looks at her and says, "Being a nigger." All the children and Miss Sims are silent and bow their heads in collective guilt.

Charles, meanwhile, tries to track down Solomon's parents. At home, Laura tells her mother how badly Solomon wants to learn in school and how she feels guilty that she has a family and a school to go to.

> CAROLINE: You mean you suddenly realized there's a lot you take for granted?
> LAURA: I guess so.
> CAROLINE: Everybody takes things for granted from time to time. You are no different than anybody else. The important thing is you realized it, and you're doing something about it.

That night in bed, Caroline turns to her husband. "You know, Charles, it's funny. We worry so much about our children. Look over them. Protect them. And here's this little boy, no bigger than a minute, doing for himself."

On the school steps the next morning, Charles and Solomon encounter snooty Mrs. Oleson, who reminds Charles that no child may attend school whose family doesn't live in the township. In one of the show's lighter moments, Charles tells off Mrs. Oleson when she says the boy stated his parents weren't from Walnut Grove.

In the barn, Charles talks to Solomon, who complains about his condition in life. Times have changed a lot, Charles tells him. The youngster, in his innocent wisdom, tells Charles that laws like the Emancipation Proclamation don't change anything. "Let me ask you something, sir. Would you rather be black and live to be one hundred, or white and live to be fifty?" Charles just stares off, a disturbed look covering his countenance. He bows his head and walks off.

Later, Charles tries to explain discrimination to the boy. "When people spend their whole lives thinking a certain way, it just takes time for them to change." Solomon protests that he goes to the same school and learns the same lessons as whites but nothing changes, and in the end all he's good for is working behind a plow. Charles counters that *he* works behind a plow. "That's your choice," Solomon retorts. "I ain't got a choice. Don't make no difference to learn something if you can't use it." In the finale, the boy breaks down and confesses that he has a family living nearby. He realizes that he must go back to them and make do with reality as it faces them. Solomon then says a tearful goodbye to Charles; they both weep and embrace; and the boy marches off, now a very mature eleven years old.

After eight seasons and numerous cast changes, Landon could see that the program had reached its zenith. The girls were grown and married; Laura had become Mrs. Almanzo Wilder; Little Carrie was joined by another sister, Grace; Mary moved to the Dakotas with her husband, Adam Kendall. Walnut Grove suffered an economic collapse, and Charles packed up the family and also headed for the Dakota Territory, where he and Caroline took on hardship jobs working in a hotel. Before long they were all back in Walnut Grove, where an orphan named Albert was adopted by the family, becoming the first man-child of the Little House.

Still, sweet memories linger—the ever-present warmth and affection of the Ingalls household, their abiding neighbors, the ever-present innocence and innate kindness of the children. The dangers when the crops were threatened by hailstorms, when Charles took a job as a demolition expert, mining a tunnel for the railroad, working eighteen hours a day to get money for Mary's urgent operation. The time Laura was leaving her tomboy stage and moving into young womanhood, when she went to school with little apples stuffed into her dress top to make her look older, was painful and precious and real, thanks to Mr. Landon.

In the final episode, Landon decided the show should go out with a bang—literally. From the beginning, the show had been shot in Simi Valley, rolling farm country about forty miles from Hollywood. "There was one main reason I decided to blow the town up," said Landon in 1984. "We leased this land and built every house, office, church, and hut used in the show [Ed. note: He painstakingly recreated the look of the 1870s using photographs of the time and copying everything]. There was

Going out with a bang! was the way star and executive producer Michael Landon wanted the show to end, and so it did. In the two-hour "Little House—The Last Farewell," the town of Walnut Grove is destroyed by explosions and fire.

nothing here when we started. We were notified that when the lease was up, we had to return the property in the same condition we received it—in other words, all the buildings had to be removed.

"So I thought for a while and came to the conclusion that Walnut Grove was as much a part of *The Little House on the Prairie* programs as the actors were, and I just hated the idea that a bulldozer would come in and knock everything down. Believe me, you get attached to an area, even if it is just false-front 'pretend' buildings, if you spend ten years of your life near them, in the company of people you like, doing work you enjoy. I decided to write a script where the town goes out in a blaze of glory." Many of the actors cried as they watched the blast and fire that followed, destroying the entire town. "It's like losing an old friend," said Victor French.

MELISSA GILBERT

Born May 8, 1964, in Los Angeles, she grew up in front of the TV camera, starting in commercials at age three. She did guest shots on *Gunsmoke, Emergency,* and others. Jonathan (he played Willie Oleson on *LHOTP*, 1975–83). Both Melissa and her brother, were adopted by her mother, Barbara, during the latter's marriage to late comedian Paul Gilbert. In 1982, when all others had left the cast, the show was renewed as *Little House: A New Beginning,* starring Gilbert and Dean Butler as her young husband. Gilbert fared well in TV-movie remakes of *The Miracle Worker* (1979), *The Diary of Anne Frank* (1980), and *Splendor in the Grass* (1981), made by her own company, Half-Pint Productions. When her series ended in 1983, she went on to try feature films, her first, *Sylvester* (1984), a girl-and-her-horse story, was a flop. A slew of TV-movies followed, then in 1987, she headed for New York City and theatre work. She starred Off Broadway in a traditional Jewish play, *A Shayna Madel* (Gilbert was raised a Jew). Her longtime off-and-on romance with actor Rob Lowe ended in 1987. She married screenwriter Bo Brinkman in 1988 and gave birth to a son, Dakota, in 1989.

She remains as career-oriented and ambitious and driven as ever. "Every role I've done has a piece of me in it. They've called me peppy and half-pint. I'm lively and mischievous, I'm giggly, I'm flirty. I'm no introvert." Like her mentor Landon, Gilbert would like to direct, "do films and theatre, and do everything now!" she said in 1987.

MELISSA SUE ANDERSON

A native of Berkeley, California, born September 26, 1962, blue-eyed, golden haired Melissa also began her career in commercials, followed by work in episodes of the TV series, *The Brady Bunch,* and *Shaft,* and was then cast in *Little House on the Prairie.* Whereas Laura was always the spunky, independent child, Melissa's Mary was self-sufficient, obedient, and more serene. In real life, Anderson describes herself as "a very private person. I'm very shy." During her years on the show, she tried to follow one cardinal rule: "I never socialize with the people I'm working with. Your feelings about them as friends start to affect the way you relate to them as characters."

She left the show in 1981— "it was taxing to play the same character for so many years, and especially monotonous since she was blind. They ran out of things for me to do." Afterward, she found work in TV movies and won an Emmy Award for her starring performance in an ABC Afterschool Special, *Which Mother Is Mine?* She starred in a horror film, *Happy Birthday to Me* (1981), and formed her own company, MSA Enterprises. Tabloid papers rumored she had left *Little House* because she was jealous of costar Gilbert, a story she vehemently denied. Another tabloid report about her romance with Frank Sinatra, Jr., eighteen years her senior, she did not deny. After she left *LHOTP,* she admitted, "I'll miss the people. They're all very nice. Not family, but friends." As for the future, the show made her "financially independent and will keep me that way." She is paid residuals on all foreign sales and on all syndications of the program.

KAREN GRASSLE

Shortly after leaving *LHOTP,* Grassle wed for a second time. She and her real estate-developer husband, Allen Radford, adopted a baby girl, Lily, and Grassle devoted herself to being a wife and mother. Three years later, Grassle divorced Radford (1986). Like the others in the cast, Grassle is financially set because of residuals from the show, and occasionally works in a TV movie. She won the role of Caroline Ingalls over forty-seven other auditioning actresses.

ALISON ARNGRIM

"Just because I like hang gliding, snakes, and New Wave music, and played nasty Nellie doesn't mean I'm not nice," said Arngrim in 1982, after she had left *LHOTP.* Born in 1962, Arngrim has always been outgoing: "I'll do anything if you pay me or dare me." At fifteen, she heckled a stand-up comic who then challenged her to do better onstage; she did. She also used to keep a fifteen-foot pet boa constrictor. Arngrim ultimately became a Las Vegas showgirl, appearing scantily clad in the "Casino de Paris" revue at the Dunes Hotel. She's also worked as a stand-up comedienne, has had a few TV-movie roles, and has hosted her own cable-TV program in Los Angeles. She is an ardent vocal supporter of AIDS research.

VICTOR FRENCH

Born December 4, 1934, in Santa Barbara, California, the hulking (six-foot-one, 200 pounds), brown-eyed, brown-haired actor spent the first twenty years of his acting career usually playing a heavy. But French always had a passion for theatre and for years directed the Victor French Drama Workshop, a weekly get-together of pro actors in Los Angeles. In the early 1970s, he began directing for TV on such series as *Gunsmoke* and *Petrocelli*. He quit his role as Isaiah Edwards after three seasons in 1977. He then had his own series, *Carter Country* (1977–79). He returned to *Little House: A New Beginning* (1982–83), then joined his pal Michael Landon on *Highway to Heaven* in 1984 until his death from cancer on June 15, 1989.

In the spring of 1991, Michael Landon was diagnosed to be suffering from inoperable cancer of the pancreas. In keeping with his valiant spirit, Landon appeared on national television to openly discuss his condition and to say that he was going to fight against the disease. With his family gathered around him, Landon died on July 1, 1991.

CAST LIST

FAMILY: The Ingalls

MEMBERS:

Charles Ingalls . . . . **Michael Landon**
Caroline Ingalls . . . . **Karen Grassle**
Laura Ingalls . . . . **Melissa Gilbert**
Mary Ingalls . . . . . **Melissa Sue Anderson**
Carrie Ingalls . . . . **Lindsay Green Bush or Sidney Green Bush**

SIGNIFICANT OTHERS:

Lars Hanson (1974–78) . . . **Karl Swenson**
Nels Oleson . . . . **Richard Bull**
Harriet Oleson . . . . **Katherine MacGregor**
Nellie Oleson Dalton
  (1974–81) . . . . **Alison Arngrim**
Willie Oleson . . . . **Jonathan Gilbert**
Dr. Baker (1974–78) . . . . . . **Kevin Hagen**
Reverend Alden (1974–78) . **Dabbs Greer**
Eva Beadle Sims
  (1974–78) . . . . **Charlotte Gilbert**
Isaiah Edwards
  (1974–77, 1982–83) . . . . . **Victor French**
Jonathan Garvey (1977–81) **Merlin Olsen**
Albert Ingalls
  (1978–82) . . . . **Matthew Laborteaux**
Alice Garvey (1977–80) . . **Hersha Parady**
Andy Garvey
  (1977–81) . . . . **Patrick Laborteaux**
Adam Kendall
  (1978–81) . . . . **Linwood Boomer**
Grace Ingalls
  (1978–82) . . . . **Wendi Turnbeaugh or Brenda Turnbeaugh**
Eliza Jane Wilder
  (1979–83) . . . . **Lucy Lee Flippin**
Almanzo Wilder
  (1979–83) . . . . **Dean Butler**
Jenny Wilder
  (1982–83) . . . . **Shannen Doherty**

THEME SONG: **David Rose**
TIMEFRAME: **1974–83**
NETWORK: **NBC**
ADDRESS: **Walnut Grove, Plum Creek, Minn.**

201 episodes
(Including "Little House: A New Beginning")
plus three two-hour wrap-up movies in 1984

ONE DAY AT A TIME

Pat Harrington, Jr.'s comic turns as the bizarre building super, Dwayne Schneider, won him a well-deserved Emmy in 1984. Seen here are Schneider and his adopted family (from left): Barbara (Valerie Bertinelli), Ann (Bonnie Franklin), and Julie (Mackenzie Phillips). A One Day spinoff, with Schneider as the main character, was attempted with a pilot that aired in 1984, but the idea didn't fly.

"Mom, you're sooo *medieval,*" cries Julie. "I'm surprised you don't want me to wear a chastity belt!"

Such a device would be a little ungainly in twentieth-century Indianapolis, but Julie's point is well taken. Why would a contemporary mom forbid her sixteen-year-old daughter to go on a sleep-away camping trip with two other girls and three guys?

The answer is that Ann Romano is old-fashioned. She doesn't believe it is right for Julie, or any other girl her age. And no matter how scared and insecure Ann feels in her new role as a single parent, she is going to hold the line.

After accusing Julie of being too rebellious, even

from babyhood ("You wouldn't let me go the full nine months, but tried to get out in seven"), and watching Julie storm out of the house, Ann has weathered her first crisis. This premiere episode ends with her sad confession: "For half my life my father made the decisions. For the next seventeen years, my husband. The first time in my life I make a decision of my own, and I blow it."

But over the next nine years, she does do much better. She establishes her authority over Julie and younger daughter Barbara, while making her way through a career and her own romantic relationships.

The Romano family represented something new for network TV, a single-parent household that managed to hold on to old-fashioned values, and to big Nielsen numbers too. Although there were male authority figures on the show, the final decision on any matter was always *Ms.* Romano's.

"Ms. Romano." That is Dwayne Schneider's always respectful way of addressing Ann. He is the very eccentric, pseudo-macho building super, and self-appointed man in the Romano family. He uses "Ms." not because he knows anything about feminism, but because he is fascinated by this "liberated" woman and wants Ann to think he is "with it." Schneider, as all the characters call him, is one of TV's great comic creations. He is a swaggering blue-collar blusterer, a mixture of John Wayne-wannabe and Ed Norton. He wears a pencil-thin mustache, a tattoo on his biceps, and T-shirts with a cigarette pack rolled in one sleeve, and keeps a blowup of Dolly Parton, showing plenty of cleavage, on the wall. When he isn't listening in at the apartment door to the Romanos' latest crisis, he is clunking about the building wearing his ever-present—and potentially maiming—tool belt.

When we first meet Schneider, he is the would-be Casanova who comes sniffing around the new, red-headed divorcee's apartment. Perhaps because he is too dense to take Ann's none-too-subtle hints and beat it, he stays around to become a platonic friend and, finally, a member of the family.

For the first season, Schneider and a chubby, cuddly-bear lawyer, David Kane, are the only men in Ann Romano's life. Although she's already confronted her eldest child's raging libido, she isn't ready yet to deal with her own sexual needs. And CBS wasn't ready in 1975 to show a single woman

with two daughters, sleeping with her boyfriend. David spends a fruitless year parked on the threshold of Ann's bedroom, but he never gets inside. After tantalizing Julie and Barbara with stories of golden California (he's just landed a job there), to get them on his side, he asks Ann to come with him as his bride. In their final episode together, despite her daughters' pleas, Ann refuses. She's just started to test her wings, she explains to David. She doesn't yet know how strong she is and how far she can go. And she'll never gain that knowledge if she remarries so soon after her divorce.

When Ann's Dad, a loud, volatile Italian, comes to see her, he complains, "Your cousin Rosalie got a Ph.D. You got a divorce." He wants her and the girls to come back to Logansport to visit "for a year." "All I know is that you need a man now to handle these kids," he gripes, after discovering that Julie has two dates for the same evening. He isn't pleased, either, when a cop shows up with young Barbara in tow. Her boyfriend had been drinking beer at the local drag strip, says the officer. "If she was older, she'd be spending the night in the slammer."

This is all the ammunition Dad needs. But Ann isn't conceding anything. She must tread softly now in rejecting her father's advice, and she must keep her own anger in check over his unwanted interference. "I am a thirty-five-year-old woman pleading with her father," she says in disgust. Then, "You've got my love, but my life is mine. You wrapped us in a protective cocoon, but that isn't the way the world is." Her children have to be free to make their own mistakes. She has raised them with the right values, now it is up to them. Barbara and Julie are pleased with this vote of confidence. And Dad is secretly impressed with Ann's new-found assertiveness.

Bonnie Franklin, who played Ann, faced her own real-life struggle for independence. "I know how Ann feels," she told an interviewer in 1977, "because I've been there." Raised in Southern California in a close-knit Jewish family (during her years on *One Day at a Time,* they faithfully attended every Friday night taping of the show), she was taught that a girl "got married, had babies—and somewhere in there got a teaching certificate as 'something to fall back on.'" But Bonnie wanted something more. "I'm a chronic overachiever. At age four I was taking piano, ballet, and tap dance."

Beautiful Shelley Fabares joined One Day *in 1981 as the catty and conniving Francine Webster, Ann Romano's business partner. Here she dishes with Barbara at the Romano breakfast table.*

She appeared as a dancer on *The Donald O'Connor Show* when she was nine. After studying theater at UCLA, she met her first husband, actor-director Ron Sossi, while they both were touring in *Carousel* for the USO in 1967. Their marriage lasted three years, bringing to the surface all of Franklin's conflicts about career versus marriage. "I wanted to get out in the world again. I wanted to be someone again. If I'd stayed married I wouldn't have been honest with Ron or myself." She went to New York and spent seven years as a musical comedy actress, winning a Tony nomination in Broadway's *Applause* in 1970. She was spotted by Norman Lear, playing opposite Judd Hirsch in the TV movie, *The Law,* and was brought aboard *One Day,* which was still in its early stages of development. (Other titles considered during this time: *Emerging Woman* and *Three to Get Ready.*)

As he had done on *All in the Family* and his other hit shows, Lear invited the actors' input during story and script discussions. "He's a good mixer," said Franklin. "He makes people express themselves. He makes us create." This often led to fights—or "collaborative conflict," as Lear preferred to call it. But he didn't mind if his actors were "difficult" as long as something creative resulted.

A pilot was to be produced with Franklin as a single mother with one sixteen-year-old daughter, Julie (Mackenzie Phillips). Franklin didn't like the idea. She thought Phillips was too tall to be her daughter, and too old (twenty). "I knew one of us had to go." But after meeting the young actress, Franklin found she was only eighteen and charming. "We get along great," said Franklin. "She's a loudmouth like me." That pilot didn't sell, so another daughter, Barbara (Valerie Bertinelli), was added.

Although the girls are only two years apart in age, they are a world apart in personality. Julie is headstrong and intense; she has her mother's hot temper and the same urge to be independent. Keeping Julie a virgin is a long and tiring battle for Ann, and in the end, she loses. After plenty of hollering and name-calling, Julie winds up living with her boyfriend of the moment in a camper. Later, unrepentant but wiser, she returns.

Cute as a kitten, with her little upturned nose, her baby-fat cheeks, and blue eyes, Barbara is the shy and sensitive one. When she decides she isn't popular enough, despite her good looks, she starts a rumor at school that she "goes all the way." This gets her plenty of dates, all of them disappointed. She will remain virtuous until her wedding night, in 1982.

The show's writers were able to use Julie, as the adventurous daughter, in stories about contemporary subjects like cults (she joins one), the pill (she takes it), and intergenerational conflict (she writes angry poetry about her mother as a tigress with sharp teeth).

Norman Lear remembered the story conferences as "group therapy for the fathers." One of the best shows was based on a true incident involving Lear's own daughter, then sixteen. Her boyfriend was trying to have his way with her, and she was resisting. Lear had a man-to-man conversation with the lad, who faithfully promised henceforth to be a gentleman. "The next night my daughter came home crying—he had all but stripped her. And that's how a show came about in which Julie faced the same problem."

Then there is the time Julie falls for an older man. This story is played out over four episodes. When Paul Curran arrives at the Romano apartment it is because Julie dented his parked car and left a note. She says she will start paying him back as soon as she finds work. Impressed by her pluck, the forty-two-year-old veterinarian offers her a job as his assistant. Julie takes him up on it.

She has just finished telling Barbara how disappointing her dates with men her own age have been. She has them all categorized by numbers. She calls a "1" single-minded. "I've dated a lot of ones." "8" is symmetrical, trustworthy, all filled in. "4" is empty-headed, while a "5" goes every which way, mercurial. It is clear she is ready for someone better.

Soon she is calling Dr. Curran "Paul" and staying late at work. Schneider, of course, is suspicious of Curran. Any forty-two-year-old man who drives a sports car is looking for younger women, he tells Ann. His personal age limit with women is thirty, "although I can drop it to twenty-five for late on a Saturday night."

Barbara is against Julie's infatuation for aesthetic reasons. "Isn't this like falling in love with Lawrence Welk?"

Then Julie drops her bombshell. She is going with Dr. Curran to Toledo. "It's for a dog show. We'll be back the same night."

Barbara's reassurance to her mother: "All she can catch is fleas."

Schneider gets drunk, worried about Julie's trip. Reeling into the Romano apartment he drawls, "I must look a mess." When his concern does not prompt a respectful response from his adopted family (they think he's a comical sight—which, indeed, he is), he sobs, "I'm not good enough to mend your hearts, just your toilets," and staggers away. End of comic relief.

Julie's fantasy of being "Mrs. Paul Curran" irritates Ann. Go slow, she warns her daughter, until she is reminded that she herself was only seventeen when she married. And that was "part of the problem," counters Ann.

Later, when Ann finds Julie and Paul embracing, things turn ugly. "What are you going for?" Ann asks Paul. "Blue Ribbon for Pick of the Litter?"

"Shut up, Mom. You lonely? You want him?" For this, Julie gets a slap in the face.

This whole story, the sight of Paul and Julie kissing, was heady stuff for TV in the late seventies. Think about it: how many teen sitcom characters have been in a situation like this? Not many. But *One Day* was always pushing the boundaries of what was acceptable. (In the end, of course, Julie and Paul Curran do not get married. And what Ann told her own father is proved right—youngsters have to be permitted to make fools of themselves before any learning takes place.)

When some organizations like the New York City Catholic Archdiocese found Julie and Barbara's flip remarks about sex objectionable—presumably because the girls were "role models" for the nation's youth—*One Day* producer Perry Grant defended the show. Sex was "one of the things that's going to get discussed" by teens, he said, "but I don't think it's been overdone."

Valerie Bertinelli and Mackenzie Phillips became close friends while playing sisters Barbara and Julie, and continued so after the show ended. They both took rock musicians as life partners: Valerie married Eddie Van Halen in 1981, and Mackenzie had a son, Shane, with guitarist Shane Fontaine in 1987.

Valerie Bertinelli (left), as the spunky Barbara and Mackenzie Phillips, as fiery Julie, were instant hits with teen viewers. Phillips's recurring problems with drugs during One Day's *run were a source of deep anger and despair on the part of Bertinelli, who wanted to help her dear friend but didn't know how.*

163

By temperament and background, Bonnie Franklin was ideally suited to play feisty, liberated divorcée, Ann Romano. One Day's co-creator, Norman Paul, said of Ann: "She's tough, she's out there scrapping." And of Bonnie: "She is perfectly cast in that her own life parallels the basic premise of Ann Romano's."

In an episode in 1976, the notion that motherhood was the "natural" destiny of every woman is challenged. Ginny, a cocktail waitress and Ann's next-door neighbor, is filled with guilt because she doesn't have the maternal feelings she thinks she ought to have. She's "unnatural," she says, and Schneider agrees. "Eight million men did not go off to war for *Dad*'s apple pie," he pronounces. Ginny's ex-husband has custody of their ten-year-old daughter, Lori, because Ginny is afraid of the responsibility. "I love her," says Ginny, "but she's better off with Frank. I just can't hack mothering, and Lori knows it. We run out of conversation.'" She's taken Lori to Kentucky Fried Chicken so many times on their weekends together, Lori's wound up "calling the Colonel Daddy." Ann reassures Ginny that mothering isn't all it's cracked up to be ("Twice a month I want to sue the hospital for giving me the right kids"), and that she's still a great person.

For a while it looked as though Ginny might become Schneider's permanent tootsie, but Ginny was gone after one season. There was also talk of a possible Schneider spin-off, but nothing happened.

Two other notable cast additions were Grandma Katherine Romano, in 1979, played by Nanette Fabray, and Francine Webster, in 1981, Ann's business partner, portrayed by Fabray's real-life niece Shelley Fabares. As both were strong-minded characters, they helped preserve the continued dominance of the feminine perspective on the show. At the same time they were also those time-honored caricatures, the busybody grandmother and the catty, conniving seductress. After all, we *are* talking about mainstream television.

Gradually, the show changed Julie's image from rebellious teen to a more mature, responsible college student. In 1979, Julie falls in love with a bearded airline flight steward, Max Horvath (Michael Lembeck), and they marry. Unfortunately, at the time, actress Mackenzie Phillips's own personal life was beginning to unravel.

Her problem was drug abuse, and it dated back to 1977 when she was found "sprawled" on a West Hollywood street and booked for investigation of cocaine possession. It was the public's first glimpse of a sad backstage secret. The lid blew off finally in December of 1979 when Mackenzie was ordered into drug rehab by the show's producers. After a brief return, she was suspended again. The scripts were amended to say that Max had gotten a new job in Houston and had moved there with Julie. Mackenzie Phillips was not to return until 1981. Two years later there were fresh whispers about drug use, as she appeared extremely pale and thin on-screen. For the second and last time, she was dropped from *One Day*.

Phillips estimated that during her addiction she spent approximately $400,000 a year on cocaine. Daughter of rock star John Phillips (of The Mamas and The Papas), she grew up amid the glamour and decadence of the pop music scene. "On weekends, at my Dad's place, I would find rock stars like Mick Jagger and the Beatles all hanging out," she remembered of her childhood. By fifteen, she was smoking marijuana. Her use of cocaine reportedly started a few years later.

Phillips went through a much-publicized rehabilitation along with her father, also a heavy user, and shortly after their recoveries they re-created The Mamas and The Papas with two other singers. In 1987, Phillips was in the newspapers again, this time for a happy reason. She gave birth to a son, Shane, named after his father, rock guitarist Shane Fontaine.

With Mackenzie Phillips absent for long stretches on the show, new characters were created. Barbara got a new "brother" in the person of teen Alex Handris (Glenn Scarpelli), the son of Nick Handris (Ron Rifkin), a divorced advertising man with whom Ann had formed a new partnership—both in business and in love. (She had previously jump-started her post-divorce romantic life by having a fling with a married man.)

The show had done stories on teen runaways, epilepsy, teen suicide, and mental retardation, but it galled Bonnie Franklin that they wouldn't touch anything to do with teen drug use, especially in light of Mackenzie's problem. "Some people don't want to face the fact there's a tremendous drug problem among middle-class kids," she said in 1980. She hoped the issue would be raised through the character of young Alex.

Bright-eyed, button-nosed Barbara found true love with young dental student Mark Royer (Boyd Gaines). He was just right for her: studious, polite, gentle, and he didn't put any moves on her till their wedding day in 1982—although they *did* think about it. But the show was about the Independent Woman with old-fashioned values who raised an old-fashioned daughter. The fact that Barbara decided to keep her virtue apparently was welcome news to many teenage girls. According to Valerie Bertinelli, "We got thousands of grateful letters from high school girls after that." The producers had even gone so far as to initiate a survey of Midwest college campuses, asking if Barbara should retain her virginity. The answer was an overwhelming yes.

In a strange twist, as Barbara was losing her heart to Mark, Mom was being courted by Mark's father, Sam (Howard Hesseman). For Ann it had to be exactly right. She wasn't going to risk marriage

VALERIE BERTINELLI: THE MAKING OF A TEEN QUEEN

Blessed with cuter-than-cute good looks and a perky, Miss Congeniality-type personality, Valerie Bertinelli was at fifteen the most popular TV star among the nation's youth. In this exalted position, she found herself surrounded by press agents and other network types eager to mold and preserve her image for public consumption. As it furthered her career, she was willing to play along. When an interviewer, in 1981, found her smoking a cigarette on the sound stage, she panicked, pleading, "Please don't write that I smoke." But when the molded image got in the way of her having some fun in her private life, she rebelled. When she was sixteen, she had a crush on her twenty-four-year-old *One Day* costar Scott Colomby (he played Barbara's boyfriend, Cliff Randall) and they began dating. The show, of course, wanted to keep the couple's age difference a secret, but the relationship lasted three years, and Valerie talked about it freely. Then there was the matter of Valerie's marriage on April 11, 1981, to rock superstar Eddie Van Halen. *One Day* imagemakers tried to suppress news of the happy event so attention could be focused on Valerie's fictional romance on the show. Needless to say, after a brief media blackout, the story, complete with wedding pictures, exploded in the tabloids, with the blessings of Valerie and "Edward" (as she prefers to call him). Today, after starring in many successful TV movies (two of which had grown-up bedroom scenes) and one unsuccessful sitcom *(Sidney)*, Valerie Bertinelli hopes she's finally overcome her cute Teen Queen image.

only to be divorced again. But when Sam came on horseback to ask for her hand, riding straight into her apartment, she was convinced. They wed at the end of the 1982–83 season.

The show wound down the following year. Ann had accomplished all she'd tried to do as a single parent. When *One Day at A Time* had begun, Bonnie Franklin had spoken with admiration of

Grandma Romano (Nanette Fabray, left) and Grandma Cooper (Priscilla Morrill, right) didn't have to worry about granddaughter Barbara (Valerie Bertinelli) remaining a "good" girl. Polls by CBS found that most American teens wanted Barbara to remain "pure" until her wedding night. And that's what she did.

another mother on another family show. "I used to watch Sada Thompson on *Family*," she said, "and I thought she had a terrific relationship with her children." She clearly wanted to emulate that performance. And, by 1984, she had. (Ironically, Franklin had no children of her own. "I don't know where I got the insight to play a mother except to say I have a great mother myself." In 1980 she married TV producer Marvin Minoff, who had two children from a previous marriage).

The next-to-last episode sees Ann take a job in London. It is an emotional farewell. "Look at you," she says to Barbara, teary-eyed. "You're all grown-up and married." And Barbara, her cute face dimpled into a quivery, sad smile, answers, "And look at you. You're all grown-up and married."

Schneider is there, of course, all the macho gone out of him. For the first time he drops the "Ms." Romano and calls her "Annie."

In the final moments, alone in her apartment, Ann Romano pauses in the doorway, remembering (in a flashback to the first episode) how she'd explained to her daughters so long ago what life was going to be like without their father, and how they all had to pull together to make it work.

Then, gently, she closes the door.

(The following week, a pilot was aired showing Schneider starting a new life in Florida as maintenance man for a boardwalk carnival, and as foster parent for two young children.)

After *One Day at a Time,* Bonnie Franklin returned to the musical stage at the head of several touring companies of shows like *Annie Get Your Gun,* and has become a well-respected TV director. She has done most of the shows in the syndicated series, *The Munsters Today.*

VALERIE BERTINELLI

Millions tuned in to one of TV's biggest events of 1982: the marriage of Barbara Cooper (Valerie Bertinelli) and Mark Royer (Boyd Gaines). News of Miss Bertinelli's real-life wedding to superstar Eddie Van Halen was harder to come by since One Day at a Time *tried to impose a media blackout on the happening.*

With Mackenzie Phillips absent from One Day *in 1980 because of drug problems, the character Alex Handris was added as a new "sibling" for Barbara. Here Pat Harrington as Schneider welcomes Glenn Scarpelli, as Alex, to the show. Note Harrington's garish period costume: flared pants and platform heels.*

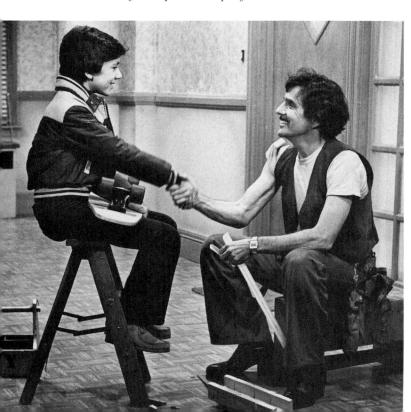

CAST LIST

FAMILY: The Romanos

MEMBERS:

Ann Romano Royer . . . . . **Bonnie Franklin**
Julie Cooper Horvath
  (1975–80, 1981–83)   **Mackenzie Phillips**
Barbara Cooper Royer . . **Valerie Bertinelli**
Katherine Romano
  (1979–84) . . . . **Nanette Fabray**
Max Horvath (1979–80,
  1981–84) . . . . **Michael Lembeck**
Annie Horvath
  (1983–84) . . . . **Lauren or Paige Maloney**
Mark Royer (1981–84) . . . . . **Boyd Gaines**
Sam Royer
  (1982–84) . . . . **Howard Hesseman**

SIGNIFICANT OTHERS:

Dwayne Schneider . . . . **Pat Harrington, Jr.**
David Kane (1975–76) . . . **Richard Masur**
Ginny Wroblicki
  (1976–77) . . . . **Mary Louise Wilson**
Nick Handris (1980–81) . . . . . . **Ron Rifkin**
Alex Handris (1980–83) . . **Glenn Scarpelli**
Francine Webster
  (1981–84) . . . . **Shelley Fabares**

THEME SONG: **Jeff and Nancy Barry**
TIME FRAME: **1975–84**
NETWORK: **CBS**
ADDRESS: **322 Beck St. Apt. 402**
         Indianapolis, Indiana

205 episodes

GREAT PERFORMANCES

Emmy Winner

Pat Harrington, Jr.

Outstanding Supporting Actor (Comedy)

1983–84

No matter what crisis is brewing in their lives, the Lawrences always paste on a WASPy smile for the outside world, and muddle through their difficulties with dignity and restraint. Here they pose for the family Christmas card, complete with Christmas tree and Willy (Gary Frank) as a bearded Santa, along with (from left): Annie (Quinn Cummings), Kate (Sada Thompson), Doug (James Broderick, seated), Nancy (Meredith Baxter Birney), and Buddy (Kristy McNichol, kneeling).

The Lawrences, from the left: Willie Lawrence (Gary Frank), Nancy Lawrence Maitland (Meredith Baxter Birney), Buddy Lawrence (Kristy McNichol), Annie Cooper (Quinn Cummings), Doug Lawrence (James Broderick), Kate Lawrence (Sada Thompson), and Timmy Maitland (Michael Shackelford).

They were the only well-to-do American TV family who had candlelight dinners when there was no energy blackout, a housekeeper who kept her nose out of family business, and a front yard with a small, tasteful guesthouse for the grown children.

Yes, the Lawrences were different. They were well-bred and proper even when they were arguing or going through a crisis, whether it be an audit by the IRS or a change-of-life hysterectomy. And they did it all without a laughtrack tittering or howling in the background.

The show's creators had strong ideas about what they wanted *Family* to be. Producer Leonard Goldberg had seen the PBS documentary, *An American Family*, about the joys and heartbreak of a wealthy California family. Impressed by its cinéma-vérité style, Goldberg determined to create as authentic a TV drama as possible. In 1973 he asked novelist and screenwriter Jay Presson Allen to do a sample script. They both agreed they would go against the TV trend of divorced or single-parent households and create a warm, loving, supportive family. The result was the Lawrences, Doug and Kate, and children Nancy, Willie, and "Buddy" (actually Letitia), and later, an adopted daughter, Annie.

For all their good manners and civility, the Lawrences are far from perfect. When the series opened on ABC on March 9, 1976, for a six-episode experimental run, daughter Nancy discovers that her husband, Jeff Maitland, has been unfaithful. She is forced to move with her newborn son, Timmy, back to her parents' guesthouse to try and put her life together again.

Beneath the antique frame and photos of WASPy ancestors that hang on their stately home's walls, the Lawrences must cope with divorce (Nancy's), a death in the family (Grandma's), and other traumatic matters.

No subject was taboo in the Lawrence house. After all, the parents are educated and progressive people (Doug is a lawyer and Kate a schoolteacher) and raise their brood to be tolerant of "different" ideas and lifestyles. For example, the subject of homosexuality is introduced via a story of fourteen-year-old Buddy's attachment to a woman teacher. The teenager's life is turned topsy-turvy when she discovers the teacher is the target of an anti-gay campaign by local parents. There is anger, hurt, and confusion on Buddy's part and a need for answers from her own parents. But they can't decide whether or not they support this "moral crusade." As usual on *Family*, there are no easy solutions.

The show quickly made Kristy McNichol (Buddy) a star because of her amazing naturalness and charm. Buddy's relationship with her big brother, Willie, is especially heartwarming. Being at that awkward age, she feels her parents' control is oppressive, and she despises her sister Nancy as

Can it be? Mater and Pater Lawrence laughing? Actually, Doug and Kate's WASPy reserve is one of the charms of this show. Its scripts studiously avoided the sudsy melodrama of the Dallas *variety in favor of a slow story exposition. And its cast consistently underplayed.*

being the "Perfect Princess." Only Willie understands her, she believes, and she includes him in all her tomboy activities. He calls her "Peaches."

There comes time, of course, when Buddy must choose a college and move away from home. Afraid of this big change, she takes comfort in the fact that Willie is a high school dropout. She eagerly agrees with his thesis that the best education is in the School of Life. She pretends all her college applications have been rejected and talks Willie into promising to take her on a cross-country auto trip. As they pack in the garage, they unearth many memories, like an old croquet set and a couple of bedrolls.

> BUDDY: We used to go camping every year. Why'd we stop?
> WILLIE: We grew up.

Kate soon discovers Buddy's deception from the high school guidance counselor. Buddy has actually been accepted at all four colleges she applied to. Buddy then explodes at Willie, accusing him of "keeping me your little sister. All my life you never let me grow up." But even this is a deception. Kate realizes that Buddy *does* want to go to college but can't stand the thought of saying good-bye to brother Willie. By lying to her parents and causing herself to be caught, she can explode at Willie and thus avoid a farewell.

It was sad watching Buddy hang up her skateboard and grow up that season. But watching Miss McNichol was always a joy. Her popularity was at its zenith in 1978, when Mego Toys, the creators of the Farrah Fawcett-Majors doll, brought out one in Kristy's likeness. She was the All-American Girl that year. And Jane Fonda, who watched *Family*, called her a "marvel." And Esther Rolle (Florida on *Good Times*), with whom Kristy costarred in the TV movie, *The Summer of My German Soldier*, said, "There isn't another young woman in acting who can touch her."

By the time Buddy turned seventeen in the storyline, producer Leonard Goldberg announced, "We're writing shows that will deal with her new maturity. Some of the younger members of our staff feel she should have a relationship with a man that results in her losing her virginity."

Teen rock idol Leif Garrett, as Zack, became her romantic interest. Fortunately for Buddy's whole-some image, when Zack pops the Big Question, our heroine thinks it over and decides she "isn't ready." Participation in the Sexual Revolution is left to Willie and Nancy.

Here's Buddy, looking like a refugee from The Waltons *in her overalls, cuddling up to her favorite big brother, Willie. Their special "best buddy" relationship is one of the most heartwarming aspects of* Family.

KRISTY McNICHOL: THE PRECOCIOUS PRINCESS

"The minute she came in, the search for Buddy was over," said Jay Presson Allen, writer and *Family* co-creator, in 1977. And Kristy's outstanding quality? "Honesty."

Kristy McNichol, all of fourteen, had never taken an acting lesson. Yet she was able to get inside her character, Buddy, with such ease and completeness that she astounded viewers and critics alike. Writers called her the All-American Girl, the reign-ing princess of prime-time TV.

Burt Reynolds, who costarred with her in his black comedy, *The End*, said, "I fell in love with her on *Family*. She's vulnerable; she's like an open wound. You don't need any long-winded speeches about what her relationships are, you just sense them by the way she looks and talks."

Kristy was refreshingly unaffected and straight-forward with interviewers. She admitted to one that the show, in its search for realism, once made

KRISTY McNICHOL

her wear a "false retainer" on her teeth. "It was very dumb. You didn't see it, but it made me lisp." She asked to have it written out of the script. She also said, impishly, that her "mother," Kate (Sada Thompson), looked too fresh in the morning. How could a mother be so well-dressed and well-groomed so early and still have time to cook breakfast?

Family ended in 1979, but Kristy was left to cope with the pressures of stardom. An expanding movie career, the start of her own production company, and other problems put her under the weather in 1983, with depression. Still, she was able to finish a feature film, *Just the Way You Are*, for release in 1984. In 1989, Kristy finally shed the last vestige of her wholesome Buddy persona by going topless in the little-seen film, *Three Moon Junction*. She had low visibility through most of the 1980s, but bounced back with her second TV hit, *Empty Nest*, showing another side of her remarkable talent: comedy.

James Broderick, as Doug, gives Kristy McNichol (Buddy) a stern look in this scene. Backstage, however, Broderick was the show's self-confessed "clown," keeping his fellow actors entertained. His son is movie and stage star Matthew Broderick.

Willie is the underachiever of the family. He strikes a rebellious pose astride his motorcycle, and moves restlessly from job to job. Although given to periodic bursts of temper, he is basically a sweet, vulnerable guy. Women are drawn to him, perhaps because of that brooding quality. After Nancy and baby Timmy move out of the guesthouse, Willie inherits it, and into his life steps a succession of young women, keeping his love life in turmoil. His longest relationship is with an unwed mother, Salina Magee. (That year there was talk that these lovers would spin off into their own series, but nothing came of it.) When the idealistic Willie finally marries, it is for altruistic reasons. His new wife, Lizzie, has a terminal illness.

Gary Frank drew on his own inner reservoir of rage to play Willie, the outsider. "He's a passionate, angry person," said Carroll Newman, his wife and associate producer of *Family*, in 1977. Gary himself told the story of how he once got into a shouting match with a stranger in a grocery store and challenged the man to step outside (the argument eventually fizzled). "I used to have romantic illusions about being Irish and getting drunk and brawling," he remarked, referring to a one-time

alcohol problem. "Since then I've learned most Irishmen who get drunk just fall asleep." (Actually, Frank's father was German-Jewish, his mother Irish Mormon.)

A student at New York's Lee Strasberg Theater Institute, Gary worked as a truck driver and busboy while waiting for acting work. He landed his first starring role as Jeff Reed on the short-lived prime-time soap opera *Sons and Daughters* (1974). Gary's Irish was up when ABC decided to drop *Family* in 1979 (its cast's five-year contracts came up on December 1, 1979, and were not renewed). He complained about the "ungracious and unceremonious" fall of the ax. But he was also philosophical. "I've long since stopped worrying about the next part," he said. "That's something I learned from Jimmy Broderick—not to worry about time, money, or the next job. I really did grow up on that show."

Compared to the other Lawrences, Nancy is not a very sympathetic character. One TV critic found her to be "like any ordinary, confused, rather flighty young divorcee with an unwanted baby on her hands." She is also self-centered, according to Meredith Baxter Birney, "to the point where she'll dismiss others' problems." She hardly seems to be Kate Lawrence's daughter at all.

Birney's task was to find some human quality in Nancy, and it wasn't always easy. She objected to the way the scripts made Nancy promiscuous after

Smile for the birdie, Lawrence children! Quinn Cummings (right) was added to the cast in 1978 as the precocious little orphan, Annie, joining Kristy McNichol and Gary Frank. Alone among the Lawrence kids, Annie is the overachiever. She reads Roget's Thesaurus *for fun.*

her divorce. "They had me meeting a guy one day," she remembered of one story, "and in the next scene I'm having lunch in his apartment. Next, I'm sitting on the bed, buttoning up my blouse. Can you imagine? I just met the guy. It was so tacky...." Her protests got that scene cut, but there would be other men in Nancy's life. Nancy uses her various unhappy affairs as a way of fending off responsibility. She often leaves son Timmy in Grandma's care.

Throughout Nancy's tribulations, Doug and Kate are patient. They understand that meddling usually doesn't work, that letting your child make his or her own mistakes is better. Only Kate's cool, probing stare—and the disapproving frown—tell Nancy that she can do better. Eventually, she does, leaving the guesthouse and getting an apartment for Timmy and herself. She also decides to follow her Dad into a law career. Bravo, Nancy! But there was one good thing about Nancy's flighty character. According to Birney, "it makes her more interesting to watch."

The daughter of film actress Whitney Blake, who costarred as Hazel's employer, Dorothy Baxter, on *Hazel* (1961–66), Birney studied theater at Hollywood High School and voice at Michigan's Interlochen Academy (she's a lyric soprano). Her first hit series was *Bridget Loves Bernie*, and she married her costar, David Birney, in 1974. They are now divorced.

In 1978, someone new joins the family. Annie Cooper (Quinn Cummings), age twelve, is added in the time-honored TV tradition, for the sake of fresh "youthful" storylines (now that Buddy is older). Her parents, best friends of the Lawrences, have died in a car crash, and Doug and Kate are named Annie's guardians in the Cooper will.

After a requisite period of adjustment, in which she is sullen and doesn't respond to the Lawrences' displays of affection, Annie becomes a full-fledged member of the clan. But she doesn't suffer from the underachieving syndrome of the other Lawrence kids. She is an A-student, an intellectual, who analyzes everything. According to her ex-tomboy sis, Buddy, "She reads *Roget's Thesaurus* for fun." Naturally, Annie's classmates hate her. They pretend to like her only to humiliate her. They invite her to Elissa's party, saying, Go ask Elissa's boyfriend, Peter, if it's okay. He snickers. "Sorry, Elissa's mother doesn't allow dogs in the house."

Like Buddy before her, Annie runs to Willie for comfort. What does she have to do to be accepted? "If you treat people nicely, they usually respond," is Willie's sage advice. "What if it doesn't work?" "You learn karate."

Annie begins her campaign by becoming the class jokester. "What can you tell me about Turkey?" asks her geography teacher. "It goes great with cranberry sauce," says Annie. "Do you want me to call your Mom?" the teacher inquires with some annoyance. "No, I'll do it for you. [Shouts] Hey, Mom!"

This gets big laughs in the classroom. Suddenly, Annie is a very popular girl, but at a price. Her new girlfriends want to be able to copy from her during a test. Instead of going along, Annie plays hooky, with Willie's help. When Kate finds this out she confronts Willie in a cold fury.

"Why did I let Annie ditch school?" Willie asks. "I remember all the times I felt different."

This isn't good enough for Kate. It is very important for Annie to like herself for herself, and not to try to make friends by being someone she's not. Annie gets the message—framed with such quiet passion and clarity in Kate's inimitable style that she can't miss it. She returns to school. "So what if I'm smart and I like school," she reasons. "Everybody has something crazy about them...."

Coming from her Tony Award-winning stage performance in *Twigs* as four different women in four generations of the same family, Sada Thompson was perfectly cast as the Lawrence

*Although they worked for rival networks on rival series, Kristy McNichol (*Family*) and Esther Rolle (*Good Times*) found time to work together in the acclaimed TV movie,* The Summer of My German Soldier. *McNichol played a young Southern girl and Rolle the wise and loving family servant in this coming-of-age drama set in the America of World War II. Said Esther Rolle of TV's then most precocious wunderkind: "There isn't another young woman in acting who can touch her."*

Kristy McNichol's natural athleticism is put to good use as the Lawrence's skateboard-loving tomboy Buddy in this on-location scene in a Los Angeles playground. For some time after Family *ended, she tried to shed her wholesome image, which she felt was typecasting her. After a decade of TV movies and feature films—and time off for what was described as "emotional exhaustion"—Kristy McNichol put her career back in high gear, with her role as Barbara in the late '80s hit sitcom,* Empty Nest.

The unsympathetic character of Nancy (seen here with little sister Buddy) was a challenge for Meredith Baxter Birney, who felt that Nancy was self-centered "to the point where she'll dismiss others' problems." The actress was also bothered by her character's promiscuity. Eventually, in Meredith's capable hands, Nancy became more responsible and sympathetic.

matriarch, Kate. Of erect bearing and a commanding sense of authority, Kate has a way of cutting quickly to the heart of the matter. *Family* coproducer Carol Evan McKeand said that Thompson was the "glue" that kept the show together. "Without the fine anger she can project, without her wry reading of lines in a funny scene, without the new lines she asks us to insert, we long since could have drowned in a sea of suds."

But Miss Thompson almost didn't make it on to *Family*. Norman Lear wanted her to play the role of Archie Bunker's neighbor Irene Lorenzo on *All in the Family* in 1973. A former Lear associate told *TV Guide* in 1977, "Sada had too much genuine class and didn't yell enough for a Norman Lear show." According to Miss Thompson, "The character wasn't really formulated, and Lear hoped I'd bring in my own ideas. Finally, we both agreed it wouldn't work out and called it a day." Her good friend Jean Stapleton (Edith Bunker) was disappointed they wouldn't get to work together.

"There's a tendency in series television to get melodramatic," said James Broderick, who played the father, Doug. "But I don't think that will happen to us....I spoke to a class of high school seniors in New York and found that they take everything we say on the show as gospel. But what's interesting is how deeply we're caught up in it our-

selves....Sometimes I find myself yelling at Willie like I yell at my own kids. Sada and I get into intense discussions whether we are really good parents. Willie dropped out of school, Nancy's marriage broke up. We get really worked up about the hanky-panky that goes on in the guest house where Nancy lives....We carry the argument to the dressing room as if these were our real kids."

Broderick's character was "a man of quiet humor and steadfastness," as described in a network press release. Offstage, his humor, like his ukelele playing and his singing of Irish songs, kept everyone entertained. "I'm the clown on the set," he once said. "In a lot of ways I'm still fourteen." When Meredith Baxter Birney joined the cast, as the third actress to play Nancy (the first was Elayne Heilveil followed by Jane Actman), Broderick quickly put her at ease with a joke. What was that locked door with the red light over it? she asked him during a lull in the filming. With an air of mystery, Broderick leaned over and confided, "That's where we keep all the Nancys!" From then on Meredith Baxter Birney felt at home. (Sadly, James Broderick died on November 3, 1982.)

Impeccable casting—plus great scripts—made *Family* the class production that it was. So classy, in fact, that ABC executives weren't sure it would really fit into their prime-time schedule. From the first script development in 1973 at Spelling-Goldberg Productions, it was consistently passed over. Other shows from the same company—*S.W.A.T., Starsky & Hutch, Charlie's Angels*—were eagerly snapped up. In 1974, Goldberg brought in director Mike Nichols as executive producer to put his prestige behind the project. Nichols did not disappoint, handpicking the superb ensemble of actors, and guiding the TV pilot to fruition. In March 1975, it was screened for ABC bigwigs, who were enthusiastic. But a month later, when the fall schedule was announced, the *Family* name was missing. By the summer of 1975, Fred Silverman had taken over as network programming chief, and he added his name to the growing list of *Family* admirers. Finally, after much lobbying by Goldberg & co., the series was given a shot as a midseason replacement. The date was March 9, 1976. It aired with little fanfare and pulled an amazing forty percent share! It was off and rolling.

From then on it found a loyal audience, winning in its time slot (Tuesday night at ten) the following fall. Although it never broke into the top twenty-five shows, it still has its fans in reruns.

Everyone in the cast agreed with James Broderick that there really was a nice family feeling backstage. According to Broderick, to young Kristy McNichol, it was all very real. "Kristy thinks of the series as one long story. She refers back to things she did in other episodes like it was an event in her life."

It is interesting to note that some of the aspects of the storyline echoed in the real life of some of the cast. Meredith Baxter Birney grew up in the Lawrence's community, Pasadena, and Willie's fascination with speeding motorcycles mirrored Gary Frank's sports car enthusiasm. (He claimed to have broken his nose four times, once when his Karmann-Ghia went over a cliff in Los Angeles in 1973.) The show let Kristy McNichol (an avid skier and tennis player) show off her teen athletic skills by putting Buddy on a skateboard. James Broderick found that, by strange coincidence, the ages of all three of his TV children were exactly the same as those of his own kids, one of whom is stage and film star Matthew Broderick.

As for Sada Thompson's magnificent dignity and eloquence as Kate, we can only quote someone else in describing her maternal role in her Broadway triumph, *Twigs.* Tom Prideaux, writing in *Life* magazine in 1972, said: "She is not really beautiful; she is middle-class American commonplace. But she gives stature and radiance to the commonplace, makes it sparkle, makes it very sound and intensely human."

Yes, that's what *Family* was. Intensely human.

CAST LIST

FAMILY: The Lawrences

MEMBERS:

Kate Lawrence . . . . **Sada Thompson**
Doug Lawrence . . . . **James Broderick**
Nancy Lawrence
  Maitland . . . . . . **Meredith Baxter Birney**
    (originally Elayne Heilweil, then
      Jane Actman)
Willie Lawrence . . . . **Gary Frank**
Letitia "Buddy"
  Lawrence . . . . **Kristy McNichol**
Annie Cooper
  (1978–80) . . . . **Quinn Cummings**
Timmy Maitland
  (1978–80) . **Michael or David Shackelford**

SIGNIFICANT OTHERS:

Jeff Maitland (1976–77) . **John Rubinstein**
Salina Magee (1976–77) . **Season Hubley**
Zack (1978) . . . . **Leif Garrett**

THEME SONG: **John Rubinstein**
TIMEFRAME: **1976–80**
NETWORK: **ABC**
ADDRESS: **Milan Avenue**
          So. Pasadena, California

94 episodes

GREAT PERFORMANCES

Emmy Winners

Kristy McNichol

Outstanding Supporting Actress (Drama)

1976–77, 1978–79

Gary Frank

Outstanding Supporting Actor (Drama)

1976–77

Sada Thompson

Outstanding Actress (Drama)

1977–78

DALLAS

The proud Ewing menfolk and their ladies (from left): J. R. Ewing (Larry Hagman), Sue Ellen Ewing (Linda Gray), Jock Ewing (Jim Davis), Bobby Ewing (Patrick Duffy), Lucy Ewing (Charlene Tilton), Pamela Ewing (Victoria Principal), Ray Krebs (Steven Kanaly), and, seated, Miss Ellie (Barbara Bel Geddes).

It was toward the end of the 1970s when *Dallas* caught the public fancy. Americans weren't feeling so good about themselves then. What was needed was a little feel-good jingoism, so we embraced this fantasy of wealth and power. We liked its implicit message that we could walk tall in the world again. And what better figure to represent our nation's can-do spirit (or was it "Do it to them before they do it to you" spirit?) than J. R. Ewing, petroleum tycoon. Right smack in the middle of the global oil crisis stood J. R. Ewing, in Stetson hat and cowboy boots, leveling his beady eyes at the country's enemies. The family whose business interests he'd sworn to protect now became our family.

And what images of strength and masculinity assailed us as the show's famous opening montage flashed on the screen: phallic oil rigs gushing crude, tall glass towers of the Dallas skyline glinting in the sun, herds of longhorn cattle, and, in the show's later years, an explosion of flying debris and foaming water.

"There are as many deals made in the bedroom as in the boardroom," remarks one character, and that neatly sums up the storyline. But this is not only the saga of the corporate maneuverings—and philanderings—of the super-rich. In the figures of J. R. (Larry Hagman) and his father Jock (Jim Davis), we see represented the mythic dynamism and power of America, where everyone who works hard can make a better life for themselves. And where amoral wheeler-dealers like J. R. can get richer and richer.

What we are witnessing is pure soap opera hokum, but it is powerful hokum, and it draws us in. We are fascinated by the Ewing clan and the ebb and flow of its fortunes. Little by little, we are filled in on how the family empire came to be, and what it all means. How Jock Ewing's relentless drive to find oil as a hardscrabble wildcatter, and his winning of Miss Ellie and her father's vast ranch holdings, were done with one thought in mind: To pass this empire onto his four sons, to have and hold forever.

And their inheritance is the Ewing Oil Company, the largest independent petroleum producer in Texas, and Southfork, their big cattle spread. Big Daddy Jock built it all practically from scratch while scrapping over the years with his rival,

That human swamp rat J. R. Ewing plots another dirty business trick with his accomplice-of-the-month Leslie Stewart (Susan Flannery). Of J. R.'s beady blue eyes, wife Sue Ellen says, "They always seem to be hiding secrets." Or envisioning plans for one of his many enemies' ruin!

Linda Gray (right), former fashion model, cover girl, and product of an all-girls Catholic school education, spent twelve years playing J. R.'s long-suffering wife, Sue Ellen. As J. R.'s long-suffering mother, Barbara Bel Geddes (left) brought to her role a wealth of acting experience from the New York stage. Following quadruple bypass surgery in 1984, she returned to Dallas *in 1985 and stayed through the next-to-last season.*

Ranchhand Ray Krebs' (Steve Kanaly) main interest was horses until he ran into this classy little filly, Donna Culver (Susan Howard). Miss Howard, who is a native of Marshall, Texas, and a member of the Foursquare Gospel Church, refused to let her character follow the script and have an abortion in 1986. Instead, the baby—which had Down's Syndrome—was lost to a miscarriage.

With mean ole J. R. two-timing her all over town, Sue Ellen decides to so some dirty dancing with cowboy Dusty Farlow (Jared Martin). Someone actually calculated that 94 percent of all TV sex activity takes place outside of marriage, leading one critic to call for the placement of ads for birth control on prime-time soap operas like Dallas *and* Dynasty.

"Digger" Barnes (David Wayne, then Keenan Wynn), and Miss Ellie (Barbara Bel Geddes) is the guiding spirit. "We may be right, we may be wrong," she says, "but we're Ewings. We stick together. That's why we're unbeatable."

J. R. often seems to forget this deep truth. While baby brother Bobby is a chip off the old Jock, swaggering J. R. seems to be filled with nothing but ruthless egoism. Still, he claims whatever reprehensible deeds he does he does to keep Ewing oil safe in Ewing (read J. R.'s) hands.

That, of course, is not the only thing J. R. wants to keep his hands on. Any pretty young thing who will put out is fair game, just as anything any of his business competitors owns is his by right of conquest, if he can take it. J. R.'s many affairs are a staple of *Dallas* plots. They run parallel to, and sometimes overlap and join, J. R.'s life as a corporate buccaneer.

Which brings us to J. R.'s own long-running nemesis, Cliff Barnes (Ken Kercheval). It was Cliff's Daddy, "Digger" Barnes, who claimed that Jock Ewing had cheated him out of his half of the oil profits when they were wildcatting partners in the 1930s. This left Cliff and his sister, Pam, to grow up poor. An unpardonable sin on *Dallas!*

Cliff is probably the only oilman capable of matching J. R. sleazy trick for sleazy trick. Their rivalry extends to the most personal aspects of their lives. Women are prizes to be flaunted at each other, especially if they can be stolen property. When J. R.'s wife, the long-suffering Sue Ellen (Linda Gray), gets fed up with her husband's infidelities, she has a fling with always accommodating Cliff, whose political career J. R. has just finished ruining. "What's my charm?" Cliff asks Sue Ellen. "J. R. hates you," is her reply.

In a typical scene, the Ewings confront each other with their sordid betrayals. "Which slut are you sleeping with tonight?" demands Sue Ellen. "Does it matter?" snarls J. R. "Whoever she is she'll be more interesting than the slut I'm looking at right now."

Little wonder that the 1980 birth of John Ross Ewing III (Tyler Banks originally, then Omri Katz) could not save their marriage. For a time, J. R. was haunted by the thought that young John Ross was

Cliff's son—that would have been the ultimate humiliation. Fortunately for J. R., blood tests proved the baby was his, and his subsequent adoration of the child became his only redeeming quality. Still, there followed a bitter custody battle, with alcoholism, kidnapping, and J. R. bedding his wife's sister Kristin (Mary Crosby) thrown in for good measure.

All these shenanigans, and more, were a staple of *Dallas* storylines for more than a decade. In 1989, J. R. was going through yet another threat to his control of Ewing Oil from Cliff. Like every other time before, he managed to squirm free at the last minute. "Never a doubt in my mind that I would be completely vindicated [of an offshore oil spill]," J. R. said. "Is this a great country or what?"

The first two seasons were devoted to setting up the characters of the four Ewing sons. We've already seen why J. R. (short for John Ross), the eldest, was not the best-loved. (Even Miss Ellie thinks he is a tad pushy.)

Second son Gary (Ted Shackleford), might have been a rival to J. R., but his weakness for liquor took him out of the running. As soon as J. R. could decently do so, he shipped Gary to Southern California, where he now does his own *Dallas* spin-off, *Knots Landing*. The pert, honey-blond, peaches-and-cream complexioned Lucy, Gary's daughter, was left behind to live in the family house. Unfortunately, Lucy (Charlene Tilton) used her philandering uncle J. R. as a role model, and became one of the richest—and easiest—girls in Texas.

Ray Krebbs (Steven Kanaly) was foreman of Southfork and Jock's bastard son by a long-ago dalliance with a nurse. Although he was recognized by Jock as a son and heir in 1980, it took Ray a long while to get the hang of operating in the world of big money. Ray liked busting broncos more than he did busting chops.

Bobby (Patrick Duffy) is the baby of the clan, a college football hero who also knew how to score touchdowns with the ladies. Inside this family of oil barons, he is the White Knight to J. R.'s Dark Prince. When Jim Davis (Jock) died suddenly in 1981 and his character was written off as having been killed in a helicopter crash in South America,

Britain's Prince Charles and Lady Di couldn't be prouder of their heirs-apparent than oil tycoons Bobby and J. R. of their respective sons in 1982. That was the year J. R. and Sue Ellen remarried (J. R. did this to foil one of Cliff Barnes's plots!). After the second breakup of their marriage, there was a helluva custody battle for little John Ross, Jr.

it was inevitable that Bobby and J. R. would cross swords. Jock's will stipulated that they would have to fight for control of Ewing Oil. Whoever made the most money for the company during the next year would become boss.

This didn't endear Bobby to J. R., who thought this whole question had been settled long ago. Hadn't Jock raised him as fanatically as a kung fu warrior to be the fierce competitor that he was? Bobby was too much of a gentleman to survive in the back-stabbing oil industry. This led to more of J. R.'s machinations.

Bobby had a handicap in his battle with J. R., having married a member of the enemy camp, Pam Barnes (Victoria Principal). When Pam announced she was pregnant, J. R. saw this as a threat. At the annual Ewing Barbecue, he and Pam got into a heated argument in a hayloft. (Actually, she interrupted him with one of his "sluts.") Pam lost her balance and fell (some say J. R. pushed her) and had a miscarriage.

It is Bobby's function on *Dallas* to rein in big brother J. R. periodically and remind him that the Ewing's good name can stand only so much tarnishing. To his role as spoilsport, Patrick Duffy brings a certain stoic manliness. (This goes against the basic nature of Duffy, who is reportedly a cutup offstage. His pal Larry Hagman [J. R.] adds that playing a nice guy is an infinitely tougher acting job

After divorcing Sue Ellen, then remarrying her and divorcing her again, J. R. (Larry Hagman) found happiness for a time with a dirt-poor country gal, Callie (Cathy Podewell), whom he married in 1988. But soon it was back to his old wicked ways, and Callie had the gumption to dump him in 1990. J. R. spent his last days at Southfork embittered and alone.

than being a lowdown, rotten snake in the grass, which is a fun job.) Bobby, then, is absolutely essential, as he represents J. R.'s conscience, the small voice that infrequently wakes up and causes J. R. a fit of remorse.

In 1980, J. R. was almost brought down, being shot by a mysterious assailant. By that time he had left behind so many discarded mistresses and angry business competitors that the list of suspects ran to about fifteen names. *Dallas*-mania reached its height as newspapers and magazines around the world speculated, "Who shot J. R.?"

THE TEN COMMITMENTS OF SOAP OPERA WRITING

1. THERE SHALL BE AT LEAST TWO MAIN FAMILIES, ONE RICH AND ONE POOR. LET THE WICKED BE RICH, BUT LET THE POOR HAVE NICE WARDROBES.
2. THERE SHALL BE NO BLACKS AND WHITES, ONLY GRAYS. THE VILLAIN/VIXEN SHALL HAVE SYMPATHY, THE HERO/HEROINE FLAWS.
3. THERE SHALL BE DRINKING TO EXCESS AND ALL THE CONSEQUENCES THEREFROM (UNWANTED PREGNANCIES, FISTFIGHTS, HEADACHES).
4. THERE SHALL BE CORRUPTION, BLACKMAIL, EXTORTION, AND MURDER.
5. THERE SHALL BE ILLNESS AND INJURY AND COURTROOM DRAMA.
6. THERE SHALL BE BEAUTIFUL FACES, FIGURES, AND SETTINGS.
7. THERE SHALL BE BYZANTINE PLOTTINGS, SURPRISES, AND CLIFF-HANGERS.

◄

Mary Crosby, only daughter of legendary singer Bing Crosby and actress Kathryn Grant, landed the juicy role of Kristin, Sue Ellen's slutty, drug-addicted sister, in 1979. By 1980, she was the center of a major Dallas *storyline, as she was thought to be carrying J. R.'s child (later proved untrue). Anyway, the answer to 1980's burning TV question: "Who shot J. R." was, of course, crazy Kristin.*

8. "GOOD" CHARACTERS SHALL RESIST TEMPTATION, BUT ONLY UNTIL THE LAST MINUTE.
9. SINNERS SHALL SUFFER, BUT NOT UNTIL THE VIEWERS HAVE HAD THEIR FILL OF FUN.
10. WICKEDNESS SHALL BE SPREAD AROUND. "GOOD" CHARACTERS ARE DULL, AND ACTORS HATE PLAYING THEM.

Security on the Dallas set was airtight. Several alternate scenarios had been filmed, so even the cast was in the dark. The largest audience in television history to that time was on hand when the new TV season belatedly opened on November 21, 1980, when Kristin was revealed as the culprit. Believing that she was pregnant with his child, J. R. refused to press charges (how could a Ewing be born in jail?). Later, it turned out that Christopher (Joshua Harris) was not J. R.'s issue. When the child's mother died of a drug overdose, he was adopted by Pam and Bobby. J. R. agreed to give him up only if Bobby voted his shares of Ewing Oil the way J. R. wanted! As Larry Hagman (J. R.) remarked in an interview with the *Los Angeles Times*: "He's the biggest, most unmitigated and dastardly &%$!! on television…. He has women tucked away all over the country. He has millions of bucks. He's a business genius with a heart of lead…"

LARRY HAGMAN:
THE ANTIC MINSTREL OF MALIBU

Larry Hagman relished his role as J. R. and approached it with gusto, both on- and offstage. During public appearances, he used a drawl perfected during childhood in Weatherford, Texas, doffing his Stetson to the ladies and happily passing out fake money. He also has a Texan's love of grand display. In fact, his eccentric behavior has made him something of a legend in the Malibu colony. When he feels like he wants to have an impromptu parade down the beach, he raises a flag on one of the nine poles that stand on his $5 million property. Flags include the Lone Star of Texas, of course, and a custom-made pennant with the words "Laurence of Malibu." If invited to a party or other social function, he's likely as not to turn up in some distinctive headgear (he has a

LARRY HAGMAN

collection of five hundred hats) or costume (anything from a coolie to a London bobby to a sumo wrestler).

When the Smithsonian Institution in Washington was ready to enshrine J. R.'s famous Dallas Stetson as part of its "Americana" collection (which also includes Archie Bunker's chair and The Fonz's leather jacket), Hagman was on hand for the festivities. For propriety, he was dressed respectably, and not in one of his many gorilla suits. He also gave a speech, this being one of the days in which he *will* use human speech. He reserves at least one day out of every seven to observe complete silence, communicating through written notes or pantomime only.

There is a method to all this quirkiness, however. First, it makes for great copy in the media. Second, it really does seem to express a philosophy of life, a sort of fearless self-expression, and to hell with what anyone else thinks. In short, kind of like good ol' J. R.

The publicity drums were beating again in 1983 when Priscilla Beaulieu Presley joined the cast as Bobby's long-lost childhood sweetheart, Jenna Wade (originally played briefly by Francine Tacker). "Being on the show took me out of Elvis's shadow," she was quoted in a tabloid. The producers had been leery of hiring her at first because of her thin acting experience. But she proved herself and stayed in her role for five seasons.

It must be said of *Dallas*'s women characters that they are seen primarily as playthings or victims, despite some spine-stiffening given to Sue Ellen and Pam in the later years. Some of them have managed to double-cross J. R. in business deals, but he always manages to have the last laugh. And when he sets his beady blue eyes on one of his "Darlin's," as he calls them, his smooth moves, ability to fake sincerity when it's in his interest are an irresistible combination.

Evil as he is, J. R. had nothing to do with the most infamous episode of *Dallas*: "The Resurrection of Bobby."

Having seen him run over by a car in 1985, cradled in a weeping Pam's lap, expire with J. R. at his bedside, and then laid to rest on Southfork land in a flower-decked casket, one might reasonably assume that Bobby was dead.

Patrick Duffy wanted him to be. He found Bobby had become "boring," and was leaving to find more challenging parts. After a year of forgettable TV movies and a pilot that flopped, Duffy clambered back on board the *Dallas* express at the urging of friend Larry Hagman. Surprising numbers of *Dallas* viewers had lost interest after Bobby's demise. The problem now was, how to revive him?

Returning from the dead is an old soap opera ploy, but it usually works only when the person died far away and no one actually saw the body, or if the body was misidentified by foreigners. Neither was the case here.

Three different segments were shot to reintroduce Bobby: 1) Bobby explains the man they buried in Southfork's Boot Hill wasn't him. An orderly had revived him, and he had spent the past year recovering in a sanitarium. 2) An impostor returns, resembling Bobby, to get his hands on the Ewing loot. 3) The entire 1985–86 season was Pam Ewing's bad dream.*

Number one was rejected. Too long-winded. Number two was better, but still not right. The producers picked number three: Pam wakes up one morning and walks into the bathroom to find a cheerful Bobby taking a shower!

According to executive producer Leonard Katzman, *Dallas* had strayed too far from its Southfork roots, becoming a "woman's show" (meaning too much like *Dynasty*). Bobby's reentry signaled a return to preeminence of the menfolk and their doin's. *Dallas*'s ratings began to climb.

With the departure of Victoria Principal (Pam) in 1987 and Linda Gray (Sue Ellen) in 1989, new characters and storylines had to be added. J. R. got a new wife and Bobby finally married his love interest, April Stevens (Sheree J. Wilson). But the glory days of the show were over. And the soap opera genre itself was fading. According to a *TV Guide* poll published in January of 1990, only sixteen percent of the respondents wanted to see

---

*A 1986 three-hour made-for-TV prequel to *Dallas* was concocted apart from the series to dramatize how the Ewings and the Barneses, initially partners, had their long-ago falling out, and how the current story evolved from the Depression through the 1930s. David Grant, Dale Midkiff, and Molly Hagan were Jock Ewing, "Digger" Barnes, and Miss Ellie, respectively. Larry Hagman turned up at the beginning to spin the tale.

more prime-time soaps.

Measured by the total number of viewers worldwide at its height of popularity (200–300 million), *Dallas* was the most successful soap opera in history. The last successful soap in prime time was *Peyton Place* (1964–69). After *Dallas* became a hit, others were produced, including *Flamingo Road, Falcon Crest, and Dynasty.* Only *Dynasty* approached *Dallas*'s cult status, reaching number one in the Nielsens in the 1984–85 season. *Knots Landing* is still running as the last of the eighties' "glitter" soaps.

Dallas used every convention of the genre: disputed paternity (was John Ross J. R.'s or Cliff's child?), kidnapping (Bobby was mistaken for J. R.), long-lost loves come to menace new romances (Jenna versus Pam), mysterious disappearances and returns (people thought to be Pam and Jock turned up), legal shenanigans (Miss Ellie versus J. R. over Jock's will), adultery (don't ask), illegitimate children arriving full grown on the doorstep (J. R.'s son James) and bizarre plot twists (Bobby's "reviving" shower).

Ironically, *Dallas* was never meant to be a serial. It was conceived by David Jacobs and produced by Leonard Katzman as a miniseries to run in May of 1978. But the story of the Ewing family was so compelling to viewers that it was decided to add it to the CBS fall schedule. It went from Sunday nights at 8:00 to Sundays at 9:00, and then into the toughest slot in television, 10:00 on Fridays. Its audience was devoted but small that first year. The future TV giant did not even crack the top twenty-five. But that no-account, evil slug J. R. kept winning new converts. People identified with Bobby and Pam, but secretly they admired J. R. What he gave them to envy was a high lifestyle lived with gusto, plenty of sex without the slightest hint of guilt, and a safe sense of moral superiority. Quite simply, he was indispensable.

Dallas went out at the end of the 1990–91 season with a special two-hour finale, a strange mixture of *It's a Wonderful Life* and *A Christmas Carol.* Guest

Although they often clashed as the oil-mad Ewing brothers, Patrick Duffy (Bobby) and Larry Hagman (J. R.) were great pals offscreen. When Duffy left Dallas *in 1985, it was a tête-à-tête with friend Hagman at a Los Angeles bistro that helped lure him back the following year.*

Time *magazine called Bobby (Patrick Duffy) and Pam (Victoria Principal) the "Romeo and Juliet" of* Dallas, *meaning that the two lovers came from feuding families, the Ewings and the Barneses. In fact, Pam's brother, Cliff, is J. R.'s mortal enemy—which makes Pam his enemy as well. In this photo we see a happy Pam and Bobby on their wedding day in 1978.*

It's a cinch these two know the difference between "crude" and "refined" in the oil business, but not in their personal lives. Watching J.R. and his nemesis, Cliff Barnes (Ken Kercheval), feud over virtually everything was one of the continuing joys of Dallas.

Pamela Barnes Ewing (1978–87)	**Victoria Principal**
Lucy Ewing Cooper (1978–85, 1988–90)	**Charlene Tilton**
Ray Krebs	**Steven Kanaly**
Donna Culver Krebs (1979–87)	**Susan Howard**
Gary Ewing (1978–79)	**David Ackroyd**
Gary Ewing (1979–81)	**Ted Shackleford**
Valene Ewing (1979–81)	**Joan Van Ark**
John Ross Ewing III (1980–83)	**Tyler Banks**
John Ross Ewing III (1983–91)	**Omri Katz**
Christopher Ewing (1984–91)	**Joshua Harris**
Jack Ewing (1985–87)	**Dack Rambo**
Callie Ewing (1988–91)	**Cathy Podewell**
April Stevens Ewing (1986–90)	**Sheree J. Wilson**
James Ewing (1989–91)	**Sasha Mitchell**

SIGNIFICANT OTHERS:

Cliff Barnes	**Ken Kercheval**
"Digger" Barnes (1978–79)	**David Wayne**
"Digger" Barnes (1979–80)	**Keenan Wynn**
Clayton Farlow (1981–91)	**Howard Keel**
Jenna Wade (1982–83)	**Francine Tacker**
Jenna Wade (1983–88)	**Priscilla Presley**
Kristin Shepard (1979–81)	**Mary Crosby**
Dusty Farlow (1972–82, 1985)	**Jared Martin**
Jamie Ewing Barnes (1984–86)	**Jenilee Harrison**

THEME SONG: **Jerrold Immel**
TIMEFRAME: **1978–91**
NETWORK: **CBS**
ADDRESS: **Southfork Ranch**
         Dallas, Texas

356 episodes

star Joel Grey appears as a kind of spiritual guide, forcing J. R. to look back at how the world would have been had be never existed. A fitting wrap-up for a memorable character who was larger than life.

CAST LIST

FAMILY: The Ewings

MEMBERS:

Jock Ewing (1978–81)	**Jim Davis**
Ellie Ewing (1978–84, 1985–90)	**Barbara Bel Geddes**
Ellie Ewing (1984–85)	**Donna Reed**
J. R. Ewing	**Larry Hagman**
Sue Ellen Ewing (1978–89)	**Linda Gray**
Bobby Ewing (1978–85, 1986–91)	**Patrick Duffy**

*The Keaton clan, clockwise from top: Steven Keaton (Michael Gross),
Mallory Keaton (Justine Bateman), Elyse Keaton (Meredith Baxter Birney),
Andrew Keaton (Brian Bonsall), Alex P. Keaton (Michael J. Fox), and
Jennifer Keaton (Tina Yothers).*

Alex is comforted by his mom, Elyse, (Meredith Baxter Birney) after hearing of the death of a friend in this special one-hour episode of 1987. Presumably, Michael J. Fox was using this episode to showcase his dramatic talents just as his film career began to take off. So far, he's won no Oscars, but he did get a well-deserved Emmy in 1986.

Steven and Elyse Keaton of Columbus, Ohio, are not your typical 1980s couple. They live a comfortable upper-middle-class existence, being professionals (he is a public TV journalist, she is an architect), but they are neither status-conscious nor trendy. They are rather endearing in their old-fashioned commitment to the enduring values of the Flower Power era: loyalty, equality of the sexes, fair play, and respect for the environment.

Imagine their dismay when their firstborn, Alex, takes to a suit and tie, laptop computers, and free market economics as easily as Ronald Reagan to teleprompters and staged photo opportunities.

"This is the eighties," pipes Alex, the diminutive capitalist dynamo. "It's a dog-eat-dog world out there." Money and influence are the only protection in such an environment, Alex preaches, and he's prepared to be the toughest S.O.B. on the block.

Such macho posturings cause Steven to wince and Elyse to fume. "Selfish," "insensitive," "egotistic," "pompous," and "greedy" are just a few of their accusatory descriptions.

For dim-bulb mall-shopping sister Mallory, he is an insufferable know-it-all. President of his high school student body, straight-A scholar, and winner of many academic awards, he never lets her forget her intellectual inferiority. (When test-taking, Mallory confesses, a "gray fog" settles over her mind. Does her mind go blank? No, it's filled with distracting images: boys…)

The youngest Keaton for the first four seasons was pubescent Jennifer, and Alex tried to run her life as well. Fortunately, when she reached high school, it was discovered that her IQ was higher than his. From then on, a somewhat deflated Alex rapidly lost his Svengali-like influence.

The birth of little brother Andy in *Ties'* fourth season gave Alex a newfound opportunity to display fraternal tenderness. He gives Andy a model of the Reagan ranch, made entirely out of glued

◄

During their days at Berkeley, Steven and Elyse drove a Volkswagen mini-van, had a dog named Beckett, and helped organize student protests. Today, Elyse is the eternally chipper Earth Mother, while Steven is the hand-wringing, but socially conscious, patriarch. They haven't lost any of their idealism.

popsicle sticks, and teaches the kid to read using the *Wall Street Journal*.

When the Keatons enroll Andy in preschool that is noncompetitive and emphasizes sharing and cooperation, Alex is horrified. He does some quick brainwashing, and the next day, as he escorts Andy into his class, he does some last-minute coaching. "Whose lunchbox is this?" Alex prompts. "Mine!" says Andy. "And what do you think of sharing *your* property with other kids?" Andy gives the idea an emphatic raspberry.

Alex's triumph is short-lived, however. As happens in virtually every episode, his parents curb his worst excesses, and he gets to learn, along with Andy, Hollywood's version of the great Liberal lesson: other people *are* important.

When producer Gary David Goldberg created *Family Ties* in 1980 (it didn't start airing until September 1982), he sold it to NBC with this "high concept": imagine a former hippie couple still committed to antiestablishment ideals, while their children, strangely, have become straighter than white bread.

It was to be Steven and Elyse's struggle to maintain those ideals in an era of brie, Perrier, and Reebok worship, that was to be the sitcom's focus. The star was to be Meredith Baxter Birney as Elyse. In contrast, Michael J. Fox was an unknown quantity. The producers originally approached Matthew Broderick to play Alex. But by the filming of the third episode (in front of an audience of one hundred), Goldberg saw that Fox was getting big laughs. "I knew then he was going to be my heavy hitter."

Not everybody was happy with this abrupt change of focus. Reports surfaced in 1987 that a "bored" Meredith Baxter Birney was ready to turn in her love beads as Elyse, and it was only Michael J. Fox's intervention that kept her on the show. (Perhaps it was part repayment for the kindness she'd shown him in the first year, when, since he was without wheels, she would pick him up every day on her way to work. "My roommate saw this beautiful blonde in a Mercedes with a sunroof and figured I had it made," reported Fox.)

Alex's girlfriend for the final two seasons was pretty college psychology major, Lauren Miller, played by Courtney Cox. Miss Cox came to national attention for her cameo on a Bruce Springsteen music video. A native of Birmingham, Alabama, she began her career as a model, and got her big chance on Ties *after Alex's previous gal, Tracy Pollan, decided not to return in the role of Ellen.*

THE REAL ALEX P. KEATON

Gary David Goldberg found the inspiration for his Alex P. Keaton character while visiting the office of his friend, newspaper editor James Bellows. As the two men—both sixties survivors and dressed informally in sweat suits—chatted, Bellows's teenage stepson, Mike Sohigian, came by. The talk turned to politics, and Sohigian—dressed conservatively in suit and tie—revealed his admiration for Ronald Reagan, big business, and making money. Struck by how far to the right the opinions of many of the younger generation had drifted, Goldberg used Sohigian as the prototype for *Family Ties*'s Alex. (Goldberg adds that Jennifer Keaton is, in fact, based on his daughter, Shana.)

Postscript: Sohigian went on to become a production assistant on *Ties* and, according to Goldberg, wound up going to Berkeley (Goldberg's own alma mater), where he was "radicalized."

Despite the malicious joy with which the witty Alex (Michael J. Fox) attacks others, he is actually a rather stiff and repressed character. In this scene from the episode "Little Man on Campus" (1985), Alex outdoes himself in his eagerness to impress his college professor, and winds up making a fool of himself in front of the class.

There still remained a worry for Goldberg and the producers: how to maintain Alex's likability. His sharp wit was often caustic and hurtful. The idea that the audience might turn against him made everybody nervous.

Since Goldberg liked to run a set where there was a genuine feeling of "family," and suggestions were taken from all levels, including stagehands and crew, he deputized everyone to make sure Alex didn't "go too far."

Goldberg remembers one particular episode, "You've Got a Friend," in which Mallory tries to befriend a troubled teenager (played by Martha Plimpton) with a proclivity for shoplifting. In the course of their conversation, we discover the girl is ignored by her parents, trusts no one, and is "acting out" her emotional problems. Enter Alex, who spots her and snaps, "What is this, bring-home-a-felon night?"

After hearing crew members complain about that remark and others like it, Goldberg had most of Alex's lines rewritten twenty-four hours before the show was scheduled to be taped. "We had to tread a fine line between humor and nastiness. Sometimes we crossed that line."

Most often, however, Alex was ultimately re-deemed in the viewers' eyes. How could it be otherwise? Michael J. Fox was the smoothest, sassiest, most personable deliverer of zingers and squelchers in TV by the mid-eighties.

His put-down would start with a pause, to take the measure of his target. No need to rush—he is supremely relaxed, confident. Then the blue eyes narrow and crinkle (especially if he has just taken a shot himself), and the mouth curls slightly in a sneaky, smirky smile. And then the salvo, followed by a crooked grin of triumph. Alex has struck!

But the future Wall Street whiz had his own insecurities. Consider his relationships with women.

In one episode, we watch Alex look for a girlfriend for his freshman college year. Taking an orderly, businesslike approach, he checks the frosh photo album, targets his prey (a cute blonde dish), and goes about his rather tacky seduction. Since the blonde has corn muffins for brains, he is successful.

His father, taking this all in, comments drily, "You've taken romance and made it into a science."

For Alex, this is high praise.

Fortunately, Fate manages to disrupt Alex's pre-fab love life in the person of another comely coed, Ellen Reed. He is fascinated by the artistic, bohemian Ellen. What kind of person would study art history, he wonders, when they could be casing the art *market?*

She becomes Alex's first "full-season" girlfriend (1985–86) on *Ties* (and, in 1988, Michael J. Fox's real-life wife, Tracy Pollan.)

The fact that he and Ellen have little in common doesn't bother our charming chauvinist. Alex goes with Ellen to poetry readings and dance recitals, and then takes her to seminars on monetarist theory. In this way, he chirps, they "support" each other by pretending to like stuff that they really hate.

More fun comes when Ellen joins Alex's first class as a teaching assistant. The text he uses is "Money: Keep It Coming."

"I think you'll get used to being totally subservient to me," he cracks, relishing his new power.

His competitiveness and perfectionism drive him to be strict with all his students, including Ellen.

"Any calls for me?" he asks his Dad when he comes home.

"Just the usual death threats from your students."

His mother cuts in. "You had a relationship based on trust and love, and now you're in a position of complete authority over Ellen."

"So?" says Alex.

With the introduction of a new "steady," Lauren Miller (played by Courtney Cox) in the final two seasons,* Alex's chauvinism is on shakier ground.

Lauren is a psychology major, and she quickly sees through Alex. His self-boosterism and antic enthusiasms, she realizes, are all a smoke screen, covering his vulnerability. She encourages him to "get in touch" with his feelings. Dutifully, Alex looks at the books she's recommended, "so I can find out what my feelings are, and then memorize them."

Warming to the idea and his new relationship, Alex enters a therapy group with Lauren. When he is slow in baring his soul, she is encouraged: "You're repressed! That's wonderful! Now we're getting somewhere!" To which Alex retorts: "I'd be happy too if I wasn't so repressed."

And again: "I'm a very private person. There are things about me that even I don't know." (No wonder he cherishes his framed, autographed picture of Richard Nixon!)

Typical is a scene in which a frustrated Alex

While audiences were laughing at Alex P. Keaton's antics, Alex was laughing at Mallory and her stumblebum boyfriend, Nick (Scott Valentine). Although Nick was to be a one-shot role, the producers liked Valentine so much they brought him aboard as a recurring character. Valentine says Nick is based on Sylvester Stallone in The Lords of Discipline.

slams his fist into the kitchen table. When his Dad asks what's wrong, Alex quickly covers up. "Nothing, Dad. I'm studying how to be a judge." He strikes the table again. "Guilty!" he pronounces. "Death by hanging!"

Still, Steven and Elyse have not toiled in vain in Alex's case. Most *Ties* episodes find Alex's pretensions deflated, his prejudices exposed. But not before he's gotten in some good licks himself!

For the show's entire run, Mallory was a favorite whipping girl. Deftly played by Justine Bateman (who had been plucked, at fifteen, out of high school, with virtually no acting experience), bru-

*Tracy Pollan left the show, so "Ellen" went to Paris to pursue her art career.

Ex-flower child Steven (Michael Gross) and his money-mad, reactionary son, Alex (Michael J. Fox), are not on the same wavelength, politically or culturally. When Steven brings out his ancient album of Dylanesque protest songs, and forces his kids to listen to its scratchy moanings about the downtrodden, Alex rolls his eyes and smiles sarcastically, saying, "Gee, this is fun."

nette Mallory almost singlehandedly erases the cliche of the "dumb blonde."

For example, Alex giving a phone message to Mallory (who had brashly requested name, time, and content of message): "Somebody stupid called, sometime this afternoon, about something trivial."

Mallory (exasperated): "That could be any one of my friends!"

Mallory's boyfriend, Nick, was equally fog-bound. Played by Scott Valentine as a combination of Rocky Balboa and The Fonz, leather-jacketed Nick swaggered through the Keaton household with his dangling earring and a clenched-fist salutation, "Hey-ay!"

But what Nick lacked in polish he made up for in street-smarts. After taking a lot of verbal abuse from Alex, he found the perfect revenge. Whenever he spotted Mallory's big bro, Nick would throw his arm around him and say, "Hey-ay, my *little pal!*" Alex would seethe.

When the Keatons press Mallory to enter college, she counters with her dream: she means to be a clothes designer someday. Straining to present the best argument she can, she cries, "A lot of people who were successful didn't go to college: Thomas Edison, Abraham Lincoln." And then, digging deep, "Moses."

Perhaps the best is the time Mallory, fed up with parental rules at home, decides to marry Nick. Nervously trying to do the right thing, Nick approaches the Keatons for their permission, "if you have a moment, that is." After he has blurted his proposal, and Steven and Elyse have thawed from their frozen postures of horror, Steven quietly speaks, "My wife and I are going to step out of this room, then step back in, and you are going to ask us something else."

(This is vintage Steven Keaton. Even in the most trying moments, he maintains his composure. Or, as Elyse once observed of him, "You're taking on that let's-be-reasonable slouch.")

Determined to have her way, Mallory decides to elope. Alex listens to her plan with mounting delight. To be rid of Mallory! To be rid of Mallory *and* Nick! It's too good to be true.

Ultimately, Alex's better nature asserts itself, and he warns them against this. Deep down, he is still the loving brother, more caring than he would like to admit. He is, in short, Steven Keaton's son.

And who is Steven Keaton? Sometimes the very caricature of the befuddled sitcom father. But mostly, in the capable hands of Michael Gross, a decent guy trying to do the right thing.

What Alex takes from him is a kind of jittery energy, a puppy-like eagerness to tackle new challenges—and a tendency to go off the deep end when he does.

For instance, take the time Alex was left in charge of the household. Elyse is on a business trip, and Steven is about to go and visit her. As he leaves he admonishes Alex not to let Mallory drive the family car; she only has a learner's permit. Alex solemnly promises, but soon after succumbs to Mallory's whiny pleading.

Presently, the car has a dent, and Alex must find a quick way to raise the money to fix it.

An item in the newspaper gives him an idea. Alumni from a local college are streaming into town to support their football team against their perennial rivals. These grads need a place to stay, reasons Alex.

Soon there is a flashing neon sign proclaiming VACANCY; Skippy (their incredibly dippy next door neighbor, played by Marc Price) is decked out as a bellhop; Mallory and sister Jennifer (Tina Yothers) are in the kitchen (where else?) doing womanly work, and Alex is in the foyer, where he's converted a table into a check-in counter and installed a metal postcard rack.

Inevitably, Dad returns unexpectedly to find valet parking in the driveway and partying football fans, complete with captured mascot.

His eyes white with rage (one of the few times we see him this way), Steven mutters, "There's a kangaroo in my living room!" Pause. "A kangaroo in my living room!"

Now it is time for Alex to present his patented "insanity defense." "I guess I went overboard," he allows, trying to explain, among other things, the billboard advertisement Dad saw en route from the airport. "I could hear the money calling to me, 'Alex, at last we'll be together.'" As a last ploy, he declares himself "a money-holic." "Dad, I need help."

Other incarnations of Alex, besides the over-achiever, are the possessor (he gallantly becomes the Lamaze coach for a single coed, then im-properly infers the unborn child will be "ours"); the manipulator (pretends to be a feminist to impress a pretty girl); the know-it-all (takes over Jennifer's school presentation of a history paper, complete with plastic replica of Washington, D.C., etc.); the deflated chauvinist (his mother excels in an auto maintenance class they take together).

Which brings us to the show's crowning relation-ship: Alex and his Mom.

As Alex tells Elyse in the final episode, "You are the hippest, coolest, classiest person around. And the one who always listened."

In that special one-hour summing-up, we see Elyse as we've seen her all along, as the strongest, most focused character.

It is the day of Alex's liberation. He is going to New York, to a job as an investment banker. "It's my ticket outta this dump," he smirks.

Our little operator soon has his sisters busy with

Michael J. Fox and future real-life wife Tracy Pollan hold hands in this scene from 1986.

his packing and preparations. While his father tries to reach out, asking whether "$75,000 a year can be fulfilling," Alex looks at his watch.

Finally, Elyse erupts. "You've been acting like an ungrateful, arrogant, selfish young boy, ignoring your family and acting like this job makes you the most important person in the world."

They argue bitterly. But what is really happening is that they are both devastated, he with leaving, she with seeing him leave.

"I see part of me breaking away," says Elyse, "and I don't want to let go."

It was a classy and fitting farewell to the second-most-watched sitcom of the eighties.

When the show first aired, much was made of the "Reagan Connection." It was reportedly the President's favorite TV show, and Alex was taken to represent a callow new generation, concerned only with money, without compassion or a social conscience.

Alex, however, only represented himself. *Family Ties* was not inspired by Reagan's election. It was simply a reflection of what happened to 1960s kids like creator Gary Goldberg. They had grown up, become gentrified, and now faced the problems of raising their own children and clinging, if they could, to some of their youthful ideals.

MICHAEL J. FOX

Another erroneous perception, perpetuated by an admiring media, was that *Ties* was a hit from the very start. The truth is that, for the first two years, it did not crack the top twenty-five. Moving it to the 8:30–9:00 Thursday night time slot, right after *Cosby,* in 1984, made it a solid Number Five. Then, in 1985–86 and 1986–87, it was Number Two. A change to Sundays, in 1987–88, saw it drop to Number Seventeen. 1988–89 was its last season.

PROFILE:

MICHAEL J. FOX

What makes Michael J. Fox run? Armchair psychiatrists and supermarket tabloids might say he suffers the "Short Man Syndrome"—a high energy, overriding need to prove himself as good and as worthy of attention and adoration as taller men. Cynics would say he's trying to prove himself "better" than those taller than he, but Fox is just too modest, too much the real-life nice guy to prove their unkind assertions.

This five-foot-four, 120-pound, Edmonton, Alberta, Canada-born (June 9, 1961) and bred, American-adopted multimillionaire media icon, *is* truly the nice kid/boy/guy next door, even if he is rich and powerful, and does sometimes hobnob with Steven (Spielberg, that is) when he's not working.

Coming from a large, blue-collar family—he's fourth of five children born to Bill, a Canadian Army career soldier, and Phyllis, a payroll clerk— Fox always has been driven, ambitious, and highly motivated to achieve. According to his mother, he always wanted to "be in every group, play in every sport, do everything." She acknowledges his being short "perhaps bothered him. He was trying all the time to please everyone, show that he could do everything."

Competition was a natural state of being in a conservative household run in military style, where Fox vied for attention along with his three older sisters and younger brother. In school, Fox was a class clown who quickly learned that being "funny" was an excellent way of surviving being smaller than most of his classmates. "I was getting attention because I was so small," he told *People* magazine in 1985, "[so] I might as well make it

positive attention…might as well be the funny guy…with the size four shoes. Girls think you're cute and the bullies want to thump you, so you've got to be pretty funny, or you'll get thumped."

Fox's drive also made him nearly fearless. On his high school hockey team, multiple injuries and more than fifty stitches in his face never diminished his fierce competitive spirit. Movie and television makeup and clever photo airbrushing now cover his facial scars. His pugnacity is in keeping with the persona of his idol, Jimmy Cagney. One of Fox's secret frustrations is that he didn't have the bulk or height to play pro hockey.

The work ethic ran strong in the Fox household, so when bitten by the acting bug, Michael dropped out of high school at fifteen and went to work. When he auditioned for the lead role in the Canadian television series, *Leo and Me,* he lied to the producers, telling them he was ten years old. He won the part and stayed with the series for two years. "I was always kind of a hyper kid. Acting gave me a creative outlet for all my energy. I'd be a little longshoreman with a bad back if roles hadn't popped up so easily for me. I could never pound the pavement with eight-by-ten glossies in hand. The opportunities just came my way, and I fell in love with the work. I still can't believe I'm getting paid to show off. Luckily, I have enough of an inferiority complex to compensate for any ego problems. Because I come from a lower-middle-class working family, the whole thing is still kind of dazzling."

Work has always been the key for Fox, not money. Although he earned $15,000 per episode early on in *Family Ties* (Meredith Baxter Birney, according to the tabloids, was making perhaps ten times as much) and reportedly $500,000 for *Back to the Future* and $1 million for his thirty-second Diet Pepsi commercial, he's still insecure and his own severest critic.

"I really haven't been satisfied with anything I've done. I work hard; obviously I'm driven, but the success has come so easily that I'm suspicious of it," notes Fox. The success hasn't come that easily, nor have the comfort and ease with the money he's earned.

"When I was a teenager," Fox recalls of the days of his two-year starring role on Canadian televi-

In part two of this 1987 episode, "Mrs. Wrong," Steven Keaton (Michael Gross) slumps on the floor after hearing the fateful news: his daughter, Mallory, has eloped with the garbage sculptor, Nick Moore. "I have the reputation as being sweet, kind patient loving Steven Keaton," Gross told TV Guide. *"I could be found with five naked woman and a can of Crisco and the* National Enquirer *would say, 'Michael Gross was discovered baking cookies.'"*

sion, "the money blew me away."

Instant Fox-mania made it quickly clear who the real star of *Family Ties* was. Although their relationship was initially warm, supportive, and cooperative, Birney and Fox grew apart as the years passed. Creator Gary Goldberg described Fox on stage as "like a white light…awesome!" Not everyone agreed. Brandon Tartikoff, head of NBC Entertainment, griped, "You'll never see that face on a school lunchbox!" Subsequently (and happily) proved wrong, Tartikoff kept a lunchbox with Fox's likeness on his desk till the end of the series' run.

To this day, Fox remains wary of success. He still worries that he doesn't deserve the acclaim, and works all the harder to prove he's worthy. He insists he doesn't ever want to come off smug, and wants to continue to grow as an actor. According to intimates, Fox is lovable, modest, and fun to be around, and he's well known for his self-deprecating humor. Upon winning his Emmy in 1986, he quipped, "I feel four feet tall!"

Fox told *People* magazine in 1987, "I'm going to marry a Jewish woman...I haven't met one I haven't liked." Raised an Anglican, Fox romanced *Facts of Life* star Nancy McKeon and Helen Slater, filmdom's *Supergirl,* who is Jewish. Fox eventually made his premonition come true when he married *Ties* costar, Tracy Pollan, on July 16, 1988. The following summer, a son, Sam, was born to the couple who have homes in Hollywood and Vermont.

When the curtain finally rang down on *Family Ties,* Fox recounted his imaginary conclusion to the show during an interview on ABC's infotainment series, *20/20.* "Alex goes to New York, gets recruited by the CIA, but doesn't like that. He changes his political party affiliation to Democrat, gets elected to Congress, and is promptly run out of town on an ethics charge."

Alan Poul, associate producer of Fox's 1987 film, *Light of Day,* offers the last word on Michael J. Fox: "All the schmaltz you've heard about him...is true."

Meredith Baxter Birney's real-life pregnancy was written into the storyline in the 1984–85 season, providing the show with another child, Andrew, while Meredith herself gave birth to twins Mollie and Peter in October of 1984. Thus the actress continued to wear pregnancy padding as Elyse Keaton after she'd already given birth to her own children. In this scene Alex tries to talk to his as-yet unborn sibling in the episode "Fabric Smarts."

SIGNIFICANT OTHERS:

Irwin "Skippy" Handelman . . . **Marc Price**
Nick Moore (1985–89) . . . **Scott Valentine**
Ellen Reed (1985–86) . . . . **Tracy Pollan**
Lauren Miller (1987–89) . . . **Courtney Cox**

THEME SONG: **"Without Us"** by Tom Scott and Jeff Barry (sung by Johnny Mathis and Deniece Williams)
TIMEFRAME: **1982–89**
NETWORK: **NBC**
ADDRESS: **Columbus, Ohio**

CAST LIST

FAMILY: The Keatons

MEMBERS:

Alex P. Keaton . . . . **Michael J. Fox**
Elyse Keaton . . . . **Meredith Baxter Birney**
Steven Keaton . . . . **Michael Gross**
Mallory Keaton . . . . **Justine Bateman**
Jennifer Keaton . . . . **Tina Yothers**
Andrew Keaton (1986–89) **Brian Bonsail**

GREAT PERFORMANCES

Emmy Winner

Michael J. Fox

Outstanding Actor (Comedy)

1985–86, 1986–87

KATE & ALLIE

The McCardle-Lowell clan, clockwise from bottom left: Chip Lowell (Frederick Koehler), Jennie Lowell (Allison Smith), Kate McCardle (Susan Saint James), Bob Barsky (Sam Freed), and Allie Lowell Barsky (Jane Curtin). Missing—away at college is Emma McCardle (Ari Meyers).

When Allie Lowell (Jane Curtin) arrived on the doorstep of her once-married girlfriend of high school days, Kate McCardle (Susan Saint James), trailing her divorce papers, two children, and tattered self-esteem, the viewer was asked to decide: can two divorced women live together in a Greenwich Village duplex apartment along with their offspring without driving each other crazy.

Seven seasons of sharp and snappy dialogue, delivered with panache by two seasoned comedic actresses, supplied a positive answer.

The role of the upbeat, spontaneous Bohemian, Kate, was a natural for Saint James, who once had plunged into the counterculture, Hollywood-style, with gusto. Colorful, animated Kate wears life's experiences with an easy grace, her voice richly rounded with a husky-raspy undertone.

Allie, of course, is the exact opposite. She is the simpering, sheltered WASP, a role which Curtin was not unfamiliar with, having played cheerleaders and Young Republican-types as an original cast member of *Saturday Night Live*.

Taped before an audience in New York's Ed Sullivan Theater, the show emphasized its urban setting in the (out-of-studio) opening of every episode, which found Kate and Allie walking through Central Park, or buying a hot dog from a street vendor, etc. These scenes set the tone of down-to-earth realism, mixed with comedy, that the two stars wanted.

Their formula worked, proving that two single mothers could be nurturing and, at the same time, witty, sophisticated, catty, man-hungry, tipsy—in short, most of the things mothers aren't allowed to be on network television.

In one vignette, we see them in front of a newsstand. Allie, the traditionalist, complains about all the smutty magazines. Kate, the tolerant sixties survivor, reminds her that that's the price we pay "for living in a free country."

> ALLIE: Whatever happened to good old-fashioned brown wrappers?
> KATE: The ones the *National Geographic* used to come in?
> ALLIE: I thought I was the only girl who did that
> KATE: That's how I got my interest in being a travel agent!

Jane Curtin got to have a husband on the show. Susan Saint James only got to have an on-again, off-again relationship with sexy Italian plumber Ted (played by Gregory Salata). On their first date, Kate found Ted "rude," while he thought she was condescending. Naturally, they fell in love.

The first season saw the roomies decide on a division of labor. Kate will keep her travel agent job, and Allie will stay at home, cook, and clean. But they must also start meeting people, Kate insists.

Allie is resistant, however. She would rather brood over the wreckage of her failed marriage.

When Kate's teenage daughter, Emma, asks her help in doing some biology homework, Allie demures. "You *were* married to a doctor," Emma reminds her. "Yes, and I can tell you what part of the anatomy *he* is," snaps Allie.

After dropping out of college to put her husband through medical school, Allie has every right to be angry at Charles (played with just the right callousness by Paul Hecht) and at the "other woman," Charles's new girlfriend Claire, as well.

"Don't you think you can stop hating Claire?" asks an exasperated Kate, on the eve of Charles's remarriage.

"That woman had an affair with my ex-husband. I *like* hating her."

And again: "I can't believe that woman is up in Connecticut, wandering around with *my* charge cards."

After several years of divorced loneliness and Dates from Hell, Allie (Jane Curtin) finally finds happiness in the arms of sportscaster Bob Barsky. Sam Freed (Bob) knew Jane from the time they'd both auditioned for Saturday Night Live *in 1975. Sam made two previous appearances on* K&A, *playing a director and a philandering politician.*

But there are other things holding back Allie's emancipation, besides bitter memories. Take the awful advice given to her by her mother, long ago: "Sex is something you do to keep a man. If you like it, that's a bonus." Allie winds up staying at home eating chocolate cake.

Kate has a different problem. Dates she has plenty of. But finding someone to hold her attention for more than five minutes is something else. Perhaps that's why she's attracted to the offbeat type. Take, for instance, Dennis, the painter-turned-cabbie. She doesn't mind that he picked her up in the back of his taxi. Or that, for their first date, he suggests a trip to Brazil ("All you need is your passport," he purrs, "and your bikini."). It takes a strong dose of Allie's patented skepticism to finally break the spell. Kate decides that they will go to Boston, not Brazil.

We hear no more of Dennis, the taxi driver, but Max, the Italian-American plumber, becomes Kate's longest-running relationship. Their first date is not auspicious, however. He thinks she looks down on men who work with their hands. She thinks he's got a gigantic chip on his shoulder.

Later, she describes him to Allie: "So rude, so defensive, so gorgeous!" Then, neatly reversing a sexist stereotype: "I kept looking at him arguing and thinking how cute he looks when he's mad!"

Allie, doubtful the attraction can last, says, "I hope you know this is purely physical." Kate, with a smirk, "I'm counting on it."

These conversations are always held in either Kate or Allie's bedroom, of course, never in front of the children.

Still, Kate's flirtatious nature has its downside. In one episode, she is taken to task by daughter Emma for "bopping." A mortal sin, it seems, when Emma is trying to impress an older (twentyish) man named Walter.

Walter had exclaimed to the beautiful Kate, "I would have thought you were Emma's sister." Then

The extraordinary chemistry between stars Susan Saint James (Kate) and Jane Curtin (Allie) was a key to the show's success. In this dream sequence, Kate imagines herself and Allie as spinsters, still living together in their eighties, and still driving each other crazy. Thankfully, she soons awakens from this nightmarish vision.

he turned to Emma: "She really looks young."

"She rubs stuff on her face at night," fumed Emma.

Stricken, Kate went to Allie for advice. Is it true? Does she flirt like an eighteen-year-old, when she should be acting like the thirtysomething mother she is?

Does she want the truth, asks Allie, or shall they remain friends?

A chastened Kate later has a heart-to-heart with Emma in her room. "I walked in cute," she concludes. "I'm walking out mature."

Allie, however, has to face the fact that she will never "bop." And she cringes when she hears Emma complain to Kate "Why can't you be a plain old mother like Allie?"

HOW CBS GOT SUSAN TO BE KATE, AND HOW SUSAN GOT JANE TO BE ALLIE...

The show's genesis began when Susan Saint James read a script by Sherry Cohen for an idea developed by Mort Lachman. The actress had done a CBS pilot, *After George,* which had flopped, and now was looking for a new property. The story of two divorced women living on their own with an extended family of kids appealed to her. She saw something of herself in the feisty Kate McCardle and thought she knew who could be a perfect Allie Lowell. Unfortunately, her good friend Jane Curtin was not interested, Still, Susan Saint James kept after her. It would be fun, she said. And the working conditions would be ideal.

The two actresses, lives had touched in many ways in the preceding years. They were both basically committed to working on the East Coast, and their Connecticut homes were only fifteen minutes apart. They had done a film together *(How to Beat the High Cost of Living),* and had given birth to children within a month of each other, in 1983. Also, in 1982, Saint James had married Dick Ebersol, former director of *Saturday Night Live,* a TV show with which Jane Curtin, an original "Not Ready for Prime Time Player," had had some acquaintanceship (although she'd never worked with Ebersol).

If they did this show in Manhattan, Saint James told Curtin, they could still be home for dinner most nights. That was the clincher that won Curtin over, plus the fact the two roles seemed tailor-made for their respective talents.

In the show's first year, the two stars were both nominated for an Emmy as Best Actress in a Comedy Series. Because she'd had a longer track record in TV, Susan Saint James truly expected to win, if anyone from the show *did* win. Imagine her surprise when Jane Curtin's name was announced. But her surprise turned to dismay at Curtin's victory speech. "I should really thank Susan Saint James," she said, "because you can't do it with a trained poodle."

Nervous, and trying to be funny, Miss Curtin had hurt her costar's feelings deeply. She explains her botched "thank you" by saying she was in "shock" at winning. It took some time for the two to become friends again.

"Plain old mothers" was exactly what Susan Saint James and Jane Curtin didn't want to be. They knew that most of the top-rated eighties sitcoms were dominated by glib, smart-alecky teen characters. And if anyone was going to have the joy of being glib and smart-alecky, it was gong to be *them,* not their kids. And though the kids' roles gradually expanded as they got older, they always remained secondary.

In fact, there is very little mother-child conflict on *Kate & Allie.* The kids are, for the most part, well-scrubbed and well-behaved. If anyone is the disciplinarian, it's Allie. Kate's idea of punishment is to send the kids to bed without their take-out pizza. And she doesn't hover over her daughter. If Emma could survive a childhood toddling alongside her backpacking parents in Europe, she can cope with anything.

It is the Lowell children who are taught to say "May I?" and not sass their mother. ("I don't need to be reasonable," Allie is fond of saying, "I'm your mother.") She also preaches Allie's Great Dictum of Life: "If you like it, it must be bad for you." No transgression escapes her laser-like, lock-on-target eyes. And no scam is clever enough to escape her vigilance. (When adolescent Chip, winningly played by young Frederick Koehler, spills catsup on his shirt, lies back on the kitchen table, and

Susan Saint James and Jane Curtin were best pals before they ever got to play best pals on TV. They lived within a few miles of each other in Connecticut and gave birth to babies within a month of each other. In this scene, Kate looks puzzled and Allie is skeptical as building super Lou (Peter Onorati) helps them prepare an Italian meal.

tucks a knife into his armpit, Allie is not impressed. "Nice try, Chip," she snaps. "But what if I were really dead?" he demands. "I'd send you to school with a note: 'Excuse my son, he's feeling a little dead today.'")

Chip's teenager sister Jennie (Allison Smith), and her roomie, Emma (Ari Meyers), attend a public school in New York City where no one is ever mugged or threatened. Their biggest hassles are, as usual, dating guys and competing for the same role in a school play. As high school teens, the girls are, in fact, boring. The only dangerous thing Emma gets to do she does offscreen. Her mother and Allie reminisce about a "greaser" she once brought home: "Eddie Spermatozoa." Says Kate, "He carried a knife." Presumably, he didn't use it.

As odd-boy-out in an all-female household, Chip is the more demanding, childish character. Trying to prevent Allie from finding out he flunked science, Chip tries to get on her good side, volunteering to take a package to the post office. Not used to this kind of helpfulness, Allie eyes him suspiciously. "What's the matter?" she demands. "Nothing!" he answers, his voice an octave higher. Later, on the verge of confession, he weakens and substitutes a more forgivable transgression: "I didn't make the baseball team…." Allie, who'd sought solace in the refrigerator, gripes, "I ate chocolate cake for *that?*"

As the kids get older, the problems become spicier. Sex rears its ugly head, and Allie is ready and waiting to knock its block off.

Warning signs flash when she visits Jennie's college dorm room and finds a host of male clothes in the bureau. "I'm paying for you to share a room with a girl, and that's what you're going to do," she screams.

Jennie then announces that she and her boyfriend, Ben, will leave college for jobs so they can support themselves in their own apartment, as a married couple. This, for Allie, is even worse than living together. Back home, she pleads with Kate for advice. Kate is flippant at first: "Let your kid go to school out of state," she counsels, "and pray." Finally, they decide to use reverse psychology. They will give the young lovers a boxful of "engagement presents" for their new habitat: rubber gloves, toilet brush, disinfectant, and roach spray.

In the end, Jennie and Ben get cold feet and decide it is probably wiser, and cheaper, to respect Allie's wishes and live in separate rooms. And Allie, for her part, doesn't try to pull her little scam on the kids. She realizes Jennie is a grown-up, and merely expresses her opinion that marriage is something for the future. When Jennie and Ben quickly accept this wisdom, Allie is stunned, but happy. The kids leave, smiling slyly.

It remains for Allie to endure one more shock to the maternal system, this time provided by a much-matured but still squeaky-voiced Chip. She finds a

Kate & Allie tackled subjects like interracial dating, lesbianism, mental retardation, and, of course, life-after-divorce, without being preachy. Here Chip (Frederick Koehler) learns to value the friendship of Louis (Michael Countryman), a homeless retarded man given shelter by the family in this 1986 episode.

condom in his pocket.

ALLIE: Where could he have gotten such a thing?
KATE: Probably from a vending machine.
ALLIE: Vending machine? Whatever happened to bubble gum?
KATE: Doesn't work as well.

As luck would have it, the two, who now own a catering business, are hosting a dinner that night for a group of psychiatrists. And the main topic of dinner conversation is sex. Allie, already in an angry mood, starts drinking the wine instead of serving it. Thoroughly smashed, she lurches through dinner, listening to the shrinktalk.

Psychiatrist, discussing a case of repression: "So, you think it's the mother?" Another, unctuously: "Isn't it always the mother?"

Allie, scowling: "Why are you attacking mothers?"

The next morning, albeit with a headache, she approaches Chip. Their discussion makes him very anxious. At one point he clutches his head, crying, "My mother said 'condom!'"

It is all for his own good, explains Mom. Embarrassment can't kill him, but ignorance can. (Of course, Chip had no real plans to actually use the condom, but the message of safe sex in the age of AIDS was clearly made.)

Kate envisions what she and Allie might be like should she marry Ted and raise a house full of children, and Allie uses her newly-won college degree to become a glamorous career woman. Other "daydream" sequences included the pals as eighty-year-old roomies, and as Lucy and Ethel from I Love Lucy.

But safe sex wasn't the only issue to be tackled by *Kate & Allie*. There is the time Kate is caught at her dentist's deserted office during a power outage. In the ensuing darkness she hits it off with another stranded patient. He invites her to a hockey game. She accepts. Then the lights come on, and we discover the personable fellow is a black man, George. True to her liberal ideals, Kate does not try to back out. Later, she confesses to Allie that she felt awkward. "Does that make me a bigot?" she frets. She hopes not. On their subsequent date, George confesses to the same self-consciousness. This upsets them both because they are "Kennedy's children" out "to change the world." Eventually, they find reassurance when Jennie and Emma say they think it's "cool." To the new generation, George proposes a toast. Perhaps *they* will live in a more open-hearted society.

During the first season (1984), Allie (Jane Curtin) was the stay-at-home housemother, while Kate (Susan Saint James) went out to be the breadwinner. Kate & Allie *was the first TV sitcom to show two women successfully running a two-family household, with nary a male authority figure in sight.*

EPISODIC WEIRDNESS
GABRIEL'S FIRE

It all starts innocently enough. Kate and Allie wish for a new catering job, as they are low on money. Suddenly the doorbell rings, and a man wearing a derby hat appears. He saw their ad and wants them to cater an expensive charity event. They happily accept. "I can believe our wish came true," gushes Kate. "It's like it came from Heaven."

"Well," says Allie, "he did say his name was Gabriel."

Their smiles vanish, however, when a $2,000 check they needed for the job is lost in the mail. They decide Mr. Gabriel wasn't Heaven-sent. "We're in Hell," remarks Allie. They take to their respective beds, depressed.

Suddenly, Gabriel appears in Kate's room. He can grant her any wish, he says. The ex-hippie doesn't have to think twice. "World peace," says Kate. And for herself?, prompts Gabriel. Well, first, Kate wants Allie to stop giving her unwanted advice. Then she wants Emma back from college in California. And third, she decides, she wants to be married.

Next morning, Kate finds her wishes granted and her world changed, but not in the ways she wanted. First, she finds a diamond ring on her finger. She's married, but to her obnoxiously macho building super, Lou. She cringes as he hugs her and whispers, "By the way, you were terrific last night!" Noticing Allie's absence, she discovered that her roomie's moved away. Then comes notification of her Nobel Prize for Peace. And last, Emma returns as a blonde California Valley Girl, completely changed in appearance from having her tummy, eyes, nose, and chin fixed. "You're not Emma," insists Kate. "You're Michael Jackson."

Gabriel reappears, asking for devil's food cake and tipping his derby hat to show two horns on his head.

"I don't want to be married, ever" complains Kate. In a flash she finds herself in a nun's habit.

Allie's wishes are granted as well, and turn out no better. When she asks simply that Chip be "strong" and Jenny be "full of life," she finds her son a pumped-up steroid hunk and her daughter pregnant. When she asks that her ex-husband Charles's second wife have an affair, she does. Allie finds her on the couch necking with her own husband, Bob! When Allie miserably asks for her old life back, she finds herself back in bed—with Charles!

Next morning, the roommates find out they had the identical dream about Mr. Gabriel. The $2,000 check is recovered, and when Mr. Gabriel tips his hat, there are no horns.

In another "controversial" episode, the rather imperious lady landlord of their duplex announces that the rent is being doubled. Reason: *Two* separate families are using one apartment. She will not be persuaded it is really one household. Finally, the girls come up with a clever scheme. They will tell the landlord that they are lesbian lovers: one is the breadwinner, the other the housekeeper. This division of labor, they claim, makes them just like any other traditional family. Sometime later, the landlord returns with a friend. This is *her* better half, she says, introducing *her* female roommate. Now that everything is out in the open, she invites them to make a foursome at a gay-lesbian dance.

In the end, Kate and Allie confess their deception, and their landlord agrees there is room for all

kinds of non-traditional households. There is tolerance on both sides.

It is refreshing to note, in this regard, that when the writers tackled controversy, they did not take the easy way out with glib, formula scripts. Nor did they hit the viewer with an anvil to make their point, or stand on soap boxes. They assumed a certain sophistication in their audience, and the resulting stories were thoughtful and underplayed.

In 1987, there occurred a mini-crisis. Miss Saint James was pregnant with her second child. Her and Ebersol's first child, Charles, had been born fifteen months before production on *Kate & Allie* commenced. (Miss Saint James also has two children, Sunshine and Harmony, from her marriage to makeup artist Tom Lucas.) With no one wanting Kate to be expecting in the storyline, they decided on the only course possible: camouflage. Kate became more and more stationary. They had her sit behind the kitchen table. When she had to stand, it was behind the kitchen counter. And when she was required to move, she carried something in front of her.

Finally, the writers had Kate break her leg and wind up in a hospital, and there have a brief flirtation with an amorous doctor. Then Allie arrives, scheduled for minor surgery. This proves to be one of the funniest episodes. Absolutely terrified, Allie slips off the gurney and wanders, in a drugged stupor, through the corridors, until she reaches a waiting room, where she lifts her hospital gown and moons the visitors.

A more ladylike Allie finds true love in the arms of sportscaster Bob Barsky (Sam Freed), and they are married in the broadcast booth during a football game, in the next-to-last season. (Freed had made a previous appearance as a politician who puts some smooth moves on his naïve volunteer, Allie. When Allie discovers he is married, she rips his button off her lapel and storms out of the campaign office.)

There are wedding bells in Kate's life as well, but she isn't the bride. It happens when her divorced Dad arrives in town to get her opinion on Rita, the woman he means to marry. Kate finds she can't stand her. Dad takes her advice and dumps Rita, but is miserable. Kate is miserable, too. Finally, Jennie provides the solution. She doesn't like *her* father's new wife, Claire, but she pretends to be friendly because she doesn't want to lose her relationship with her Dad. Kate gets the message, and urges her father to do what will make him happy. The ceremony takes place in their apartment, with a gamely smiling Kate muttering under her breath: "Do you believe that dress? This is a wedding, not a cocktail lounge...." (Susan Saint James's real-life father, Charlie Miller, a retired manufacturer, does a cameo role as the officiating minister, speaking one line.)

After Bob and Allie's marriage, the family moved to a new duplex in an uptown high-rise. Jennie was still in college, but Emma was written out of the story, having gone to live with her father and attend college, in California. The household now contained the newlyweds, plus Chip and Kate, and Bob only came home on weekends from his broadcast job in Washington, D.C.

In this way, the show tried to keep the main focus on the interplay between the two women. Already, however, *Kate & Allie* was running out of steam. The marriage, obviously meant to strengthen the show, had actually weakened it. The following year, it went off the air.

There aren't many successful sitcoms based on a "best pals" extended-family situation.

Some, it is true, become 800-pound gorillas in the Nielsen ratings, like *Laverne & Shirley*. Some are hailed, Emmy-ed, and then bid farewell, like *Cagney & Lacey*. And some are kept on the network schedule only through the kindness of a TV executive who loves them (*The Odd Couple* is one example), often finding their audience later, in reruns.

But they all have one trait in common: the incredible chemistry between the two pals. It's not something you can buy, manufacture or pretend. It's just there. And Jane Curtin and Susan Saint James had it. Along with some of the best comedy writing in television.

Although the show focused on two women trying to make their way in the world after shattered marriages, it was warm and funny and upbeat. It didn't really create a trend, but, in its quiet way it proved that two actresses could carry a comedy without much visible male support, and without being either buffoons or sexpots.

That in itself, for American television, is a fine accomplishment.

CAST LIST

FAMILY: The McCardle–Lowells

MEMBERS:

Kate McCardle . . . . . . **Susan Saint James**
Allie Lowell Barsky . . . . **Jane Curtin**
Emma McCardle (1984–88) . . **Ari Meyers**
Jennie Lowell . . . . **Allison Smith**
Chip Lowell . . . . **Frederick Koehler**
Bob Barsky (1987–89) . . . . **Sam Freed**

SIGNIFICANT OTHERS:

Dr. Charles Lowell (1984–86) . **Paul Hecht**
Ted Bartelo (1984–85,
   1987–88) . . . . **Gregory Salata**
Lou (1988–89) . . . . **Peter Onorati**

THEME SONG: **"Along Comes a Friend"**
   by John Leffler
TIMEFRAME: **1984–89**
NETWORK: **CBS**
ADDRESS: **Greenwich Village**
   New York City

GREAT PERFORMANCES

Emmy Winner

Jane Curtin

Outstanding Actress (Comedy)
1983–84, 1984–85

One of the comedic highlights of the early years were the Huxtables lip-sync renditions of jazz classics such as Ray Charles's "Night Time Is the Right Time" (pictured here from a 1985 episode, "Happy Anniversary"), for birthday or anniversary celebrations. Seen here: Theo (Malcolm-Jamal Warner, on staircase), and (left to right) Sondra (Sabrina Le Beauf), Denise (Lisa Bonet), Cliff (Bill Cosby), Clair (Phylicia Rashad), Rudy (Keshia Knight Pulliam), and Vanessa (Tempestt Bledsoe).

Maybe it's that Old Yeller protective instinct that makes Cliff want to take his daughter's boyfriend, Elvin (Geoffrey Owens), to the mat. Watching is Theo, in this 1987 episode, "Monster Man Huxtable." In real life Cosby was quite an athlete, attending Temple University in Philadelphia on a track scholarship.

In 1984, critics and viewers alike were blindsided by the quick rush to success of *The Cosby Show*. Bill Cosby, former "last string" fullback on the Temple University football squad, captained his TV team to four successive championship seasons in the Nielsen ratings (1985–89). His try for an unprecedented fifth win was blocked by the Refrigerator Perry of TV, Roseanne Barr. And even then, he only lost as the clock ticked down to the last second of the season. (The ratings share for *Roseanne* in 1989–90 was 23.4 to *Cosby's* 23.1.)

The playing field Cosby found in his premiere year was not friendly toward situation comedies. They were considered too soft to compete in the increasingly muscular world of lust, glitz, and greed represented by *Dallas* and *Dynasty* (TV's Number one and Number Two shows). Family-oriented shows got by using cute gimmicks, like white parents raising an adorable black youngster (*Diff'rent Strokes, Webster*), or kids of diverse backgrounds living together with a guardian (*Facts of Life*), or children who weren't even human (*Punky Brewster*).

Cosby's winning strategy was to sense that people were growing tired of all this unreality. What he would deliver was a simple story based on the familiar situations of everyday life (breaking up with a boyfriend, lying to one's parents, etc.) and leavened with enough humor to make the underlying moral slip down smooth and easy, like a Jello Pudding Pop.

The commercials Cosby made for Jello Pudding Pops, in fact, may have paved the way for the early success of the show. First we were grinning at his warm and winning persona as TV pitchman, then we saw this same warm and winning guy as paterfamilias of a black yuppie New York (actually Brooklyn Heights) family. How could we not be delighted with his puckish sense of humor, his amazing rapport with children?

There is equality in the marriage of Heathcliff and Clair Huxtable. They share household chores and raising the children (from oldest to youngest: Sondra, Denise, Theo, Vanessa, and Rudy). Not that they are Mr. and Ms. Perfect. Cliff will still uphold the honor of his sex when it comes to arguments about who is better at what task. And at Thanksgiving, he passes on the honor of carving the turkey to his only son, instead of the eldest girl, Sondra.

But what viewers see when they tune in this show is the revival of a "kinder and gentler" type of sitcom exemplified by *Father Knows Best*. In it the parents are firmly in the driver's seat, and the children are ready to take direction.

On *The Cosby Show*, Cliff uses his considerable charm to nudge—and sometimes shove—his four daughters and one son to maturity. (It is imperative he do this, or else the worst thing in the world will happen: His kids will *never* leave home!)

Rudy (Keshia Knight Pulliam), as the littlest Huxtable, was the darling of the first season. Unbearably cute, she is a wonderful foil for her bemused, indulgent father. When her pet goldfish dies, she is heartbroken. Cliff, progressive father that he is, decides to hold a funeral in the bathroom. It is a full-dress affair, with everyone in black. As Cliff pronounces a poignant eulogy, he finds his shirt repeatedly yanked by Rudy. "What is it, dear?" "I want to watch TV." "But we're not

Cliff and Clair Huxtable (Phylicia Rashad) flank their children (from left) Theo (Malcolm-Jamal Warner), Vanessa (Tempestt Bledsoe), Sondra (Sabrina Le Beauf), and Rudy (Keshia Knight Pulliam). Seated is Sondra's fiancé, Elvin Tibideaux (Geoffrey Owens).

After twenty years of marriage, is it possible any two adults could be as goofy about each other as Cliff and Clair Huxtable? Here they enjoy a private, at-home cheek-to-cheek on the night of son Theo's senior dance, in the episode, "The Prom," from 1988.

In this episode from 1984, fourteen-year-old son Theo tries to convince his dad that his poor grades don't necessarily mean a bleak future. Cliff sets Theo straight with a simple economics lesson using Monopoly money and common sense. (A few years later it is revealed Theo's bad report cards came from a learning disability, dyslexia.)

LISA BONET:
THE *COSBY* KID AS REBEL

Rocketed to stardom in 1984 at the age of sixteen, as one of the *Cosby* kids, Lisa Bonet seemed to always play against the squeaky-clean image of the show. Like her headstrong character, Denise, Lisa marched to a different drummer.

There was her controversial choice of her post-*Cosby* movie role, a Voodoo devotee in 1987's *Angel Heart*. The part included a nude love scene with Mickey Rourke, although she insists that a body double was used. But no stand-in was used when Lisa posed topless for Andy Warhol's *Interview* magazine that same year, followed by another sultry shot in *Rolling Stone*.

Then came "Bad Times at Hillman College," as her first year on *A Different World* might have been called. Having been handed the starring role by Bill Cosby in this *Cosby* spin-off, she seemed to squander the opportunity with a lackluster performance. The then-unknown Jasmine Guy (Whitley) stole the show, and Lisa dropped out to have a baby with musician husband Lenny Kravitz. She returned to the *Cosby* fold in 1989, provoking an item in *TV Guide* with the unsympathetic title: "Denise is back—but why?"

Although her character was no longer a "flake," rumors of her being a backstage "problem child" on *Cosby* continued to circulate. At the end of the 1990–91 season, her contract was not renewed.

finished." "I want to watch TV." Soon the whole bathroom clears, and the poor goldfish gets an unceremonial flush down the toilet.

Then there was the time Cliff took Rudy and four of her friends to their first fancy restaurant. In mock seriousness, Cliff lays down the first rule: "We will not act like heathens." "No heathens!" the kids repeat. "And no mad dogs when the bread comes." The kids promise—and then act like mad dogs.

A watching waiter catches the spirit of the moment. "Don't you ever feed these kids?"

One little girl has two front teeth missing. "You can't have anything to eat," Cliff pronounces, scanning her, "because you haven't got any teeth."

As the kids squeal and squirm, the salad comes. One girl cannot eat beets "or my eyes will swell shut." She shows Cliff a list of other allergic reactions. Turning to another, he asks, "Do you have a list?" "No, but I can't have olives...But I feel alright so far." "Okay, but if you feel the olives kick in later, let me know." (This is one of the few times Dr. Heathcliff Huxtable, obstetrician, offers future medical assistance. Magically, he never gets calls in the middle of the night from women in labor.)

Despite the fine fare available, the kids order hamburgers but are disappointed when they come. "They're too big." "There are no buns." Cliff is reduced to ordering fast food from Circus Burgers next door. He comes home with two Circus Burger balloons tied to his ears, and the uneaten restaurant burgers in a paper bag. After giving them to son Theo, who disappears into the kitchen, Cliff removes his coat and follows. "Do you love your father?" "Yes." "If you really love him, can he have a burger?" "I can't. I ate them." "You ate four burgers in forty seconds?" "Yeah. But, Dad, I still love you." "Thank you, son." "And one more thing." "Yes?" "Burrrrrp!"

This is *Cosby* at its best, getting the most laughs out of the thinnest of plots. The wild energy of youth, and the voracious appetite of one teenager, are satirized, but in an affectionate way. No one's feelings are hurt, not even when Theo burps in his Dad's face.

By making Heathcliff as puckish and adorable as his youngest daughter, Bill Cosby has opened up the lines of communication between generations. In fact he never talks down to his children. Even if they let their impulses get the better of them most of the time, he still treats them as responsible and rational.

Second-youngest child is Vanessa (Tempestt Bledsoe). Self-possessed and not at all awkward for her age, this junior high schooler is the household's chatterbox and Little Miss Know-It-All. When Cliff challenges her to read a book instead of "going to the mall," she outmaneuvers him. "Malls have nothing to do with the intellect," says Vanessa. "I go there to relax." "And meet boys," prompts Cliff. "No doubt about it. Denise married a boy. Sondra married a boy. I hope to be married but if I

It's time for Cliff and daughter Rudy to kiss and make up, while mother Clair looks on. Keshia Knight Pulliam (Rudy) says, "Rudy is very different from me. She gets into a lot of mischief like cutting pictures out of her dad's encyclopedia. I wouldn't dare do something like that at home."

don't go out and meet boys I may spend the rest of my life in this house." Bested by this Philadelphia lawyer, Cliff mutters, "Go to the mall."

Theo (Malcolm-Jamal Warner) is by far the most engaging of the children, and the light of his father's eyes. (The character is based on Cosby's real-life son, Ennis.) He has the usual teen male preoccupations: being stylish to impress the girls, and conning Dad for cash. Dad, however, knows all the scams.

When Theo tries to get his college expenses in

advance (tuition plus "incidentals"), Cliff tells him the family can't afford it. There are always hidden college costs, he explains, citing the extra money he spends for Theo's older sisters Denise and Sondra (Sabrina LeBeauf). They're the "askadentals," he continues, the money you ask your parents for after you squander your "incidentals."

Another time, Theo announces he will not be attending college, but plans to be an "ordinary" person getting "ordinary" wages. Cliff and wife Clair agree now is the time to teach him about the cost of living. They calmly figure out what Theo's hypothetical salary might be, and when he returns home that evening, they give it to him in play money. The Huxtable residence has now become the Real World Apartments. Cliff introduces himself as Harley Weewax, the super, and asks for a month's rent and one month's security. Clair is introduced as Millie Farquhar, who runs the Chuckwagon Restaurant (otherwise known as the Huxtable kitchen). Even Rudy joins in as the very businesslike Mrs. Griswold, the building owner, complete with pince-nez. By the time the evening ends, the bare necessities of life have consumed Theo's "ordinary" income, and a lesson has been learned.

Let's face it, The Cosby Show *would be more appropriately named* Bringing Up Daddy. *After all, this Daddy is more cute and cuddly than all his kids, plus their friends, combined. In this scene, big kid Cliff leads a lot of little "heathens" to luncheon in a fancy restaurant, where they all order fast food burgers.*

But money is still a divisive issue as when Cliff asks Theo to babysit for Rudy. Instead of doing the right thing, Theo asks, "How much does it pay?" Doing his famous slow burn, Cliff decides to tell Theo a parable. Years ago there was a farmer who told his son that there was plowing to do. His son asked, "How much does it pay?" So the farmer went off, got the plow, "and ran it over his son...."

But Cliff never stays angry at Theo for long. You just can't help liking the kid. There is a special sparkle in their scenes together. In one episode, they even created the Huxtable Men's Club so that Cliff could eat a hoagie sandwich—one of the foods the cholesterol-conscious Clair had forbidden. The club rules were as follows: "One— Whatever we eat remains a secret. Two—If you can find a good woman to be with, the meeting is adjourned. Three—If you can get rid of the other members, you can have all the hoagies for yourself."

Cosby emphasizes this mischievous, never-quite-grown-up quality in Cliff. In many ways, Clair plays mother to Cliff's bad boy. She smiles and shakes her head when he insists on fixing the dishwasher when she knows he can't fix things. She wants him to eat healthy foods and must scold him when he tries to scarf down a spoonful of ice cream or a piece of cake. (Long before Roseanne and Dan Conner on *Roseanne* were talking dirty to each other, Cliff and Clair Huxtable were playing footsy in bed, and nibbling on each other's earlobes. They are so cute doing it, and work so hard to keep the romance in their marriage, that we don't feel embarrassed watching them. After forty years of TV sitcoms, Mother and Father were finally openly being sexy.)

In one of the show's funniest episodes, Theo decides to join the fad for earrings and has his ear pierced. Entering his residence with a manful strut, he announces, "When people look at this, they'll know they're dealing with a man!" Older sister Denise thinks otherwise. What she sees is a young boy with an impending ear infection.

When Cliff comes home, Theo's manliness deserts him. He rushes to his room. Dad soon finds his son on the bed, bopping to music and wearing large earphones. He turns off the juice, forcing Theo to abandon his camouflage. They sit side by side, with Theo careful to keep his swollen ear away from Dad's sight. When Cliff leans forward to look at him, Theo leans forward too. When Cliff leans back, Theo leans back. In a swaying, synchronized ballet, they play cat and mouse until Theo is caught red-eared, as it were. "Have you been tagged by the Wildlife Federation?" smirks Cliff.

But Cliff's laughs at Theo's expense are short-lived. Grandpa Huxtable has come by. And in a scene repeated many times, with variations, we learn how foolishly Cliff acted when he was Theo's age. When Cliff was fifteen, Grandpa explains, he and his friend Lex decided they'd straighten their hair to impress some girls. But since they had no money, they concocted a mixture of potato peels, corn syrup, and nitroglycerine. The potion left Cliff with scorched hair, nearly bald.

THEO: You burned off all the hair on your

All of five years old in 1984, Cosby's premiere year, Keshia Knight Pulliam became an audience favorite as Rudy, the most adorable Huxtable (after Bill Cosby himself, that is!). Seven years later, her place in the cuteness hierarchy has been taken by Raven-Symone, who joined the cast as Olivia in 1989.

head for Mom?
CLIFF: (trying to stop his son) Someday you're going to need some money…
DENISE: You men are crazy.
CLIFF: But we always get our women.
CLAIR: Not because of the things you do but in spite of them!

(In 1987, Bill Cosby allowed Malcolm-Jamal Warner to wear a small stud, barely visible, in his left ear lobe. The following season, Cosby gave way again as Warner appeared with a carefully cultivated mustache and a small "tail" of hair at the nape of his neck.)

Another time, Theo spends a small fortune on a designer shirt that he simply must have. Dad, of course, must shell out the bucks. "How much?" he demands. Theo tries to impress with labels. "It's a Gordon Gartrell!" But Dad is relentless. "How much?" "With quality like that you have to pay more!" "How much?" Theo finally breaks down. "Ninety-five dollars." Cliff, laughing disdainfully, says, "Do you want to trade your *room* for that shirt?" (Harley Weewax couldn't have said it better.)

But Theo isn't the only teenage spendthrift. Denise, the family's resident flake and clothes-

Cliff's trademark cute expression (pursed-lip smile and coy eye-roll) are mimicked by his two daughters, Denise (Lisa Bonet) and Vanessa (Tempestt Bledsoe, right), as they try to psych their father up for a foot race against an old college sports rival, in this scene from 1986. Bill Cosby's real-life career as a college athlete at Temple U. forms the basis of many sports-related Cosby *storylines. (He ran in track and played basketball and football.)*

horse (her wardrobe contains baggy harem pants and a cloche hat), runs afoul of Mom when she insists, a little too vehemently, that it's *her* money in *her* bank account and she can spent it on whatever she pleases (a car). After all, "Isn't this America?"

Clair coldly glares at her daughter: "If you ever take that attitude again, you can take all that money and go *discover* America!"

Clair, who erupts in righteous fury from time to time, is the perfect counterpoint to the laid-back Cliff. Clair's frosty look can freeze-dry any miscreant in his tracks, whether it be a disrespectful child, a sexist son-in-law, or her own misbehaving husband.

When eldest daughter Sondra became involved with husband-to-be Elvin (Geoffrey Owens), the show turned its cheerful eye on the battle of the sexes. Elvin has the misfortune to wonder aloud why Clair bothers to work (she's a partner in a law firm), when a woman's duty is clearly to stay at home. By the time Clair has finished straightening him out, Elvin is ready to park himself in the kitchen, wear an apron, and dry dishes.

Clair Huxtable is indeed a Supermom. She does most of the cooking and most of the disciplining, and has a flourishing career as a lawyer to boot. When there is a family disagreement, she's been known to question the various members, as though she were in court. Sometimes, she conducts mock trials, assigning her children various roles as attorneys, witnesses, and jury. That's not to say that she is starchy and humorless. She's sensuous and fun-loving as well. But for many TV-viewing Moms, she's a tough act to follow.

The rest of the Huxtable clan has drawn fire for much the same reason: They're seen as being too "perfect." African-American social critics, in particular, complain that the show is not "black" enough, that the family lives too well and is thus not representative. (In fact an average of $3,000 per

Cliff (Bill Cosby) shows son Theo (Malcolm-Jamal Warner) a few slick basketball moves in this moment from 1985. Away from the show, Warner presented a thoughtful, personable image, and penned a teen advice book, Theo and Me: Growing Up Okay *in 1988 for E.P. Dutton. Although one storyline poked fun at Theo for trying to wear an earring, Cosby permitted Warner a small stud in his left ear in 1987.*

episode was spent on clothes for the characters by Sarah Lemire, the show's costume designer, according to *TV Guide*. And Bill Cosby's eye-catching knits—lambasted by celebrity fashion expert Mr. Blackwell as "psychedlic ski sweaters"—can run as high as $500 apiece.) Clearly, the Huxtables are more than middle class, with the two well-adjusted parents highly paid professionals.

As for the complaint that they aren't "black" enough, Cosby snaps, "Which is to say that Cliff isn't poor and doesn't go around exchanging high fives each time he delivers a baby…."

The Huxtables' ethnic pride is shown in subtle ways, he contends, as when Cliff and Clair decide to buy a painting by a famous black artist, or when they help Theo do his history homework by relating their personal memories of the march on Washington. (And all *Cosby* scripts are reviewed by African-American psychiatrist Alvin Poussaint to assure their "authenticity.")

More important than their social class, says Cosby, are the Huxtables' values. They are the same as those for most Americans, and they are spotlighted so the message is crystal clear. The formulaic hard work equals good grades is impressed on Theo, for example, who is the family's underachiever. And when Denise spends her last night before going to college with a group of friends, the family pretends disinterest in her leave-taking, reinstructing her as to where her loyalties should lie.

All this may not be real-life, but it is how we would like family life to be—and how we remember it from the TV of the fifties. A warm and wise father; a strong, competent mother; and kids ready to take guidance.

Perhaps in answer to some of the criticisms, in the past few seasons the Huxtables have become more human. Clair now complains of fatigue and even loses her fabled composure, calling Rudy "raggedy" and Vanessa "a fool." The kids, too, have become more recognizable as rambunctious adolescents. In describing her day to Cliff, Clair relates, "Rudy threw Vanessa's book out of the window, and Vanessa tried to throw Rudy out of the window…."

The one element of *Cosby* that needs no change is Heathcliff Huxtable himself. He is a gem of a

With one stroke of the scriptwriters' pen, the show upgraded Denise's image from resident flake and college drop-out to responsible stepmother and wife. Lisa Bonet, as Denise, returned to Cosby *after one year in her own* Cosby *spin-off,* A Different World *(1978–88), and a year off to have a baby with rock superstar and husband Lenny Kravitz. Here is the happy sitcom family: Denise, husband Martin Kendall (Joseph C. Phillips), and Olivia (Raven-Symone).*

comic creation, with all the sparkling facets of his creator.

Cosby uses his full repertoire of facial expressions and postures, his mastery of the double and triple take and slow burn, to milk laughs. But beyond these skills he has conjured up an endearing and memorable character, a quirky, old-fashioned guy who loves his kids, his wife, and his collection of rare jazz albums. (In his youth, Cosby had been in a jazz band, and he was delighted to welcome, as guest stars on two separate episodes the great Dizzy Gillespie and pop star Stevie Wonder.)

Cliff can usually match any cut he hears to the album it came from, and give the artist, label, and date of recording. And the lip-syncing of his family to songs by Ray Charles and others are comic classics. However, when Denise says his old-fashioned dancing isn't "cool," Cliff lets go this diatribe on breakdancing: "They get a piece of cardboard, spin on their head, neck, and chin, and call that dancing?" In his day it was known as "having a fit."

Cliff likes to assume the identify of favorite stars from old movies from time to time. When he sees Clair working in the backyard garden, planting veggies, he feels like Gary Cooper "looking out over the back forty."

And as a man with three teen daughters, he likes to keep an eye on the men they date. He feels

(continued on page 219)

PROFILE:
THE COS

From Fat Albert and friends to the Huxtable family, Bill Cosby has used his own experiences and observations as the foundation of his comedy.

Like Dr. Heathcliff Huxtable, he is married to a beautiful, stylish woman (Camille Hanks), and they have four daughters (Erika, Erinn, Ensa, and Evin) and one son (Ennis).

Cliff's memories of his stern upbringing and his philosophy of childrearing mimic Cosby's. Heathcliff: "All [my mother] wanted was a stick, and she asked God to give her the strength to hit me into Kingdom Come…" (Cosby credits his parents' strictness with keeping him out of trouble on Philadelphia's mean streets.) As a parent, Bill Cosby wants to be "hip, have compassion, handle all situations." And through his character as Cliff, he can be Superdad. But in real life, he once had to take a "stick" to his son, who had lied. And he recalls that after one of his daughters amassed over $1,000 in parking tickets, he wanted to have her declared "legally stupid." "One of the things you learn when you become a parent," went one of his old routines, "is the horrible thought and the reality that your children will be your children for the rest of your life! That's why there's death."

Funny stuff. And true.

In fact, Bill Cosby is a TV demographer's dream: a nonthreatening individual who crosses all age, sex, and racial lines in his appeal. He is also a world-class entertainer whose fortune numbers in the tens if not hundreds of millions of dollars, and a comic with more gold and platinum comedy albums than anyone else.

A native of Philadelphia, he played basketball in Philly playgrounds. He attended his hometown school, Temple University, on a track scholarship, earning extra money as a bartender at student parties. Although he dreamed of teaching, he quit college to pursue another ambition. He went to New York City to try out his stand-up comedy routines at little cafes in Greenwich Village like the Gaslight Coffee House in the early sixties. He quickly won a following, and a few months later made his first appearance on *The Tonight Show.* From this and other appearances his career was launched.

Icy professionalism is the look the Cos sought to project as secret agent Alexander Scott in TV's I Spy *adventure series of 1965–68, which earned him two Emmys as Best Actor in a Drama. For* The Cosby Show *on the other hand, he firmly rejected any suggestion that he even be nominated for an Emmy.*

No, it isn't Santa Cos, but Cos from the "2nd Bill Cosby Special" of 1969, wherein he played the bearded Biblical hero, Noah, as (according to the 1969 press release) "ark builder, animal cupid and friend to Bill Cosby."

217

In 1966, he won a role as costar of the espionage action series, *I Spy*, for which he won two back-to-back Emmys as Best Actor in a Dramatic Series (1966–67 and 1967–68). But his family comedy series, *The Bill Cosby Show*, (1969–71) and his comedy-variety show, *Cos* (1976), were Nielsen flops. When he was set to do another television series in the early eighties, he first proposed a detective show, modeled on *Columbo*, but with a difference. This time the sleuth would be teamed with a girlfriend who was strong, independent, and an equal partner. (Shades of the soon-to-be created Clair Huxtable.) When NBC passed, Cosby convinced programming chief Brandon Tartikoff to let him rework his idea. Now his creation was to be a chauffeur. The network asked him to take a step up in class, so he became Dr. Huxtable, an obstetrician-gynecologist.

There were other issues on which Cosby wouldn't budge, however. It was to be *his* show, and he would control its content and direction. All the laughs were to be based on relationships, not plot gimmicks. "My humor isn't jokes," he once told an interviewer. "I tell stories and play the characters in the stories." And on *Cosby*, the stories would do more than amuse. His strong desire to teach (he once declared he was ready to leave show business to become a teacher in the inner city) made him scrutinize every script. His high standards wore down more than one writer. Several quit before the first half-dozen episodes were even completed.

Cosby originally set his sights on a career teaching physical education. In fact, on his first sitcom, 1969's *The Bill Cosby Show*, he played a high school phys ed teacher, Chet Kincaid. By 1977, he realized a lifelong dream when he was awarded a doctorate in education from the University of Massachusetts at Amherst for a 242-page dissertation on the use of Fat Albert and the Cosby Kids as an elementary school teaching aid. (That's why one of *The Cosby Show*'s credits identifies him as "Dr. William Cosby, Jr." He's also listed four other times in the credits: as star, coproducer, executive consultant, and coauthor of the theme music.)

Since his imprint is everywhere, he finds himself having to personally answer all the criticisms of the show's detractors. This has led to charges that he is thin-skinned, not to say irritable, arrogant, and rude.

Looking like some mad Hawaiian poker player, Cliff puts on display all the dumb presents his kids gave him for Father's Day. "Next time, give it a little more thought!" he pleads, in this December 1984 episode.

> When Fox Network threw down the gauntlet, however, challenging *Cosby* by scheduling the hot animated series, *The Simpsons,* in the same time slot, the Cos was insousciant. He let Raven-Symone (Olivia) appear in one of her scenes wearing a Bart Simpson mask. The audience roared.
>
> As the show-business saying goes, you have to have a healthy ego to survive. And Bill Cosby has flourished.

(continued from page 215)

protective toward them, like "Old Yeller." "Boys come and I bark," he explains to Clair. "Some are good, some are bad, but that's my job. I'm Old Yeller." "Cliff." "What?" "In that movie they shot Old Yeller."

As an ex-college athlete and avid sportsman, Cosby can do physical schtick, too. When Elvin quits college to open The Wilderness Store, Cliff and Clair agree to help test his camping equipment. They lie in bed in their room, encased in sleeping bags, with the window wide open (they refused to sleep in the backyard). When Cliff hears Nature's call, he finds his zipper is stuck. Since Clair refuses to come out of her own warm coccoon to help, Cliff must slip off the bed and wriggle like an inchworm into the bathroom.

Elvin, of course, eventually marries Sondra and resumes his studies. He learns to admire his father-in-law and calls him "Sir." On the night Sondra gives birth to their twins, Elvin has his first man-to-man talk with Cliff. "I've thought of you as the perfect father. I guess I shouldn't say that I've heard what your kids say behind your back." "What?" says Cliff, getting a little tense. "Oh, little things. You're stubborn. You'll never admit to a mistake. You're tight with money." Cliff, annoyed, snaps, "Alright, that's enough!"

But Cliff can rest easy. He has no real reason to be upset. His vision of life—the mainstream, upwardly mobile road to success—has prevailed. All the youngsters that strayed are back in the Huxtable fold and doing fine. Even that flake Denise, who dropped out of college after one year, returned from Africa in 1989 with a naval officer husband and an adorable, four-year-old stepdaughter, Olivia, in tow.

CAST LIST

FAMILY: The Huxtables

MEMBERS:

Dr. Heathcliff Huxtable	**Bill Cosby**
Clair Huxtable	**Phylicia Rashad**
Sondra Huxtable Tibideaux	**Sabrina Le Beauf**
Denise Huxtable Kendall (1984–87, 1989–91)	**Lisa Bonet**
Theo Huxtable . . .	**Malcolm-Jamal Warner**
Vanessa Huxtable	**Tempestt Bledsoe**
Rudy Huxtable	**Keshia Knight Pulliam**
Elvin Tibideaux (1986–)	**Geoffrey Owens**
Anna Huxtable	**Clarice Taylor**
Russell Huxtable	**Earle Hyman**
Olivia Kendall (1989–) . .	**Raven-Symone**
Lt. Martin Kendall (1989–)	**Joseph C. Phillips**

THEME SONG: **Bill Cosby and Stu Gardner**
TIMEFRAME: **1984—**
NETWORK: **NBC**
ADDRESS: **Brooklyn Heights New York City**

GREAT PERFORMANCES

(Bill Cosby consistently refused to allow himself to be put into competition for the Emmy)

A miraculous transformation you say?

Having seen one Heathcliff Huxtable, father, in action, we are believers.

MARRIED...WITH CHILDREN

What this? Al Bundy (Ed O'Neill) cuddling up to sex-driven wife Peg on the sofa! He usually tries to keep her at arm's length.

The premiere of *Married ...With Children* signaled a fresh and irreverent view of family life. The word FAMILY appears to the familiar strains of the Sinatra recording of "Love and Marriage." We see scenes of the Bundy household. Then, as the credits continue to flash onscreen, the theme music stops abruptly. The words WITH CHILDREN are stamped across MARRIED, the color a bilious green, and that green begins to run. Clearly, something has gone bad in the Bundy family. They are grotesques; a mixture of *The Munsters* and *Long Day's Journey Into Night*. A sitcom as it might have been written by the Sex Pistols.

Peg (Katey Sagal), the wife, looks like a refugee from the B-52s. All teased, fifties-style hairdo, a too-tight top, and toreador-style pants, she teeters on high heels as she walks with tiny, mincing steps, clasping her ever-present emery board. When she wants something from her husband, she purrs and wheedles, in the best pre-liberation fashion. And what she wants most of all is sex.

Al (Ed O'Neill), her disgusted-looking husband, isn't interested. He's too tired, having spent an unpleasant day sniffing other people's feet at his job as a shoe salesman. What he wants most is to be left alone.

Al and Peg Bundy are a blue-collar couple whose best days are behind them—days which were probably never that great to begin with. Fresh out of high school, they bought the American Dream: marriage, two kids, a house of their own, a dog, a car. Now they are stuck with a dream gone stale. To liven things up they insultingly poke holes into each other's illusions, and into ours as well. Therein lies the charm of *Married...With Children*, a crude, bracing antidote to *Cosby*-style fantasy.

Take Al and Peg's attitude toward their kids, Kelly and Bud. They realize they have inherited the "Bundy Curse," meaning that they will fail in whatever they try. Therefore the youngsters are tolerated with a minimum of fuss and bother. For their kids' annual school dental check-up, Al and Peg shine flashlights in their mouths. "Go upstairs," Kelly and Bud are told. "We'll forge your dental records later."

There are moments, however, when the kids' presence seems genuinely welcomed. When they're in the same room as Daddy, he uses them as a shield against Mommy's advances. Which brings

The Bundy Bunch includes the family pet, Buck (played by Michael, a five-year-old French sheepdog), probably the only nonhuman sitcom character to have his own stories and dialogue.

us to one of the show's favorite subjects: sex. *Married...With Children* is adult comedy with a vengeance.

Its studio audience seems to be drawn from the same young, "hip" pool as *The Arsenio Hall Show*, "yawping" it up at anything they perceive as lewd or suggestive. And there is plenty of that.

In one episode, titled "Her Cups Runneth Over," the story centered on Peg's need of a new bra, and it included a shot of a woman divesting herself of same (although with her back turned), plus a raunchy reference to vibrators (Peg to Al: "If you had what other men have, I wouldn't need batteries").

Marcy has her money at the ready to tip this male stripper the way male strippers like to be tipped, while Peg Bundy cops a feel. Married...With Children *is adult comedy with a vengeance.*

This was too much for Terry Rakolta, a concerned Detroit housewife and mother. She started a letter-writing campaign and appeared on several national talk shows, urging viewers to boycott *Married.* Some of the series' advertisers were scared off. The *New York Times* saw fit to run a front page story on the brouhaha, and other commentators entered the fray. The end result was little more than a slap on the wrist for the show's creators, Ron Leavitt and Michael G. Moye, and probably even a bigger audience. The producers forced The Fox Network, of which *Married* quickly became the centerpiece, to shelve an even raunchier episode, titled, "I'll See You in Court," in which the Bundys and their next-door neighbors, Steve and Marcy Rhoades, sue a sleazy motel for secretly taping them having sex in their respective rooms. But *Married* continued to serve up saucy scripts, with Leavitt and Moye given as much freedom as any creative team working in commercial television. Fox knew that to gut the show of its blazing gonads altogether would risk losing their audience.

But how much reliance on sex-for-humor is too much? Take the case of the nubile Christina Applegate. A mouth-watering sight in tank top, short skirt and spandex, she plays Kelly Bundy, the high school slut and self-proclaimed "dumbest girl in America." The camera loses no opportunity to linger on her physical charms, as when she improbably won a job as "weather girl" on a local news show, and kept dropping the chalk so she'd have to bend over and pick it up. Another time, Kelly was asked to do an interpretive dance in a school production. Although her dance talents were weak, her sense of rhythm was excellent, and her onstage writhings so aroused the audience of watching parents there was practically an orgy right on the auditorium floor. "She's our best student," sighed one flushed teacher.

Unfortunately, by making Miss Applegate's character only interested in one thing, the show squanders other opportunities for comedy. It is to the young actress's credit that she makes lusty Kelly seem equally innocent and sympathetic—a girl who just wants attention.

According to Applegate, some fans refer to her as "the blonde neutron bomb," which she finds "demeaning." When Fox sent her on the TV talk show circuit to promote *Married,* she was careful to distance herself from her character. She bases Kelly on a species of L.A. female she calls "the rock bimbo," whose greatest aspiration in life is to say, "I'm with the band." But equally demeaning to Miss Applegate—though an excellent source of humor for *Married*—must be Kelly's stupidity. Kelly makes *Family Ties*'s Mallory look like a rocket scientist. When younger brother Bud (David Faustino) tries to help her with her history homework, poor Kelly thinks Thomas Jefferson is one of the characters on *The Jeffersons.* She's not very hip about astrology either. "My birthday's in February," Kelly announces. "I'm an Aquarium." To which Bud replies, "Yes, an empty one."

And again, doing her homework, Kelly asks Bud, "What goes quack?"

Yes, quite an airhead.

Yet, for all his alleged intelligence, brother Bud isn't much of a character either. When he's not scouting through his father's impressive collection of *Playboy,* he's busy drilling a hole in the garage wall to spy on the sexy houseguest (a French exchange student), or trying to scam some money out of his Dad. His sister refers to him, disdainfully, as "Spud." And, like his sister, he remains basically one-dimensional with little to do compared with the leads, Katey Sagal (Peg) and Ed O'Neill (Al).

These two aren't exactly the most romantic couple in the world. They're both couch potatoes. Peg spends the day watching TV and eating chocolates. When Al comes home, he takes over, staring at the tube with one hand tucked into his pants, scratching. The engagement ring Peg still wears implies, "Glass is forever."

In the first season, we meet the Bundys' neighbors, Steve and Marcy, kissy-poo newlyweds, hence objects of pity. They haven't the first idea what marriage is all about. All their babbling about honesty, empathy, tenderness! Al and Peg know better. Marriage is war. Each side probes for weakness, hordes its ammunition. Truce comes only when it's time for food, sex, or sleep. (The Bundys' motto: "Anytime I can embarrass my spouse, it makes me feel better.") A few years later, Marcy finds out that Peg is right. Men are scum. Her husband Steve has left her. (Actor David Garrison

That's our Al, as usual picked clean by those free-spending vultures he calls a family.

Like all the Bundys, daughter Kelly is a caricature, the self-proclaimed "dumbest girl in America," and the "easiest" one at school. In Christina Applegate's capable hands, we also see the innocent and sympathetic side of Kelly.

Amanda Bearse and David Garrison as the cleancut preppy newlyweds, Marcy and Steve Rhoades, are the perfect comic foils for the bizarre Bundys.

was written out in January of 1990, to take a leave of absence, according to the show, so he could take the lead role in the Stephen Sondheim musical, *Merrily We Roll Along.*) His departure is in character for the dweeby Steve, who wants to become a park ranger.

This development allows the preppie Marcy (Amanda Bearse) to throw her Reeboks to the wind. She becomes the life of the office Christmas party, sitting on the Xerox machine, her skirt rucked up, as a male coworker eagerly passes out the resulting photocopies. Another time, she shows up at the Bundys trailing an ethnic-looking guy with open shirt and medallion, trying to prove she "can still get a man."

Peg knows all too well the depths to which wives must sink for a little attention. She wants to feel that she is still attractive, but when a Peeping Tom starts roaming the neighborhood and ogles everyone but her, she is frantic. What's wrong with me? she wonders. Al, sensing strong measures are needed, decides to play the peeper's role himself. As Peg sits, draped in her low-cut negligee, Al peers in gamely, only to be caught by the neighborhood patrol. The title of the episode? "Here's Looking at You, Kid."

DID AL STEAL LUCY'S "LOOK"?

There are may "looks" in an actor's repertoire of facial expressions. When *I Love Lucy* was setting the standards for television comedy on that infant medium in the 1950s, Lucille Ball honed a distinct look that came to be known as the "Spider." It is a grimace in which the upper lip would rise, exposing the canines. This usually occurred when something extremely distasteful was happening to Lucy, and it would be accompanied by a guttural noise.

If you watch Ed O'Neill as Al Bundy going through the extremely distasteful task of passing money over his shoulder to his assorted family including in the opening credit sequence, the family dog, you see Lucy's "Spider" look. The only thing missing is the guttural noise. O'Neill prefers the subtler approach of eyes narrowed darkly, and silence. It is a major expression of Al's, seen often, as with Lucy. Did he steal it?

In many ways *Married* resembles the so-called live-action cartoon series of the sixties, *The Munsters* and *The Addams Family*, in its freakish portrayal of human behavior. After all, a *real* person would never rope-tie and gag little kids in a shoe store on Christmas Eve, just to keep them quiet, as Al did. And who would believe a family that fights viciously over cooked meat at the dinner table unless that family is a cartoon?

Because of the cartoonish flavor of the show—it's been called a live-action *Simpsons*—the casting had to be impeccable. Only skillful actors can bring to life people who are essentially caricatures. That's what Ed O'Neill and Katey Sagal are able to do. (Doesn't Peg's tight outfit, and all her wriggling, remind you of Gomez's wife Morticia on *The Addams Family*?)

Katey Sagal grew up as a show-biz brat in the West Side of Los Angeles. Her father was film and TV director Boris Sagal, and her younger twin sisters, Jean and Liz, appeared in the short-lived 1984 comedy series, *Double Trouble*. (Their stepmother is Marge Champion.) Meanwhile, Katey was singing in various bands, and did backup work for Bob Dylan, Etta James, and Bette Midler (as one of the "flashy, trashy" Harlettes). Her work as the wisecracking, chain-smoking columnist on the ill-fated *Mary*, Mary Tyler Moore's comeback vehicle in 1986, caught the eye of some executives, and a year later she was offered her role on *Married*.

She thinks *Married* has the same importance, as a mold-breaker, as *All in the Family* did in its heyday. The only difference being that *Family* was very political, whereas *Married* ignores politics altogether, which is "very eighties."

Ed O'Neill grew up in Youngstown, Ohio, and aspired to be a professional athlete. He was a fifteenth round pick of the Pittsburgh Steelers football team, but was cut from the team during training camp. After working variously as a busboy, bellman, and social studies teacher, he got his first important acting job on Broadway, in *Knock Out*, a play about prizefighting. After two failed pilots, *Farrell for the People* (with Valerie Harper) and *Popeye Doyle*, he read for *Married* and won the role. "I hadn't thought of doing a sitcom," he admits, "until I read this script."

Part of the inspiration for his portrayal comes

Peg Bundy (Katey Sagal) looks sexy in her leopard-print leotard, while girlfriend Marcy (Amanda Bearse) is more subdued in her jogging outfit. Both are preparing to go to the health club. It remains a mystery why either one bothers to work out since their husbands don't pay them any attention!

from his Uncle, says ONeill. "The voice, the kind of way he talks, he's like Al in many ways. Except my Uncle is an Ohio Supreme Court judge."

He sees sourpuss Al as a "victim, in a way, of society, living a hand-to-mouth existence." Trading insults with his wife is "a way of coping with the situation." After all, couples can't love each other "twenty-four hours a day. They're out of love a lot. And our show is honest about that."

Now that blue-collar men and women have become the "in" group of the nineties (as yuppies were in the eighties), we can understand the reason: diminished expectations. When Peg tries to push the idea of graduating from high school on Kelly, because it's important for her future, and then says, "Who am I trying to kid?" she is saying in exaggerated form what many people are feeling. Will anything that anyone does really make a difference? Isn't the idea of "bettering oneself" a cruel delusion? That seems to be the message of *The Simpsons* and *Roseanne,* two shows whose blue-collar cynicism was trailblazed by *Married.*

The Fox show, is, of course, entertainment and not social commentary. Perhaps its most important contribution is the acceptance by mainstream audiences everywhere of its bawdy, naughty humor. Lines like Peg's description of sex with Al ("My thirty-second trip to the moon") would have been considered too provocative for Mr. and Mrs. Average TV Viewer, until *Married* proved otherwise.

It wasn't looking for new comedy horizons that led Fox to permit this kind of explicit pseudo-smutty humor, however. Fox began in 1987 promising "hip" programming, and then delivering the same tired old network formula: *Werewolf* (Great idea! Teenage wolfman!), *The Dirty Dozen* (Great idea! Teenage guerrillas!), *21 Jump Street* (well, you get the idea). None of these was capturing the vaunted eighteen to thirty-five crowd. The only thing with a little sparkle on its schedule was *Married...With Children,* an instant hit. People who saw the premier were impressed enough to talk to their schoolmates/colleagues the next day. It was enough to get Fox airborne.

Its creators, Leavitt and Moye, came with impressive TV resumés *(The Jeffersons, Happy Days, Laverne & Shirley).* It is to their credit that they didn't let cautious Fox executives dilute their frothy recipe for success. The brass wanted "a few thousand" changes in the pilot, Leavitt recalls, but he and his partner dug in their heels. Finally, a compromise was reached. In order that all of America not be offended simultaneously, they agreed to a tamer version of the script with the understanding they would have free rein afterward. Fox agreed—but both sides knew there would be future battles.

When those are over, one thing will remain. The knowledge that since that night in 1987 when the rambunctious Bundys first burst into our living rooms, American television has never been quite the same.

CAST LIST

FAMILY: The Bundys

MEMBERS:

Al Bundy	**Ed O'Neill**
Peg Bundy	**Katey Sagal**
Kelly Bundy	**Christina Applegate**
Bud Bundy	**David Faustino**

SIGNIFICANT OTHERS:

Steve Rhoades (1987–90)	**David Garrison**
Marcy Rhoades	**Amanda Bearse**

THEME SONG: **"Love and Marriage" by Sammy Cahn and James Van Heusen**
TIMEFRAME: **1987–**
NETWORK: **Fox**
ADDRESS: **Chicago, Illinois**

The Conner clan, from left: Aunt Jackie (Laurie Metcalf), Becky Conner (Lecy Goranson), Darlene Conner (Sara Gilbert), Roseanne Conner (Roseanne Barr), Dan "D.J." Conner, Jr. (Michael Fishman), and Dan Conner (John Goodman).

The Conner family lives in the small town of Lanlord, on the working-class side of the tracks. Their tract house, at the corner of Third and Delaware Streets, has a cozy, lived-in look. Pillows, toys, discarded socks, and sneakers are strewn about as befits a house with three adolescents living in it. The kids include the eldest, Becky, a high schooler; the middle child, Darlene, whose smart-mouthed personality is most like Mom's; and the baby boy of the family, D. J. They're a boisterous bunch, and the zingers fly back and forth, child to child and child to parent. The kids feel comfortable doing this because their parents do it to each other. When Roseanne calls Dan "Butthead," it's just the Conner way of showing affection. It is also done for entertainment and to blow off steam, with no harm meant. They are an immensely likable group.

Hard-hat husband Dan is a big but cuddly bear of a man, roly-poly Roseanne's high school sweetheart. He rode a motorcycle once when they were both rebellious outsiders. Now that they have kids they worry about acting too much like their own parents. "Didn't we vow to be hipper than that?" asks Dan. They treat the kids more like midget adults. And like real kids everywhere, their mouths are sometimes too clever for their own good. Roseanne is not amused when Darlene refers to her as "Big R."

Of course, Roseanne loves to tease the kids, too. Darlene is put into a dither when Mom explains she named her after a Mouseketeer. To sister Jackie, Roseanne reveals why she and Dan are always strapped for cash: "We live with three little moochers who suck us dry." And when Jackie agrees to keep an eye on the kids for the evening, Roseanne calls it "monster patrol." Watching the kids play "Dirty Scrabble," Roseanne and Dan don't bat an eye. Perhaps letting the kids have lots of leeway is a way of feeling young again themselves.

Dan and Roseanne love each other, but there is an undercurrent of unrest and dissatisfaction, not with one another, but with the institution of marriage itself. It seems, somehow, unnatural. It robs people of their youth and freedom.

They long for the old days when they could just jump on Dan's motorcycle and ride. All this is brought painfully home to them as Dan sits, comatose, in front of the TV, clutching a can of beer. In the distance is the rumble of a big bike. Suddenly, there is a knock on the door. It is a friend and fellow biker they haven't seen in twenty years. He is still riding, while Dan's machine lies disassembled and gathering dust in the garage. Roseanne tells Jackie what the lure of a man on a bike is: "Danger, freedom, sex, all in one." But now that is just a memory. "We used to be Dan and Roseanne," she laments. "Now we're the Conners." Dan tries to make excuses as to the neglect of his bike. They have kids now, bills and a mortgage to pay. Then he admits the real reason: "I caved." (The episode does end on an upbeat note, however, as Dan vows to rebuild his bike.)

Roseanne's ascendancy was comet-like (it premiered in the Number Five spot in the Nielsens), and its star's ranking as the highest Q-rated actress* in television tied her for first place with Estelle Getty of *The Golden Girls*. But despite this fast success, not all reaction to the show was glowing. Some viewers were disturbed by a meanness of spirit, even a nastiness, in some episodes. Perhaps *Roseanne*'s sarcasm seemed to cut too deeply at times but there were other viewers who found Barr's candor refreshing. "She says all the nasty things we have on our minds to say to our husbands, but are afraid to say," one enthusiastic supporter told a TV reporter.

And all was not sweetness and light in the second season when Roseanne suddenly finds herself unemployed after eleven years at the local plastics factory. It was a place where management would begrudge its workers two minutes off the assembly line to make a phone call home to the kids. It was this slave-driving attitude that led Roseanne to quit, proudly taking her walking papers and several colleagues with her (including her sister Jackie and her flaky friend Crystal). Her pals quickly found gainful employment. What followed for Roseanne was a succession of Jobs From Hell, as she tried her hand at telemarketing, taking

Laurie Metcalf, who plays Jackie, is liked by everyone backstage because she is a total professional and a warm personality. Her character is based on Roseanne's real-life sister, Geraldine.

fast-food orders, and being a Girl Friday. It was a rough time for Roseanne. She knew the family needed a second income desperately, but she would not suffer to work for fools (like the self-important twerp at the burger joint). After all, Roseanne was still Roseanne!

Finally, she found a congenial place. She became Sweeper of Fallen Hair at a beauty parlor (eventually to be promoted to Shampooer of Hair). This new setting prompted a new, shorter hairstyle for the star, and gave her a chance to dish with the other girls in the parlor. After Dan finds her minuscule rise in rank a cause for amusement, she turns on him. "Yes, this job is degrading. But when the people you work with treat you with respect, you forget that it's degrading." The message in this storyline was simple: that even the humblest jobs have dignity. A heartfelt sentiment, it would seem, from a woman for whom work has been the road to self-affirmation.

Like Bill Cosby, Roseanne Barr began her show business career as a stand-up comic. And as with

*In TV jargon, likability as well as recognizability.

Imagine Clair Huxtable or June Cleaver putting up with such a messy kitchen—impossible! But Roseanne and Dan Conner like a cluttered, lived-in look. In fact, Roseanne has been called the "anti-June Cleaver."

Cosby, many elements in her sitcom mirror her real life. For instance, like her character, she has three children, two girls and a boy (Jessica, Jennifer, and Jake). She also has had to work away from home to help make ends meet. Her 1980 job as a cocktail waitress, in Denver helped her get her start. That was the year a diet made her slender enough to wear her "degrading" costume. One of the occupational hazards of being a cocktail waitress, of course, is being hit on by the customers. After a time, Roseanne became very adept at fending off advances and at holding her own in flirtatious verbal sparring. Recognizing a clever wit when he heard it, a customer one day mentioned a club, the Comedy Works, in downtown Denver.

Gathering up her courage, Roseanne went there one evening and found she liked it. The audience was receptive. It was a revelation.

Her performance evolved into a mix of feminism and housewife jokes (she sarcastically dubbed herself the "Domestic Goddess"). Typical jokes were: "I have three kids. I've been married for fourteen years, so I breed well in captivity." And: "The day I worry about cleaning is the day Sears comes out with a vacuum cleaner you can ride."

It was a long road to national acclaim—which came in 1985 when a talent scout booked her on Johnny Carson. Her HBO special in 1987 was a dress rehearsal for *Roseanne,* as she played a homemaker with three kids, with her husband played by writer-comic Tom Arnold, whom she married in 1990. (He's her second husband.)

It is easy to see why audiences have loved her

John Goodman's high-energy style matches Roseanne's and they play well off each other. Roseanne insiders say Goodman is the "glue" that holds the cast together.

ways feisty. And she takes chances other TV stars don't. In order to incorporate the whole spectrum of human colors into her character, she allows us to see the darker side of Roseanne Conner, and a lot of viewers don't like it. In one controversial episode, Roseanne gets so angry at being disturbed by the family while taking a bath that she has a dream in which she roams the house murdering everyone. Not your typical behavior for a sitcom Mom, even if she is only dreaming!* But then, as costar John Goodman (Dan) says, "She wants to be the anti-June Cleaver…"

She is well-matched with John Goodman. He has the same high-energy style and plays well off her. He is an excellent physical comic and does some wonderful schtick. When he wants to do the voice of a cartoon character, he does a Mel Blanc-style wag of his entire saggy face, so that his mouth, cheeks, and voice vibrate. He can be as angry and fuming, or as cute and raunchy, as Roseanne. Their banter is some of the sexiest on television, but it is meant to be fun, and it's done in such a light-hearted way that it can't be offensive. For instance, after Dan has rebuilt his motorcycle, he shows it off: "I'm proud to present the seat of passion on which this family was founded." Or Roseanne, trying to convince her hubby to take her to the movies: "I'll let you do that trick with the popcorn box." And Jackie, taking care of the family while Roseanne works late, asks over the phone, "What does Dan like to eat?" We don't hear Roseanne's answer, only Jackie's reaction. "That's disgusting!"

Jackie is the slim-Jim antithesis of her rotund sister, but they are best friends. (When the series began, Roseanne Barr called in her real-life sister, Geraldine, to make sure they'd "get the sister character right.") They form a united front against their mother (played with prickly-pear perfection by occasionally-seen Estelle Parsons), who is always bugging Jackie about not being married. But Jackie is always running into Mr. Wrong. Normally a strong personality, she ends up letting the men she's involved with run her life. When Roseanne points this out to her, she gets angry. "You can't

The phrase "shrinking violet" is not in Roseanne Barr's vocabulary. She is by turns blunt, bawdy, provocative, neurotic, never dull. That is her unique charm.

evolving TV persona. They like her brashness, her "This is me and to hell with you if you don't like it" way of presenting herself to the world. She is by turns bawdy, blunt, provocative, neurotic, and al-

* During the season following the infamous "murder" episode, Miss Barr told interviewers the story had been "forced" on her and she hated it.

handle conflict," Roseanne continues. "That's why you drink." They are standing in the kitchen, so Jackie counters effectively: "Look at yourself, and that big pile of pancakes!" Roseanne concedes the point. But this is all leading to something bigger. Jackie accuses her sister of not supporting her ambition to be a cop. What does she have to do to convince her, Jackie asks, beat her up? Roseanne takes up the challenge. They start wrestling, rolling over the sofa, clawing at each other. Dan enters the room.

"Excuse me," he smirks. "Is this a sex thing?"

When things quiet down, Roseanne reveals her

EPISODIC WEIRDNESS
FRIGHT NIGHT AT THE CONNERS

It is the day of Halloween. Roseanne and Dan compete to see who is the Master of the Macabre. Dan rushes in from the garage, clutching his hand. "I cut it on the power tool," he croaks, and blood spurts from the wound. But before his wife can call for an ambulance, he grins. "Gotcha!" Later, Roseanne teases her hair so that it stands on end, then puts her hand into the toaster. When Dan comes into the kitchen, he sees the result of hundreds of volts screaming through her body as she shakes in convulsions. Sorry, he's not buying. He saw that the toaster wasn't plugged in!

The Conners hold an open house on Halloween. Darlene is shot through with arrows, Jackie is the screaming head underneath the cover of a silver serving dish, and Becky walks about with an empty sleeve streaming blood. When a business associate of Dan shows up unexpectedly, he finds Dan with a hatchet buried in his head. Now in cahoots with the businessman, Roseanne tries to trick Dan, but fails. Then Dan completely unhinges her. She sees a backlit figure in a leather mask coming through the screen door with a revving chainsaw! "Dan? Is that you?" Okay, she shouts, you're the Master, just quit that revving!

Next morning, Dan finds Roseanne deep in a phone conversation with her mother. Yes, she says, they'd just *love* to have her stay for a prolonged visit! Dan's face falls. Frantically he gestures—No! No!—Roseanne hangs up the phone. "Gotcha!"

---

real reason for not supporting her sister. "I'm afraid if you become a cop you might be killed." (In a subsequent episode, Jackie does join the police force.)

The idea of how people suppress rage is a staple on *Roseanne,* and a special concern of Miss Barr's. It's clear from her interviews that she spent many years pleasing other people and not thinking about what *she* wanted. Through a feminist consciousness-raising group she joined in Denver, and her burning need to express herself (first through writing poetry, then performing) she came out of her shell—to put it mildly.

No, she's not shy when the subject is Roseanne Barr's thoughts and feelings. During the tumultuous 1989–90 season when *Roseanne* went to Number One, the media—especially the tabloids—were filled with stories quoting Roseanne on every conceivable area of her life. She also published her autobiography, *Roseanne: My Life as a Woman,* in which she candidly described her first sexual experience, her mental breakdown at the age of sixteen, her strange sojourn as a Utah-born Jew in the Mormon religion, and the beginnings of her career. The picture we got from all this was of a complex, fascinating, charming, ambitious, driven woman, who, by her own description, pulled herself up from despair and poverty to become TV's biggest star.

All during her first year of network television fame, she was riding a wild emotional roller coaster in her private life. Marital problems eventually led to divorce from Bill Pentland, her husband of sixteen years, and to a romance with, and subsequent marriage to, Tom Arnold.

Despite her protests that the press would not give her any peace, she seemed to relish all the attention. There was a bidding war for the exclusive rights to photograph her much-ballyhooed wedding to Arnold. It was won by *Life* magazine, which paid the entire $300,0000 that it cost for the couple's nuptials. The bride and groom spent their wedding night onstage at the Improv comedy club in West Hollywood.

Her fans love her for her flamboyant personality and her refusal to go the usual Hollywood route of sappy press releases and attendance at all the

Blue collar bon vivant Dan Conner models for an appreciative Roseanne the latest in men's gear: a baseball batting cap with beer can and drinking tube attachment for those hot summer afternoons watching sports as a couch potato.

Long familiar as a featured player on TV and in movies, John Goodman found his role as Dan Conner was what made him a star. He's parlayed his fame into big money roles in films like King Ralph, Always, Stella, *and* Babe, *in which he plays the legendary Babe Ruth.*

"right" places. When she became the subject of a threatened lawsuit by several photographers who claimed she had paid three young toughs $50 to rough them up, her comment was vintage Roseanne. She had paid them only $20, she said, and her only regret was that the photographers had caught her coming out of Spago, the chic L.A. eatery where many celebrities hang out. "I deserve a lawsuit for even *going* to Spago," she told *People*.

Her snub by the TV industry at Emmy time in 1989 contributed to her growing image as a Hollywood outsider. She had a revenge of sorts in the same *People* interview with her theory that "skinny, chinless, balding, latent homosexuals with car phones" presumably run Hollywood and have "intense problems with women." Theory Number Two was that the *women* of Hollywood disliked her because she was fat. (She had slimmed down to a svelte size six, in 1980, but found that she didn't feel any sexier.) "(T)hey think fat erases sexuality," she sniffed.

Surely the success of *Roseanne*—and audience acceptance of Dan and Roseanne Conner as sexy despite their less-than-perfect physical dimensions—proves them wrong. After eight years on the road as "Domestic Goddess," Roseanne Barr has come home.

This can be seen in her sometimes bizarre choice of subjects for *Roseanne*. One evening it was a fart and its effect on young Becky's life that occupied the family. Dan knows something's in the air when Becky comes home from school and promptly disappears into her room. "It must be serious," he remarks, "she's not taking calls." Then sister Darlene spills the beans. "People are calling her Conner the Bomber," she says. "The only woman to break the sound barrier without a plane!" Seems Becky "cut the cheese" while giving a speech.

Dan insists Roseanne go up and speak to Becky, since this is "your area of expertise." Roseanne gives Becky her standard mother routine: Don't worry, this happens to everyone, and it will soon be forgotten. (Aunt Jackie spoils the effect of this speech by recalling a long-ago incident in which a teenage Roseanne dove in a pool and then spent time talking to a guy "with your left buoy hanging out.") But all ends well when the boy who is supposed to take Becky on a date *doesn't* fail to show up.

By the third season, the characters of Becky and Darlene are much richer. They are both young ladies now. Actually "ladies" isn't the right word. But they are dating now, and facing the world of sex (as well as that incredibly dumb parent-to-daughter talk that Roseanne and Dan don't know quite how to give). Darlene has already had a heavy petting session on the couch in the darkened living room (while her parents were out). And Becky has been grounded for going out with the local leather-jacketed hoodlum. But they are basically both "good" girls, trying to be as patient and helpful as they can, while their Mom and Dad go through the difficult time of raising two adolescent daughters....

PROFILE:

ROSEANNE: HOT & COOL

Cool. That is an oft-used word on *Roseanne,* as in "Hey, that's cool." Or *"Please,* that is *so* uncool." Like is another one: "Like, don't get all bent out of shape." Or "Like, you're not going to get all mushy on me, are you?"

And realistic. That's a word fans use most often when praising the show. "It's the most realistic sitcom...That's the way families *really* talk...."

Here are Dan and Roseanne Conner, Mom and Dad of a new generation—too young to be Baby Boomers, too old and too poor not to say too cool to be Yuppies—and profoundly ambivalent about the words "responsibility," "adult," and "parent," three profoundly uncool words. The last thing you will see on *Roseanne* is a goofy communal hug at the end of an episode. Instead you will see a truce in the continuing war of wits among Mom, Dad, and the kids.

All this should come as no surprise to any confirmed Roseanne Barr watcher. (And who isn't, with headlines screaming from every tabloid and daily paper practically every week.) Roseanne Barr would never settle for anything less than a show that allows her to be herself. And while she takes her career and her work seriously, she is too cool to take her status as "Hollywood star" seriously.

Hearing Roseanne tell the story, *Roseanne*'s tumultuous first year was anything but cool. There were heated disagreements between herself, the producer (Matt Williams), and the various writers. Basically, she claims, they told her her suggestions for script changes were "not funny" and to stop interfering in the creative side. She also charges they gave her character lines "degrading to women." Furthermore, they gave lines to John Goodman which were degrading to him, turning him into a wimp.

The addition of her husband Tom Arnold as a writer, supporter, and ally helped her find the courage to fight for the changes she felt were vital. When the battle ended the offending producer and writers were gone. This being *Roseanne,* however, the rumor mill now said Tom Arnold was running things. But the idea that any man can control her life, Miss Barr says, is "a joke."

Possibly her most uncool moment, as a public figure, came in 1990 when she screeched her way through "The Star-Spangled Banner" during a nationally televised baseball game. She finished by grabbing her crotch and spitting. The media firestorm that followed had her reeling with surprise. Watching others sing off-key at ballparks had given her the idea to go them one better. And the crotch-grabbing and spitting were supposed to be parodies of what so many players are seen doing in the dugout and the field all the time. Roseanne being Roseanne, she would not apologize for what she thought was "funnier 'n hell," except for the fact that some people had been "offended."

Then came the heartbreaking news in the fall of 1991 that two of her children had been hospitalized. Jennifer was under care for emotional problems, while Jessica was getting in-patient treatment at another facility for "alcohol problems." With husband Tom Arnold involved in his own apparently successful recovery from cocaine addiction, one can only wonder at her ability to hold all the pieces of her life together under such pressures. And to keep us, and herself, laughing.

CAST LIST

FAMILY: The Conners

MEMBERS:

Roseanne Conner . . . . **Roseanne Barr**
Dan Conner . . . . **John Goodman**
Becky Conner . . . . **Lecy Goranson**
Darlene Conner . . . . **Sara Gilbert**
Dan "D. J." Conner, Jr. . **Michael Fishman**
Jackie Harris . . . . **Laurie Metcalf**

SIGNIFICANT OTHERS:

Arnie (1990–   ) . . . . **Tom Arnold**
Crystal Anderson . . . . **Natalie West**

THEME SONG: **Howard Pearl and**
Dan Floriat
TIMEFRAME: **1988–**
NETWORK: **ABC**
ADDRESS: **Delaware & Third Sts.**
Lanford, Illinois

Roseanne, as first conceived by Miss Barr, was to be "revolutionary." Other sitcoms were too male-oriented, she thought. They were *Father Knows Best* all over again, with Mother left standing in the kitchen. Much of the turmoil surrounding the show's first year was due to her efforts to get her vision onto the screen. She fought with one co-executive producer, who has since left. Executive producers Tom Werner and Marcy Carsey *(Cosby; A Different World)* are still with her. Her success in getting the kind of show she wants, however, has been mixed. It is by no leap of the imagination "revolutionary." The boundaries of "good taste" (or shall we say "bad taste") have been stretched to include farting and dreams of murder. But Mom's domain is still as homemaker, while Dad does the heavy lifting and brings home the bigger paycheck.

But it is Roseanne Barr's willingness to take chances, to go against what is considered proper in a sitcom, that makes *Roseanne* so compulsively watchable. She made it okay for family members to be more three-dimensional, to have dark sides and yet still engage our sympathy. Not everyone has

bright things to say all the time. The dialogue isn't just a series of set-ups for jokes, but a communication between people (albeit very clever and humorous ones).

Roseanne Barr has pushed the boundaries of the sitcom structure into new shapes and she is still experimenting. She is going to be an inspiration for new television comedy for some time to come.

▶

The fifties had picture-perfect married couples, like Jim and Margaret Anderson on Father Knows Best. *The nineties demand something more down to earth, resulting in Roseanne and Dan Conner, who are stubborn, sloppy, sassy, sensuous, and definitely non-suburban.*

THE SIMPSONS

The Simpsons *home is tastefully decorated in early Motel Six. But whatever the shortcomings in decor, each episode requires more than seventy-five artists and upwards of 14,000 images to come to life every week. The* Simpsons' *success prompted a surge of new TV cartoons, including* Little Rosey (Roseanne Barr *as a ten-year-old) and* Merrie Melodies (a repackaging of Looney Tunes *classics).*

When Fox preempted its hit animated series, *The Simpsons,* on April 1, 1990, switchboards at the network affiliates lit up with complaints from disgruntled fans, and one mother explained that she used the show as a reward for her kids for being good, and now they were griping that they'd been good for nothing.

What viewers were missing most was that demonic bundle of malevolent energy, ten-year-old Bart Simpson. What would he be up to in the next episode? Would he ride his skateboard like a deadly projectile against unwitting pedestrians? Or would he take secret snapshots of his dad cavorting with an exotic dancer at a bachelor party? Whatever it was, it would be fun. Bart is considered "cool" by the twelve-to-seventeen set because he's got no respect for authority, and he often appears right not to have any.

Strange that a housewife should choose *The Simpsons,* with its rambunctious, not to say obnoxious, kid characters and its skewed view of family life, to be her electronic babysitter. But such was the instant success of this show that within a few months of its premiere, a tidal wave of *Simpsons* gear broke over America. It's likely this mother's children were using any number of Simpsons products, including, but not limited to: T-shirts, underwear, dolls, video games, buttons, life vests (approved by the Coast Guard), key rings, beach towels, snow boots, and laminated magnets.

As part of the New Wave of sitcoms based on less-than-perfect blue-collar families, *The Simpsons* scored hot numbers in the Nielsens and made Bart the idol of rebellious adolescents everywhere. In thousands of playgrounds, his catch phrases echoed on a thousands tongues: "Don't have a cow!" "Eat my shorts!" "Aye caramba!" Thanks to Bart, the show was Number One among young viewers, and the only program on Fox to land consistently in the top fifteen.

Based on the characters sired by cartoonist Matt Groening as one-minute animated segues on *The Tracey Ulman Show,* this bizarre family, with its protuberant eyes, prehensile upper lips, and jaundiced complexions, created enough of a cult following to merit their own series. *The Simpsons* are a reflection of Groening's own jaundiced view of the world as a strange, sometimes hostile place, where the young often are encouraged to stifle their individuality by embittered elders who long ago have given up theirs. This was the point of view in Groening's pre-*Simpsons* cartoon strip, "Life in Hell," which ran in college newspapers and the "alternative" press. A daydreamer and time-server in public school himself, Groening sees Bart Simpson as one agent of vengeance against a system that often promotes deadness instead of creativity.

And Bart is an expert in such guerrilla warfare. The devilish delinquent has been known to call up the local tavern to inquire of the bartender, "Is there a Jock Strap around?" And if the blackboard sentences he is kept after school to write are any indication, he is by turn mutinous ("I will not instigate revolution"), impertinent ("I will not call my teacher 'hot cakes'"), and obnoxious ("Garlic gum is not funny"). As one of the three *Simpsons* executive producers, Sam Simon, told *Newsweek,* "The combination of Bart's lack of intelligence and sociopathic leanings probably means he'll either go to jail or become a successful [show business] agent."

There is a sentimental side to Bart, however. One Christmas he got "Mother" tattooed on his arm, hearing in his imagination his Mother's fond response: "Oh, this is the best present ever, and it makes you look dangerous, too."

As befits any self-respecting young man, Bart isn't too fond of having two baby sisters. They're a pain in the you-know-what. But most of the time they're fun to tease because they get all teary-eyed and start to scream. Lisa, who's two years Bart's junior, is a caution. She's smart and sensitive, and she expresses herself by playing soulful saxophone, sometimes in duets with a raspy-voiced black musician named Bleeding Gums. Really a strange chick! (She is also a forgiving daughter. During one of her periodic bouts of existential funk, she sniffled in her mom's arms about finding a Meaning to It All. Mom's advice: "Just smile. Then you'll fit in and the boys will like you and happiness will follow." Luckily, Lisa still has her saxophone to talk to.)

Maggie, the baby of the family, with a neat little blue ribbon in her hair and an ever-present pacifier in her mouth, crawls about, the silent voice of

Here's Bart trying to battle his bad image with schoolteachers by pretending to read a book. His more favored pastime is trying to run down pedestrians with his skateboard.

The Simpsons prehensile upper lips have been a source of fascination for anthropologists—or was it orthodontists? It's no wonder, then, that the family's mud-smeared patriarch, Homer, was once mistaken for Big Foot in a Midwest national forest. But with Homer safely domesticated by Marge in Springfield, we can all rest easier.

innocence in a turbulent household. Wide-eyed, she watches everything, thoughtfully drawing on the rubber nipple.

Homer Simpson is the besieged paterfamilias in all this. His main daily communication to Bart is, "Why, you little…" All he wants is some peace and quiet after his day as safety inspector at the Springfield Nuclear Plant. Poor man, he dreams of a promotion and a better life, but he lacks that go-getter quality. With a bulbous beerbelly, a four o'clock shadow, and a balding pate, he is hardly management material. His supervisor calls him "Bonehead," and once, on a camping trip, he was mistaken for Bigfoot. No wonder his sisters-in-law Patty and Selma think that Marge's biggest mistake in life was marrying him.

Marge is too busy trying to keep her squabbling kids in line, and the mutually antagonistic Bart and Homer apart, to give much thought to What Might Have Been. (Some of her nights are spent as a rollerskating carhop to supplement Homer's salary.) Still, she tries to be there for her children as much as she can. When Marge discovers Lisa jamming on saxophone with Bleeding Gums one moonlit night, she calmly interrupts the session. Tomorrow, after all, is a school day. She is apologetic to Bleeding Gums as she spirits her daughter home. "Nothing personal," she tells the black jazz-man, "I just fear the unfamiliar." The one strength in Homer and Marge is that they know their limitations.

Still svelte, Marge's most striking feature is her hair, a Leaning Tower of a blue beehive. The romance, alas, has long since gone out of her marriage. Homer thinks it entirely appropriate to give her a bowling ball with *his* name engraved on it, as a birthday present. Little wonder that when a sleazy denizen of the bowling alley and a would-be Casanova begins to shower her with compliments, he creates the greatest emotional upheaval in her life. Will she keep their tacky rendezvous at the local motel? Marge drives to within sight of the motor lodge when her nerves fail her. It is the closest she can come to an escapade. Swinging her car around she heads instead to the nuclear plant. Rushing in, she passionately embraces Homer. She's made his day! In a scene borrowed from *An Officer and a Gentleman,* Homer sweeps her off her feet, crowing to his coworkers,"I'm going to the

MATT GROENING

Cartoonist Matt Groenings's comic strip, "Life in Hell," was a precursor to The Simpsons, *and appeared mainly in alternative weeklies and college newspapers. Its hero was a rabid rabbit with buck teeth and Simpson-like overbite, who challenged authority while trying To Make Sense of It All.*

back seat of my car, and I won't be back for ten minutes?!" (That's eight minutes more than Peg Bundy would expect from Al!)

On one occasion, Homer almost got his wish to be rid of Bart. He gets a call from Bart's principal. Seems Bart flushed an "explosive device" down the toilet of the school john when the principal's mother was seated at the distaff end of the line. This little antic has taken the principal to new heights of consternation. Bart will not only be expelled, he proclaims, he will be deported! Bart will fly to the wine country of France as part of a student exchange program, while the Simpsons

Everybody wants to get in on the rambunctious fun of this hit toon. Some big stars who add their voices to the rising chorus of new Simpsons *characters are Dustin Hoffman, Danny DeVito, Larry King, Michael Jackson, and Harvey Fierstein. Daniel Stern, who does the off-camera adult reminiscences of Kevin on* The Wonder Years, *did a vocal parody of that show's flashbacks, as an adult Bart on* The Simpsons.

They say the words father Homer most often speaks to son Bart are: "Why, you little…" But it's Bart's rebellious spirit that endears him to millions of pubescent (and adult) viewers.

will receive a little Albanian. (Homer misunderstands the principal. "You mean a kid with white hair and pink eyes?")

When Bart arrives at the French chateau, he finds it looks nothing like the beautiful picture he saw in his brochure. It is a tumbledown, rambling wreck of a place, run by two sadistic French farmers. They work Bart unmercifully in the vineyards all day. While they eat well, *his* reward in the evening is a plate of turnips. As for sleeping accommodations, the comfort of their favorite jackass is given more consideration than Bart. The jackass gets a pile of hay in a cozy corner of the room. Bart gets a corner, but no hay.

But Bart is Bart, and eventually he turns the tables. He escapes to a nearby village, accosting a gendarme to tell of the farmers' perfidy. They are making a very bad wine and trying to pass it off as a premium! As the farmers are led away in chains, Bart sneers, "Au revoir, suckers."

Back home the little Albanian, Adil, arrives and Homer takes an instant liking to him. He is polite; he flatters Homer by taking a great interest in his work. He wants a tour of the nuclear plant. "My biological children never asked to do that," sniffs Homer.

In the vast control room, he proudly displays America's finest achievements: assorted donuts in a box. "Look, Adil, American donuts. Chocolate covered, coconut, raspberry-filled. How's that for freedom of choice?"

Little Adil, tourist camera at the ready, is more interested in the "plutonium isolation module." Attentive host that he is, Homer obliges.

The next night, FBI agents surround the treehouse in the Simpsons' backyard. Little Adil is up there radioing the fatherland.

It is all too much for Homer. At the airport, teary-eyed, he watches Adil exchanged for another espionage agent, a homecoming American fifth grader. "Goodbye, Adil," he calls, "I'll send you those civil defense plans you wanted."

And so the viewer gets to learn an old-fashioned moral—the grass is always greener, etc.—in a fresh and amusing way.

As the creator of the first successful prime-time animated series since *The Flintstones* (1960–66) and *The Jetsons* (1962–63), Matt Groening finds inspiration in the cleverly satiric *Bullwinkle Show,* brainchild of Jay Ward. (*Bullwinkle* ran first as a weekday children's show called *Rocky and His Friends,* 1959–61. Then new elements were added—such as the campy Russian spies Boris and Natasha—when it was taken to prime time, 1961–62. Reruns since have raised *Bullwinkle* to cult status as an "adult" cartoon.)

When Groening was negotiating with network execs, his avowed aim was to do a Jay Ward-style show. And, as usual, this new idea was seen as too risky for mainstream television. It was only at Fox, which was looking to capture a youthful audience, that he got the green light. A formidable talent pool was assembled, including Oscar-wining director James Brooks *(Terms of Endearment)* and veteran sitcom writer Sam Simon *(Cheers* and *Taxi).*

Tracey Ullman regular Julie Kavner's gravelly voice can be heard as Marge, with costar Dan Castellaneta as Homer. Nancy Cartwright is Bart and Yeardley Smith is Lisa. The actors try to enter into the Simpsons' spirit. When the script required Homer to choke Bart, there was a vigorous laying-on of hands by Castellaneta to get the requisite strangled wheezings from Cartwright.

The logistics of putting one episode together are daunting. After the voices have been taped, the drawing commences. Timing is crucial here, to match the voices to the action. Some seventy-five Los Angeles artists, working in groups of eight or ten, start the process with some 2,000 preliminary drawings. These are shipped to South Korea for assembly-line-style production of 14,000 more im-

Such bon mots of Bart's as "Aye, caramba," "Don't have a cow," and "Eat my shorts!" have enriched the language and been the inspiration for new primetime toons, scheduled for the 1991–92 season, as Fish Police, *an underwater saga of the underworld;* Capitol Critters, *which makes monkeys and turkeys of the Washington politicians, and* Family Dog, *a comical, canine-eye view of the world.*

MATT GROENING

Bart moons America, in this sassy scene from the hit animated series. Creator Matt Groening says his inspiration came from the work of the late Jay Ward, animator of the classic Bullwinkle Show.

ages. A final step takes the episode to Brooks's Gracie Films for the finishing touches. From start to finish, it has taken some nineteen to twenty weeks for completion.

Matt Groening is proud of his toon. As charming as previous efforts have been, like Hanna-Barbera's *The Flintstones,* Groening knows *The Simpsons* are a quantum leap ahead of them in quality. The *Flintstones,* after all, were a *Honeymooners* rip-off, with Fred Flintstone in the blustery Ralph Kramden role and Barney Rubble as the good-natured, dim-witted Ed Norton. "And *The Honeymooners* did it better," concludes the artist. He prefers to think of his colorfully contentious family as both entertainment and a kind of funhouse mirror. There, on the

misshapen and twisted surface, we see something very familiar. Ourselves.

By giving Groening's vision a chance to air, with a minimum of interference, Fox was started a mini-revival of prime-time toons, with some very big names involved. As this is being written, ABC has given a thirteen-show commitment to *The Aristo-critters,* to be produced by Steven Bochco. At CBS, Steven Spielberg is developing *The Family Dog.* Also projected at CBS is an all-new *Pink Panther* series, which will combine live actors with animated characters, as in *Who Framed Roger Rabbit.*

Not since 1962, when ABC had *The Flintstones, The Jetsons, Top Cat, The Alvin Show, The Bugs Bunny Show,* and *Beany & Cecil,* all on in prime time, has there been such excitement in the possibilities of stories told with nothing but voices, lines, and color.

CAST LIST

FAMILY: The Simpsons

MEMBERS:

Homer Simpson . . . . **Dan Castellaneta**
Marge Simpson . . . . **Julie Kavner**
Bart Simpson . . . . **Nancy Cartwright**
Lisa Simpson . . . . **Yeardley Smith**
Baby Maggie Simpson . . . **(Sound Effects)**

THEME SONG: **Danny Elfman**
TIMEFRAME: **1990–**
NETWORK: **Fox**
ADDRESS: **Springfield, U.S.A.**

Marge and Homer flank their kids, Baby Maggie, Bart, and Lisa. Marge's blue beehive Leaning Tower is one of Springfield's scenic wonders, as is the nuclear power plant where Homer works—which tells you something about the safety, or lack of it, at the place! Actually, the portrayal of Homer and his coworkers as "bumbling idiots" raised the hackles of the U.S. Council for Energy Awareness!

AFTERWORD

In the early 1980s, the media pundits erected a tombstone. It read: "R.I.P. The Family Show/Sitcom." Needless to say, its reported demise was greatly exaggerated. The family show is back stronger and more popular than ever.

Like every other television genre, it simply went out of fashion for a time. But there was never any real possibility that it would completely disappear. TV shows about family life and our core experiences as humans hit too close to home to be ignored. In fact, of the thirty-nine top-rated TV programs since 1951, three-quarters have been centered on stories about the family unit.

Sitcoms and "family dramas" originated with radio programs like *The Jack Benny Show, Our Miss Brooks, One Man's Family,* and *The Adventures of Ozzie and Harriet.* When television began to look like the wave of the communications future, some of these programs made the transition to the new medium. *I Love Lucy* and *Mama* were two of the earliest, most successful television family programs based on material first aired on radio.

Then came the great handwringing of the sociologists and thinking persons: TV was destroying family life. No one sat and talked around the supper table any more because we all took our TV dinner trays and sat in front of the boob tube, isolated and insulated from each other. But what TV might take away, it also gave back, mesmerizing us with spectacles of family as fantasy-fulfillment: every problem slickly resolved within twenty-six (or, at most, fifty-two) minutes, and the happy group dissolving in a loving embrace, fade to commercial. The question remains: What was so wrong with that? As life becomes swifter and more complicated (not to say frenetic—social scientists tell us the amount of information in the world doubled in the decade from 1980 to 1990), a few solid laughs and some good feelings help us relax in the evening. And the Hollywood TV-studio fantasy-masters even throw in a few "sterling values" so it's not all follow-the-laugh-track mindlessness. Remember the words of wisdom from Jim Anderson and Ward Cleaver: Don't lie to your parents; be loyal to your friends; keep your word; and always value Doing the Right Thing Over Making a Quick Buck. (That last one, actually, sounds more like Steven Keaton.)

We never tire of the good feeling we receive when watching these programs because we want the world to be like it is on TV. And we want to pretend that we too can Do the Right Thing when it counts, and end up with a loving, forgiving hug as our reward.

These programs, of course, were created to entertain, not to instruct or edify. It is their entertainment value that keeps us coming back for more. But what is it that makes a classic family show so much better than its competition?

The best of the best always have a guiding spirit behind them, working to shape and give them direction. That spirit might come in the form of an executive producer like Leonard Katzman (*Dallas*); a team like Leonard Goldberg, Jay Presson Allen, and Mike Nichols (*Family*); an executive producer/director/star like Michael Landon (*Little House on the Prairie*); or a concerned star like Carroll O'Connor (*All in the Family*). Their type of dedication and professionalism always filters down into the rank and file.

Shows in this category—and we believe all the ones included in this book qualify—have actors who fight for their characters at story conferences, and writers who labor to make those characters sparkle. The exposés in tabloids and fan magazines about "backstage battles" are really the oft-told tale of clashing ideas/ideals. They are about *passion*—the passion to create and to express.

There is no easy formula that works every time. Just as individuality is what we prize most in our friends, in our favorite programs it is originality. We want something new. When we look at the screen, we say, "Surprise me." And that which we desire most is to find a new character to welcome, to befriend, and to *love*.

Our favorite characters are often the offbeat ones, the self-contradictory ones, impulsive, blustery types like Archie Bunker, Alex P. Keaton, or Roseanne Conner. Or the bumbling but lovable kind like Beaver Cleaver, Barney Fife, or Ozzie Nelson. Isn't it comforting to know that other people in the world sometimes can screw up, be obnoxious, stupid, and pigheaded, like us, and still be okay, even be likable?

That brings us to the final element...*likability.* That seems to be the key ingredient that pushes a show into Nielsen ratings heaven—and it's often

THE LIFE OF RILEY: *Marjorie Reynolds, Jack Kirkwood, and William Bendix.*

provided by just one actor. Those who score well in Hollywood's secretive, scientifically conducted *Q*-rating (likability) scale (yes, they *do* quantify such evanescent human qualities as that!) can often carry a show and a network to triumph. Put simply: the more characters that sparkle, the better the show.

These shows deserve our serious attention because they already have our abiding frivolous attention each week. And they *are* serious business, for they shape our hearts and minds to a far greater extent than we may realize.

—Michael Denis

In the introduction to this book, we promised you, our readers, an honorable-mention list of those favorite American television families that could not, because of format and space considerations, be accorded chapters of their own in this volume. Many of them could be dealt with at length should a Volume II ever make it into bookstores.

Other shows on our original list, and probably yours as well, include (alphabetically):

The Addams Family (ABC 1964–66)
ALF (NBC 1988–90)
Bachelor Father (CBS 1957–59, NBC 1959–61, ABC 1961–62)
The Beverly Hillbillies (CBS 1962–71)
Blondie (NBC 1957)
Blondie (CBS 1968–69)
The Brady Bunch (ABC 1969–74)
The Courtship of Eddie's Father (ABC 1969–72)
A Date With Judy (ABC 1952–53)
Dennis the Menace (CBS 1959–63)
The Dick Van Dyke Show (CBS 1961–66)
Diff'rent Strokes (NBC 1978–85, ABC 1985–86)
Dinosaurs (ABC 1991–   )
Eight Is Enough (ABC 1977–81)
Empty Nest (NBC 1988–   )
Evening Shade (CBS 1990–   )
Family Affair (CBS 1966–71)
A Family for Joe (NBC 1990)

THE LIFE OF RILEY: Lugene Sanders, William Bendix, and Marjorie Reynolds.

The Family Holvak (NBC 1975)
Family Man (CBS 1990–91)
Family Matters (ABC 1989–   )
The Farmer's Daughter (ABC 1963–66)
The Fitzpatricks (CBS 1977–78)
The Flintstones (ABC 1960–66)
Full House (ABC 1987–   )
The Ghost and Mrs. Muir (NBC 1968–69, ABC 1969–70)
Gimme a Break (NBC 1981–87)
The Goldbergs (CBS 1949–51, NBC 1952–53, Dumont 1954)
Growing Pains (ABC 1985–   )
Happy Days (ABC 1974–84)
Hazel (NBC 1961–65, CBS 1965–66)
How the West Was Won (ABC 1978)

THE DANNY THOMAS SHOW: Marjorie Lord, Rusty Hamer, Angela Cartwright, Danny Thomas, and Sherry Jackson.

BEWITCHED: Elizabeth Montgomery, Erin Murphy, David Lawrence, and Dick Sargent.

I Love Lucy (CBS 1951–57)
The Jeffersons (CBS 1975–85)
The Jetsons (ABC 1962–63)
Just the Ten of Us (ABC 1988–90)
Lassie (CBS 1954–71, Syndication 1971–74)
Life Goes On (ABC 1989–   )
Life of Riley (NBC 1949–50)
Life of Riley (NBC 1953–58)
Life With Father (CBS 1953–55)
MacKenzies of Paradise Cove (ABC 1977)
Make Room for Daddy (ABC 1953–57, CBS 1957–64, ABC 1965–71)
Mama's Family (NBC 1983–85, Syndication 1986–89)
The Many Loves of Dobie Gillis (CBS 1959–63)
Meet Corliss Archer (CBS 1951–52)
The Monroes (ABC 1966–67)
The Montefuscos (NBC 1975)
Mr. Belvedere (ABC 1985–89)
Mulligan's Stew (NBC 1977)
The Munsters (CBS 1964–66)
My Two Dads (NBC 1987–90)
The Oregon Trail (NBC 1977)
Otherworld (CBS 1985)
Our House (NBC 1986–88)
Our Man Higgins (ABC 1962–63)
The Partridge Family (ABC 1970–74)
The Patty Duke Show (ABC 1963–66)
Petticoat Junction (CBS 1963–70)
The Pride of the Family (ABC 1953–54)
The Real McCoys (ABC 1957–62, CBS 1962–63)
The Rifleman (ABC 1958–63)
The Ruggles (ABC 1949–52)
Sanford and Son (NBC 1972–77)
Silver Spoons (NBC 1982–86, Syndication 1986–87)

BEWITCHED: Dick York as Darren and Elizabeth Montgomery as Samantha.

THE GOLDBERGS: Eli Mintz (left), Gertrude Berg, and Robert H. Harris.

The Stu Erwin Show (ABC 1950–55)
Thirtysomething (ABC 1987–91)
Valerie/Valerie's Family/The Hogan Family (NBC 1986–90, CBS 1990)
The Waltons (CBS 1972–81)
Who's the Boss? (ABC 1984–   )
The Wonder Years (ABC 1988–   )

THE WALTONS: Richard Thomas as John-Boy.

LASSIE: (From left) George Cleveland, Arthur Space, Jan Clayton, Tommy Rettig, plus Lassie and Pokey.

THE DICK VAN DYKE SHOW: Mary Tyler Moore, Dick Van Dyke, Morey Amsterdam, and Rose Marie.

BACHELOR FATHER: Noreen Corcoran and John Forsythe

Compared to soap operas like Dallas *and* Knots Landing, *the bedroom scenes in* Family *were so tame as to be non-existent. Nevertheless,* Family *was the first TV family drama to deal realistically with contemporary sexual morality through the two eldest Lawrence children, Nancy (Meredith Baxter Birney, pictured here) and Willie.*

It's almost a case of Back to the Future's Past when Tony Dow (formerly Wally of Leave It to Beaver) *played a high school vice-principal trying to steer a wayward youth, Michael J. Fox (Family Ties) away from trouble in the made-for-TV movie,* High School U.S.A., *which was broadcast October 16, 1983.*

In retro-fifties wig and low-cut blouse, Katey Sagal vamps as Peg Bundy in this publicity shot. The 1991 season of Married ... With Children *opened with Peg's announcement to Al that she again is pregnant. Al responded by trying to skip town.*